From Carrie Brunton
Lucy
June 30th 1951

THE
UNTUTORED TOWNSMAN'S
INVASION
OF THE COUNTRY

ΣΑΤΥΡΟ

THE
UNTUTORED TOWNSMAN'S
INVASION
OF THE COUNTRY

by
C. E. M. JOAD

with drawings by
THOMAS DERRICK

FABER AND FABER LTD
24 Russell Square
London

*First published in Mcmxlvi
by Faber and Faber Limited
24 Russell Square London W.C.1
Printed in Great Britain by
Purnell and Sons Limited
Paulton (Somerset) and London*

ACKNOWLEDGMENTS

My thanks are due to the *Countrygoer* for permission to reprint the first parts of Chapters III and V and to *Everybody's Weekly* for permission to reprint part of Chapter VII.

I wish to thank Mr. Philip Cleave for revising the book in manuscript and for the Appendix on the Highlands of Scotland printed at the end of Chapter V. I also have to thank Mr. Francis Ritchie for putting me right on numberless points of fact and for the preparation of the very full and helpful Appendices which will be found at the end of the book.

C. E. M. JOAD

Hampstead
July 1945

CONTENTS

CONTENTS

APPENDICES

DRAWINGS

Forget the countries overhung with smoke,
Forget the snorting steam and piston stroke,
Forget the spreading of the hideous town,
Think rather of the pack horse on the down,
And dream of London small and white and clean,
And clear Thames bordered by its garden green.

WILLIAM MORRIS
from the Prologue to
The Earthly Paradise, 1868

There'll always be an England
Where there's a country lane

Soldier's Song, 1940

Chapter One

HISTORICAL RETROSPECT

I. The Towns Drain the Country

At the end of the eighteenth century, when the population of England and Wales was between eight and nine millions, 78 per cent of us lived in the country and about one-third of us were employed in agriculture. Throughout the eighteenth century the importance of the towns was growing and that of the country diminishing, but it was not until the imposition of the Corn Laws in 1815 that the balance between town and country began radically to alter. For a further thirty years the country still predominated, but after their repeal in 1846 the preponderating influence passed finally to the towns. Pessimists believed that the repeal of the Corn Laws would mean the ruin of British agriculture; their expectations were premature. Owing to a variety of circumstances, British agriculture continued to flourish and reached a peak of prosperity about 1870 when eight million acres were under corn. During the next decade, however, it began to decline and after the whole-hearted adoption of Free Trade about 1875 and the resultant flooding of English markets with cheap corn from the newly developed American and Canadian prairies, it declined very rapidly. By 1885 the acreage under wheat in England and Wales had fallen by a million; vast areas of cornland had been laid down to grass and the numbers employed in agriculture had fallen by several hundred thousand. By 1900 the corn-growing areas in England and Wales had shrunk from the eight million acres of 1870 to six million acres. The farm labourer could not be expected to remain on the land when his occupation was gone and higher wages in the towns were a magnet to draw from the countryside its best men. When the war broke out in 1939, of the forty-one and a half million inhabitants of England and Wales, less than

900,000 were employed in agriculture.[1] In fact, the 1800 ratio between country and town population had been nearly reversed. Thus, for a hundred years past the life of the great bulk of Englishmen has been divorced for the first time in our history from contact with nature. The decline in rural economic prosperity has been accompanied by a social impoverishment. Death duties and estate duties have weakened the resources of the big landowners, with the result that they have been forced to sell their country houses which have been turned into institutions and their parks and estates which have been broken up for building.

Indifference of the Towns

Most Englishmen have looked with indifference upon the decline of the countryside. As the interests of town and country came increasingly to diverge, some even regarded it with satisfaction. The interest of the towns was in cheap food which mainly came from abroad in the shape of imported corn, foreign meat and canned goods, both because it was cheap and because the lands from which we imported it provided a market for the machine-made goods which our towns were the first to produce. The townsman was certainly not going to give more for his food merely because it happened to have been produced in England, nor would he willingly pay higher taxes in order to maintain in solvency such an uneconomic luxury as British farming, merely because it happened to be on his own doorstep.

Moreover, socialists and radicals associated the landowning system with vestigial feudalism, regarded farmers as natural reactionaries and were not sorry to see the landowners humbled and the farmers impoverished. Thus, for various reasons the towns regarded the decay of rural life with comparative equanimity. As G. M. Trevelyan comments in his *English Social History*, 'The men of theory failed to perceive that agriculture is not merely one industry among many, but is a way of life, unique and irreplaceable in its human and spiritual values.'

[1] As recently as 1840 the respective populations of towns and country in England and Wales were approximately equal. In 1937 thirty-one millions were living in towns and ten and a half in the country.

14

II. The Reverse Flow

Concurrently, however, another tendency has been at work. It was in 1865 that the Commons, Footpaths and Open Spaces Preservation Society was formed. It sought to prevent commons from being enclosed and open spaces from being built upon. The great battle of Berkhamsted Common was fought in 1866 and in 1878 Epping Forest was preserved for the public by the efforts of Sir Robert Hunter. The significance of these events lies in the words 'the public', for the public for whom it was sought to preserve these tracts of country was predominantly a public of townsmen. Thus began that complicated process of ebb and flow between town and country which has gone on ever since.

It was characterized on the townsman's side by an interest in the country founded not on economic but on physical, cultural, and aesthetic considerations. It was from about 1870 onwards that a trickle of townsmen began to resort to the country for air, exercise, recreation and spiritual refreshment. With the coming in the twentieth century of the second industrial revolution, the trickle broadened out into a river; for the second industrial revolution was a revolution in transport.

Effects of the Revolution in Transport. The Towns Burst

Ushered in by the invention of the internal combustion engine, it was reinforced by a minor revolution in building materials as a result of which concrete and cement tended to take the place of bricks and mortar.

The influence of the second industrial revolution caused our towns to burst like bombs and scatter their *débris* far and wide over the surrounding countryside. Everybody, it appeared, wanted to live in the country; everybody, it also appeared, wanted to live as far as possible from his neighbours. The internal combustion engine enabled these desires to be satisfied. A man could now live in one place and work in another, travelling to and fro in his private car or in the public bus. As the years passed and the motor-car was supplemented by the motorcoach, the Green Line bus and presently the electric train, the distances over which people travelled daily to and from their places of work increased. Thus arose that strange, new life of the dormitory suburb, a place without civic centre or social consciousness, vomiting out its men morning by morning into the trains, sucking them back again evening by evening into its villas, and relapsing into stagnancy during the day, a waste land peopled only by children and bored and idle women. Those who dwelt in these places suffered in a pre-eminent degree from the disadvantages both of town and of country life. They lacked the social life of the town, for here there were no occasions for social meeting. There were few pubs, fewer churches and no assembly rooms. They lacked no less the countryman's contact with nature and intercourse with his neighbour.

But it is with the effect of the internal combustion engine upon the countryside rather than on those who travelled to seek it that I am here concerned. This effect may be most concisely described by saying that the seekers found that they had sought in vain. The idea that had occurred to them had also, it seemed, occurred to others, and where one country-seeking clerk led the way, a thousand others presently followed in his train. A man built or bought a house at the end of the last row of the last suburb; in a year there were a dozen rows beyond. He valued his view over fields and woods; before he had time to look at it twice, they were replaced by houses and bungalows. He thought that it would be pleasant to live in an old-fashioned village, but others, it seemed, thought so too and before they realized what they were doing he and they had transformed the village into a suburb. Under the influence of these desires, the towns shot out their arms into the country as though they were telescopes, and octopus-like yearly engulfed fresh areas of green within their tentacles of builders' pink.

Escape at the Week-end

But the second industrial revolution had a further effect. It enabled young people with good hearts, high spirits and comparatively empty pockets to leave the towns and for the first time to sample the joys of the country. They have shown an increasing disposition to take advantage of the opportunity. Singly, in couples, in groups or organized in clubs—in the fifteen federations comprising the Ramblers' Association there were organized in peace-time over six hundred clubs with 50,000 members—young people have formed the habit of going on Saturdays and Sundays and, increasingly, for the whole week-end into the country. You can see the living witnesses of this revolution at the Central Station at Manchester early on a Sunday morning, complete with rucksacks, shorts and hob-nailed boots, waiting for the early trains to Edale, Hope and the Derbyshire moors. Looking at them, one might be tempted to think that the whole of Manchester was in exodus; justifiably, since these northern cities are by any reckoning the ugliest con-glomerations of bricks and mortar with which mankind has ever defaced the unprotesting surface of the earth. For over a hundred years men and women stayed in these places because they must, worked in them, played in them and on Sundays, when piety forbade games, lounged in their streets and waited for the pubs to open. In our day, hiking has replaced beer as the shortest cut out of Manchester, as turning their backs upon the cities which their fathers made armies of young people make sorties at any and every opportunity into the countryside. You could in peace-time see the same sight at Waterloo or Victoria on a fine Sunday morning, although in the softer south there were fewer hobnailed boots.

For the accommodation of this new army of townsfolk seeking the country, there sprang up in 1931 a new organization, the Youth Hostels' Association. Before the war it was covering England with a chain of hostels, at which the walker or the cyclist could put up cheaply for the night, cook his own meal if he wished or at most hostels get a decent meal provided by the establishment at a reasonable charge. In any picture of England after the war the Youth Hostels' Association will have a definite and an assured place. Some indication of the size of this townsman's exodus is afforded by the number of people using the hostels for what are called 'overnights'—every time a man spends a night at a hostel, he is counted as one 'over-night'. During the years immediately before the war, the mem-bership and 'overnight' figures at all hostels were as follows:

Year	Members	Overnights
1931	6,439	—
1932	16,914	78,067
1933	27,905	157,582
1934	37,285	221,271
1935	48,057	307,811
1936	59,768	385,407
1937	70,505	463,116
1938	79,821	536,543
1939	83,418	537,986

The figures provide a fair index of the growth of the movement. At Easter 1931, it had six thousand members and seventy hostels; by the summer of 1939 there were three hundred hostels and eighty-three thousand members. Temporarily arrested at the beginning of the war, when a number of hostels were taken over for war purposes, the movement quickly recovered and is now advancing faster than ever as the following figures show:

Year	Membership	Overnights
1940	50,864	275,600
1941	55,327	331,877
1942	78,382	408,443
1943	100,907	502,632
1944	133,678	613,215

At Easter 1945 new members were coming in at the rate of 1,200 a day. In July the membership was 150,000 and by the end of the year it will probably have reached 200,000. Of the 1944 membership, 62 per cent was under 21. Thirty new hostels have been opened since the beginning of the war.

These figures cover, of course, only a small proportion of the vast army of ramblers. There are those who put up at pubs, there are those who get cheap lodgings, there are those who cannot afford a night away from a town and whose ambitions are, therefore, limited to the day in the country, there are also the campers.

When Lord Justice Scott's Committee on Land Utilization in Rural Areas took evidence in the spring of 1942, six representatives of open-air organizations, the Ramblers' Association, the Youth Hostels' Association, the Workers' Travel Association, the Holiday Fellowship, the Co-operative Holidays Association, the Cyclists' Touring Club and the Camping Club gave evidence before it.

Such, then, in effect is the second tendency, a tendency the reverse of that which I began by describing.

Attitude of the Countryside to the Townsman's Invasion

The first tendency was economic in origin; it drained the countryside into the towns. The second is cultural, physical, nostalgic, aesthetic—call it what you will; it is the reverse flow of the towns back into the country. Like all things English, this reverse movement was unforeseen and, because unforeseen, unplanned and unprovided for. The attitude of the countryside to the invaders from the towns has varied between rapacity—the townsman is rich and one can make money out of him—and resentment—one does not want a lot of 'townees' trampling over one's fields and breaking down one's hedges—but has in the main been suspicious and hostile. Notice boards sprang up telling 'Trespassers' that they would be 'Prosecuted' and the boundaries of farms and woods bristled with new rings of barbed wire fencing. A club of ramblers would go out for a week-end's tramping and find that it had nowhere to tramp; motorists would take out the car on a Sunday afternoon, find the main roads crowded with other cars and overflow on to the side roads which were wholly unsuited to their needs. Thus, the townsman has invaded a countryside unprepared for his reception and on the whole disinclined to receive him. There are subsidiary reasons for his unpopularity. He buys up the country cottages which the farmer wants for his labourers and by his superior purchasing power puts up the prices in the village shops. His morals are a cause often of surprise and sometimes of consternation; he throws his weight about in the village pub and on Sundays wears flamboyant and startling garments in the village street; his women seem particularly out of place . . . .

The Post-War Prospect

After the war what was first a trickle and then a stream will swell to a flood. People will have been penned up in the towns for five[1] or, it may be, six years. Most of them have been much too busy to get out into the country. Even if they had not been too busy, there have been few buses, while train journeys have been crowded and uncertain. They have had no petrol. After the war there will be leisure and holidays with pay; the railways promise all the old facilities, cheap fares, week-end fares and cheap day excursions; there will be Green Line buses and char-a-bancs. Above all, there will again be petrol for private cars which will increase in numbers, as they diminish in cost. How people will rush about in their cars! Meanwhile a flood of fighting men back from the war, agog for England, home and country, will ask nothing better of life than the chance to take the wife or the girl for a day's outing in woods and green fields. With what articulate longing they have looked forward to drinking English beer in English pubs—in English country pubs! Some, more ambitious, vow that nothing will content them after the war but a little place of their own in the country. They don't, they say, mind how poor they are or how hardly they live provided they can own their acre, work for themselves and be freed from the obligation to catch the 8.15 to town and office in the morning. They will want to build themselves little houses all over the face of England.

These are a few of the considerations which justify the expectation that the invasion of the country by the towns will after the war be on a scale greater by far than we have yet experienced. So will the problems that it brings in its train and, in particular, the problem of the impact of the townsman upon a countryside which having for half a century felt itself the Cinderella of our national economy is jealously resentful of the townsman and will lose no opportunity which comes its way of taking it out of him.

Purpose of the Book

It is to a discussion of these problems that this book is devoted. It is a book about the countryside from the townsman's point of view or, rather, about the countryside as it will present itself *to* the townsman's point of view. Among many disqualifications

[1] I am writing in November, 1944.

I have one qualification for the writing of it. I am equally of the town and the country. My father's people were country people working on the land; my mother's were of the town. I was brought up mainly in the country, partly in the town. Since I grew up, I have lived in London but have gone regularly and of later years increasingly to the country, so that I now spend nearly as much of my time in the country as in London. I am never for any length of time wholly happy in either. In whichever I happen to be in at the moment, the strand which binds me to the other begins to pull and, before a week is done, I am off again to town or country, whichever it may be. In this I am, I think, typical of many men of my time.

In addition to this qualification I have been associated for years with what is called the Open-Air Movement. I am identified with the work of the Ramblers' Association and have a fair working knowledge of such bodies as the Holiday Fellowship, the Co-operative Holidays Association and the Youth Hostels' Association, whose purpose it is to give the townsman some knowledge of the country and to accommodate him when he is there.

Finally, I love the English country which I think the most beautiful in the world, feel intensely patriotic in regard to it, and care passionately that it should be defended and preserved. Like all lovers of good things, I want others to love it too; but I know that, as things are, their affection will spoil the thing they and I love. From this background I have written this book. It is designed to give expression to the following convictions.

Convictions of the Author

First, that the experience of being in the country is a good, good that is to say in itself, and that, lacking it, our lives are the poorer for the lack. The nature of that good is not easy to describe nor shall I here attempt the task. It is, however, pre-eminently a good of the spirit. I content myself with again quoting G. M. Trevelyan's remark that 'agriculture is not merely one industry among many, but is a way of life, unique and irreplaceable in its human and spiritual values'.

Secondly, that to enjoy this good it is not necessary to live and work in the country, although living and working there may be necessary to its *full* enjoyment. It follows that the occasional visitor, the townsman out for a ramble, the week-end walker, even the afternoon-in-the-country walker, will receive in some small part the benison the country has to bestow. It is not necessary, moreover, for these partial enjoyers to be engaged in agriculture. The townsman, then, may in his degree enjoy and receive some part of that fullness of life and richness of spiritual experience which nature can bestow.

If I am asked how I know these things to be so, I have no answer to make. I just see them to be so. For these goods, then, I can offer neither defence nor justification; nor do they need them. If I am right, the split between town and country life which has occurred during the last hundred years is bad; it is, therefore, desirable that it should be healed, in order that the townsman may have more abundantly the chance to enjoy the goods which the country offers, the chance, that is to say, to go and to remain for a space in country *which really is country*. Thus, he will become a fuller being and his life a richer life.

Thirdly, whether or no we agree that the townsman ought to go more to and be more in the country, nothing will, in fact, prevent him from doing so. The week-end and holiday invasion of the country by the towns, great before the war, will be greater afterwards and nothing short of the exhaustion of the world's supply of petrol will avail to stop it.

Fourthly, the right attitude to and use of the country does not come by chance or nature, any more than the right attitude to any other thing that is good and lovely so comes. For we are born in original aesthetic as in original moral sin and our instinctive taste is bad and for what is bad. It is made better by training, teaching and the effect of environment. This truth, which is recognized in the moral, is not usually conceded in the aesthetic sphere. It is a truth, nevertheless, since, as Plato told us, if you bring up a soul in a gracious and harmonious environment, it will itself become gracious and harmonious; conversely, if the environment is mean and ugly, the soul will not come easily to terms with that which is noble and lovely. It follows that we cannot expect those who come for the first time in their hundreds of thousands to the country to know how to treat it or how to behave in it.

Fifthly, this is not a reason for closing the doors, putting up the fences and denying access. It is a reason for making access easy, since, if I am right, it is only by intercourse with the beautiful thing that a man will come to realize that it is beautiful, to love it and treat it as he ought to do. Thus, the education which is necessary before we can comport ourselves as we ought in the country and use it as it should be used, is an education which only the country can give.

Nevertheless, the community more particularly in its executive aspect, the State, can assist in the educative process. Indeed, it has a duty to assist not only because it is at once the purpose and the privilege of a democratic state to ensure that the lives of its citizens shall contain as many elements of value as they can be made to compass, but also because it is the modern democratic state which, by reason of the policy it has pursued in the past, is chiefly responsible for the coming to maturity of a generation which has been disinherited of its just inheritance of the loveliness which is England and deprived of that natural and instinctive knowledge of country sights and sounds which all previous generations of men have possessed as their birthright. It is, then, the duty of the State to help to heal the split which the policy of that same State has introduced. Indications are given in the following pages of the legislation and the administrative changes which are necessary to that end.

Sixthly, the indispensable condition of the retention and increased enjoyment of the goods to which I have referred is the continued existence of the country *as country*. This has been threatened in the past; the threat still exists in the present and it will increase in the future, so much so that, unless steps are taken to avert it, my grandchildren will have grown to maturity without knowing what it is that we who talk of 'the country' mean, so that the goods of which I have spoken will to them be meaningless, as sound is meaningless to a man who has always been deaf, sight to a man who is congenitally blind. The fact that they will not know that they have been deprived does not mean that their deprivation will not be real, or that their lives will not be the poorer because of it.

The Need for Legislation

It is, then, important not only that we may enjoy in the present but that also we may preserve for the future, that we should take such legislative steps as are necessary to ensure that the country remains country and the town town, and that the latter is not permitted either openly to encroach upon the former or covertly to infiltrate into it. Of the two, covert infiltration is the more to be feared.

The English countryside is a heritage of great worth that we have received from our ancestors; we owe it to them no less than to ourselves to hand it on undiminished to our posterity. This we cannot now do, since in our own generation we have already much diminished it. What has been done is, indeed, beyond repair, but fresh impairments can be stopped if we have the will to stop them.

But although the preservation of England's beauty and the continuation of the country tradition and way of life in which some of us have been brought up is a debt that we owe to posterity, it is the immediate rather than the remote future that I have had in mind in the writing of this book. My concern is with the immediate post-war world. The concern is that the disinherited of the towns should visit the country and should come to know it; that the way should be made easy for them; that they should learn how to use the country aright and to bear themselves rightly when they are in it; and that they should not in the process of visiting and coming to know ruin the thing they profess to love, which many of them do, indeed, love, and which more may come to love.

Chapter Two

THE COUNTRY'S ENEMIES

'I would sooner die than see a spire of English grass trampled down by a
foreign trespasser.'—Lord Halifax.

The Ridge of the Malverns

In the August of the last year of the war I walked along the
ridge of the Malvern Hills. I am not an enthusiast for this
West Midland country, though if I had been brought up here
or knew it well enough, I should, no doubt, proclaim it the best
in England. As it is, I find it a shade too soft and too mild. The
plain of the Severn round Upton suggests at times in its richness and lushness an over-ripe fruit. Good skylines are rare and
there is little suggestion of that starkness and bareness with
which the line of the Downs defends the Sussex Weald from a
similar charge. I venture, then, to add a stricture on the score
of featurelessness. Copse, field, small hill, pasture, meadow,
slow-moving river—they go on mile after mile until you come
to the Malverns. Go forty-five miles farther west and you come
to the Welsh border country; to that area which runs up north to
Craven Arms and Bishop's Castle and so into Wales at Welsh-
pool, south to Kington, Leominster and Knighton and west
into Radnor Forest, and you will have a very different story to
tell. This is, I suppose, the most untouched part of the whole
countryside of England south of the Yorkshire dales. It contains
the finest hill, as distinct from mountain scenery in England
and Wales, heaths, moors, rushing rivers, gorges, castles 'the
quietest places under the sun' and Ludlow, which I am often
tempted to think with Bath the loveliest town in the country.
The Teme and his tributaries run everywhere through the most
beautiful scenery. With the exception of Church Stretton, the
prey of retired persons and old ladies, nobody very much has
been to these parts, the area being protected by the unparagoned
inefficiency of the railway system, and I can only hope that no
ill-considered word of mine will take anybody there now.

But to return; I have no right to speak disrespectfully of this Malvern country. It is pleasant and agreeable enough and very English, exemplifying in a high degree of perfection all those well-known characteristics of softness of atmosphere, haziness of outline, thatched cottages, wayside flowers, hedgerows, lush meadows and slow streams, the whole in miniature, so that every quarter of a mile yields a fresh scene and a new view, which are traditionally associated with the English countryside. Distinctive are the half-timbered houses. When you go a little farther west into Herefordshire, you will find whole villages of them—Kilpeck and Weobley, for instance—and very lovely they are.

The Westward View

A walk along the Malvern ridge affords material for reflection upon the condition of the English countryside in the fifth decade of the twentieth century. It also serves as a text for this chapter. You are going northward, we will suppose, and you look to the left. You see Herefordshire; it presents all the characteristics I have so briefly and baldly indicated, plus a lake in the foreground, two or three large country houses standing in their parks and a row of sharp pointed hills stretching over to Ledbury. It is an agreeable and a restful view—you can sit for hours looking at it with continuing pleasure—and in the far distance you can see the Black Mountains guarding the confines of Wales. To say that it is untouched by man would be a falsehood. The lines of hedges, the orderly layout of field and meadow, the farmhouses and cottages pushing up their roofs from within their circles of sheltering elms, even the great trees standing solemn and brooding in the fields or lined in avenues—all these betoken the continual care and tendance of man. But not of modern man; this is England as it has been for two centuries or more and very nice too, in fact, as nice as nice can be.

The Eastward View

Now turn to look eastward; you are looking into Worcestershire and Gloucestershire. (Parenthetically, it is extremely difficult to tell which of these counties is which; Worcestershire in particular is very careless in her boundaries. Fragments of her—she is clearly a feminine county—have been cut off from the parent body and embedded in those of her neighbours, so that to get from one part of her to another you have to traverse across intervening corridors of Gloucester and Warwickshire). This view is not inherently less lovely. To the south stretches the Vale of the Severn, indisputably Gloucestershire; it is flat, fat, green and lush. To the north the country is wooded and rolling. The nearer background is filled by the long ridge of Bredon Hill, while further afield is the outline of the Cotswolds.

But upon this landscape the twentieth century has been at work and the marks of the trampling feet of progress are everywhere visible. What most prominently strikes and affronts the eye is a series of bald, white patches. They are camps, complete with concrete roads, asphalt paths, camouflaged huts, poles, posts, tin, brass, brick and barbed wire. They look like great pallid fungi spreading over the green face of the land. There are five of them in the view and between them they cover a considerable area. Immediately below lies Malvern; its buildings are of every conceivable colour, size and shape, but it itself has no shape. Surrounded by fine commons it sprawls untidily over them, shooting out in every direction tentacles of undistinguished-looking houses. If all these houses were packed together in properly planned streets and crescents, Malvern would occupy rather less than a quarter of its present space. Most of the buildings I can see look ugly—particularly ugly is the angry pink of the vast girls' school. Malvern College for boys is built of stone. From here it seems dignified and grey stone always looks well against the surrounding green. It was built in the Victorian age and is, I imagine, mock Gothic, but from here, as I say, it looks well enough.

Looking further afield, you see a number of scattered patches of pink, as if the land had caught a disease and its face had come out sporadically in a rash. These, I am told, are the suburbs of Malvern. They are set in no pattern and conform to no plan; they have apparently just broken out, broken out anywhere. Between them they cover a considerable area.

Going on to the top of the highest of the hills, the Worcestershire Beacon, I found to my consternation a wretched shed with a wrinkled roof of terracotta-coloured tin. Round it were arranged a number of tables for refreshments. Its windows contained placards announcing the sale of chocolates and cigarettes, while the premises generally were encrusted with the usual scurf of advertisements printed on highly coloured posters and painted on tin plates. From its little tin chimney smoke poured out upon the tables and those who sat at them. The whole was enclosed by iron railings through a gap in which patrons proceeded by an asphalt path to the tables. Mine is no pen to do justice to the ugliness and squalor of this little place.

Upon all the more frequented parts of the hill there was a scatter of broken glass, cigarette cartons and scraps of torn paper. As it was war-time, there was no orange peel but I am told that in the days of peace the top of the hill is white with paper and yellow-white with orange.

These four things, the camp, the unshapely sprawl of Malvern and its outlying suburbs, the tin shed and the litter of glass and paper symbolize between them the forces which in the twentieth century are making England ugly, transforming the loveliness that we have inherited into the squalor that we shall bequeath, and turning the countryside from a land of beauty into a sprawling suburb studded with preserved beauty spots. These are the forces that are eating up the country at so prodigious a rate that unless they are arrested England will in fifty years' time be neither town nor country, but only a single continuous suburb spreading from coast to coast.

This book is designed to celebrate the virtues of the country and to laud the benefits it confers upon those who live in the towns and can, therefore, visit it only at intervals. Its contention is that unless these forces can be controlled, there will presently be left no country for the people of the towns to visit. I accordingly propose to devote the rest of this chapter to a closer examination of the tendencies which camp, sprawl, shed and litter exemplify and to an indication of some of the ways in which they can be counteracted.

THE COUNTRY'S ENEMIES

(1) *Camps and Aerodromes*

First, the camps. That they are, or rather—for I hope that the war will be over by the time this book appears—that they have been necessary, nobody doubts. There may be two opinions as to the suitability of the sites chosen, the amount of land eaten up, the waste of land, of time and of labour when camps, established without adequate forethought, have been used and abandoned or never used at all because the site was too damp, or because there were no men available to fill them; but as to the necessity of these places there can be only one. What concerns me here is their removal. We are an untidy nation and it is rarely that we take the trouble to clear up the messes we have made. Each successive revolution in transport does not remove the *débris* of the last; it leaves it and adds its own. When the Southern Railway electrified its lines, it did not liquidate the traces of the steam transport it had superseded. The derelict engines, the sidings, the coal dumps, the water tanks, the pumps stayed; the paraphernalia of electrification, power houses, dynamo stations, wires, poles and so on were added. The motoring age littered the countryside with garages, petrol pumps and parking places. When we have most of us taken to flying, hangars and runways will be added to the obsolescent garages, which brings me back to the spreading aerodromes begotten upon us by the war. Will they be removed when the war is over and done with? The answer of history is not encouraging. A few years ago I was taken by a friend over Dartford Heath which runs south of the Thames some twelve miles south-east of London. It is on the edge of some very pleasant and surprisingly unspoilt country on the way to Longfield, Meopham and Sole Street. It is, indeed, in this direction that London ends most easily and abruptly and you can walk for a day within twenty miles of Charing Cross on downs crowned with small coppices and studded with yews into little valleys, where one or two or no houses are seen. I have shot pheasants here in a November mist and might have thought myself—did indeed think myself—out on the Wiltshire downs, six or seven miles from the nearest village. To the north and the west are the industrialized areas of Crayford and Dartford.

As we walked across Dartford Heath, we traversed a number of lines of shallow depression which might once have been trenches. 'What are these,' I asked, 'relics of the last war?', meaning the war of 1914–18.

'No,' said my friend, 'these were dug in the Napoleonic wars in 1805 when everybody was expecting England to be invaded. It has been nobody's job to fill them in and they never have been filled in.'

Will it be so, I wonder, with the aerodromes? Probably it will, for far more is involved here in the way of time and effort than is entailed by the filling up of a trench. To disrupt and remove these miles of concrete runways will, I am told, be an immensely laborious task. Even if the will existed, there is at present no body or department in England with the necessary authority to undertake it and so these further erosions of the already diminished area of English soil, these new scars upon its tormented face may well remain simply because it is nobody's business to take them away. Or because the War Office thinks that they are useful, or—such are the aesthetics of war departments— beautiful. The Society of Sussex Downsmen has recently published a statement by the South-East Regional Planning Officer on the subject of the numerous roads which the War Office have driven over the South Downs during the period of war occupation. Many of these are concrete and tar-macadam roads and it has been suggested by the War Department's Command Land Agent that these should be retained as 'a means by which motorists and others will have easier access'. If they are retained, the beauty and solitude of the downs will be permanently destroyed. For concrete and tar-macadam roads, reinforced by abandoned runways and embellished by convenient car parks while, from the motorists' point of view, they may in the words of the War Department's Land Agent, be 'to a certain extent improvements', will ruin the downs for walkers and those who care for solitude and beauty, as completely as similar developments have already ruined the area immediately behind Brighton. What is most disquieting is the statement by the Department's Land Agent that 'the matter will have to be referred to the War Office for a decision'. Why should the War Office decide such questions in peace-time? If any single Government department is to decide over our heads whether beauty is to be retained or destroyed, it should surely be the Ministry of Town and Country Planning.

Or the scars—the roads and the huts and the runways—may remain because it is too expensive to take them away. In June 1945, a measure known as the Requisitioned Land and War Works Act[1] was passed. Its effect is to place the future of all land requisitioned for any purpose by a Government department during the war at the disposal of the Government. The Government, which in this connection means some seven or eight different Government departments, will be advised by a specially appointed Commission responsible to the Crown. Acting on the advice of the Commission, Government departments will have power to retain in perpetuity land which has been requisitioned, paying compensation to the owners; if they do not wish to retain it themselves, they will determine how it shall be disposed of. Thus they can sell it, or restore it to private possession, or even dedicate it to the enjoyment of the public. Under the powers conferred upon him by the Act any one of the Ministers in charge of the owning department can divert a highway or footpath leading to the requisitioned area.

Arguments which have been advanced in favour of retention are: (1) that the camps and aerodromes, more particularly the aerodromes, may be useful in the next war; (2) that a substantial proportion of the war-time erections, particularly hospitals and factories, are of permanent value and benefit to the community; (3) the high cost of clearing away the aerodromes, runways, huts, block houses, anti-aircraft batteries, searchlight stations and all the other structures which the war has deposited upon the land.

It is this consideration of cost which will, I imagine, chiefly weigh with the departments. The question they will put to themselves is, will it cost more to restore the land to its former condition, or to return it unrestored to its former owners and compensate them for the fact that it has not been restored, or to buy it outright? If the relevant Government department thinks the cost of restoration too high, the fences and enclosures will remain, the fields which have been withdrawn from private

[1] For a summary of its provisions see Appendix IX.

cultivation will continue to be withdrawn, the meadows which have disappeared under sheets of concrete will remain covered. In effect, then, many areas which possess high amenity value (including areas whose beauty or wildness commends them for consideration as future National Parks),[1] to the use and enjoyment of which the public were accustomed before the war, but which have been covered with hutments and roads or otherwise spoilt during the war—obvious examples are Studland and Tyneham—may, instead of being restored to the public, be bought outright by the Government and left as they are, because to buy outright will be cheaper than to restore.

The only limitation upon this new power which the Act confers upon Government departments is in the case of common land. This cannot under the Act be retained unless an alternative area of equivalent size is presented for public use. Even here, however, a loophole is left for retention since, provided express Parliamentary sanction is obtained in each case, there is apparently power to retain even the common land. Thus, the State, which once failed to prevent the private enclosures of common land, is now given the power to make fresh enclosures in its own right. The two most disquieting features of this proposed measure are first, the secret procedure which it envisages. Land can apparently be acquired without any right of objection being given to interested persons or local authorities and roads and rights of way extinguished by secret or semi-secret methods. Neither Parliament nor the law courts nor the public will in effect control the doings of the Commission. Secondly, only the most perfunctory mention is made in the Act of the Ministry of Town and Country Planning which, it might have been supposed, would be allowed to hold at least a watching brief on behalf of the amenities. The supposition, I think, is natural enough. If the country is to survive as country, somebody must be charged with the job not only of preservation but of renovation and of restoration; somebody made responsible for the task of clearing up the mess of each successive revolution in industry and transport, of removing the *débris* of each new war and of restoring to public enjoyment or agricultural use land which, in the course of waging it, the Service Departments have destroyed

[1] See ch. v, pp. 106–109.

or stolen from the farmers or the public. But no provision is made in the Act for that necessary 'somebody'.

(2) *The Sprawl*

Our towns sprawl because it is nobody's business to confine them. The medieval town was built to a plan; it had an optimum size and a shape; often it was circumscribed by a wall. Obsessed by the modern craze for the country, we decide to live as far away from the place in which we work as we can contrive, proposing to travel daily to and fro from town. We do travel daily to and fro, but others, it appears, have been imbued with the same idea, with the result that we find we are not living in the country after all, but only in a far-flung extension of the town. Again we are suspicious of our neighbours and cannot tolerate being overlooked. Accordingly, we build our houses as far away from one another as our means will permit. This neighbour-phobia eats up space. As a result of these tendencies, desires and fears, our towns have thrown a scurf of villas and bungalows far and wide over the surrounding countryside. Every year they shoot out longer tentacles of brick, slate and concrete into the circumambient fields; every year larger areas of green are submerged beneath the tide of oncoming pink. If the country is to survive, we need legislation to determine the size of our towns. Upon the growth of large towns we should place severe restrictions; any further growth of London we should bar altogether. We should allow no towns to spread except in accordance with a planned scheme which would take into account the necessity for tracts of country—and by a 'tract of country' I mean something more extensive than a green belt—surrounding the town. Between town and country there should be a clearly defined boundary over which the towns should not be allowed to spill. Cities should not, that is to say, be allowed to surround themselves with an uncouth fringe of villas, reinforced by petrol stations, advertisement hoardings, shacks, cafés and other attendant satellites of the villas to hide and banish[1] the country from their citizens. As for the piles of refuse which our towns dump upon their outskirts, wasting good

[1] This principle entails an extended use of flats, see ch. ix, pp. 189–191.

land, annoying residents and disfiguring the landscape—these should be burnt, or made into compost and employed to reclaim the swamps and foreshores.

(3) *The Shed*

Its like may be seen in many a beautiful place up and down the country, especially if it be a high, beautiful place with a view, such as Newlands Corner, for example, which looks over the Tillingbourne valley to the pine hills of Leith, Holmbury and Pitch, or Whiteways on the downs above Arundel whence there is, or rather was, for they have shamefully cut down many of the big trees in Arundel Park, one of the best views in the south of England. There used to be a superb example of the shanty, all tin and iron and litter complete with its 'Gents' and 'Ladies' on the top of Snowdon, till Mr. Clough Williams Ellis replaced it by a comparatively seemly little hotel.

What are we to deduce from the prevalence of the shanty? That the English by and large have little or no sense of beauty or that, if they have, they allow the utterances of its still, small voice to be smothered by the blare of advertisers or the cries of profit makers; that having by the grace of God been given the loveliest countryside in the world they have done their best in the last fifty years to make it mean and ugly and that most of them, not knowing what it is to be 'mean and ugly', are quite unaware of what they are doing.

Newhaven

These observations are general; let me give them particularity by an account of one or two sample outrages which have been committed on some spot of special prominence or beauty, the summit of a hill, the top of a pass, an old ruin, a lake or the entry to a harbour. Consider, for example, the case of New-haven. As you cross the Channel from Dieppe and near the English coast, you cannot fail to be struck by the magnificence of the Seven Sisters. I must have made the crossing a score of times; yet always these seven dramatic white curves—in fact there are nine, or is it ten?—cut in the face of the green cliff make me catch my breath with their loveliness. Behind are great folds of green down stretching one beyond another, as far as the eye can see. It is, indeed, a wonderful approach, and it is reasonable to suppose that a people who valued beauty would have seen to it that it should have been left in its loveliness to welcome the stranger, as an earnest of the equal loveliness of the land that awaits him. A venturesome people might even have sought to embellish the beauty of nature with the works of man. But even the most indifferent, one would have imagined, would have been at pains to ensure that no unworthiness in the latter should be allowed to detract from the beauty of the former. . . . One would have been wrong. As one's boat approaches the land, one sees that the green of the downs is scarred with the familiar rash of angry pink. The town of Seaford has been allowed to burst its confines and to scatter its litter of bungalows and villas broadcast over the surrounding country. The houses, haphazard as they are, nevertheless contrive to suggest the malevolent design of ruining the largest possible extent of country with the smallest possible quantity of pink slate and concrete. As one runs into Newhaven harbour, one is welcomed to England by a sprawl of little mean buildings, shacks and shanties and tarred sheds, which have been allowed to proliferate over the quayside without plan or order.

The Backs

What is the loveliest half mile in England? For myself, I have no doubt as to the answer. It runs along the Backs at Cambridge from King's in the south past Clare and Trinity and ending behind John's in the north. I have gone there at all times of the year, sitting on some point of vantage or in the grass court behind King's Chapel to look at and take it in. My favourite spot is the north-western corner of this court in the angle between Clare and the river. Here I have sat many times on the grass, eaten my lunch and on occasion gone to sleep. At all times of the year the view is lovely but most of all in spring when the willows come out in their yellow-green and every tint of green is to be seen in the developing elms and beeches; or again in the autumn, when the greens deepen into their many various shades of brown and orange and gold and yellow. I was sitting there on a typical autumn afternoon in the third year of the war. The warm sunlight lay in level shafts across the lawn; in the air there was just that touch of blue, that hint of haze that somehow thickens the atmosphere of an autumn afternoon giving it an opaqueness that it lacks at other seasons, so that at moments it seems almost as if you could touch it. I got up to look northwards at the wing of Clare that forms one side of the quadrangle. After King's Chapel which it neighbours, it is, to my mind, the loveliest building in Cambridge. Behind was Clare bridge, the most graceful, I think, in the country, and below the Cam, flowing smoothly without a ripple and flanked by a miscellany of poplars and willows, elms and beeches, standing up in the green meadows in the last stages of their gorgeous decay. Among them I remember was one Wellingtonia. So much for the views in front and to the right. To the left I dared not look for on the leftward scene the twentieth century had entered— entered to some purpose. Just across the river was drawn up a long line of jeeps and lorries. They had stood there, I was told, for a year or more and were destined to remain until the end of the war. They were flanked, surrounded and infiltrated by all the accompaniment and appurtenances of the Forces, notably asphalt paths, dumps, barbed wire, sheds, latrines, portable kitchens and shanties—the whole presenting a scene as ugly as King's and Clare are beautiful. These things are the characteristic emanations of the twentieth century, as King's and Clare are of the fifteenth and the late seventeenth, and it had planted them just across the river opposite the Colleges, as if to cock a deliberate snook of derision at the beauty that our forefathers knew how to create, but which we do not know how to respect. 'Why here? Oh, why just here of all places in the world?' I asked myself. 'The Forces have all the rest of England to dump on and deploy in; they might have left this loveliest half mile alone.' But no! Wanstead Flats and the Breckland go undumped on and undeployed in; the Backs behind King's are chosen for latrines. 'Did nobody', I asked later on in the King's Common Room, 'protest?' For King's, after all, is the centre of Cambridge culture; there beats such heart of reverence for beauty and respect for the things of the spirit as Cambridge in the twentieth century still possesses. But my friend told me that against this desecration nobody had raised a voice. The King's dons, he said, the appointed guardians of the beauty of the place, were afraid of being thought unpatriotic. Thus, 'Beauty is set at nought and no man regardeth. O God! O Montreal and, also, O King's!'

I should add that in the corner between Clare and the river where I used to sit there is now an N.F.S. hut made of the most respectable concrete and a large iron pipe which stretches across the lawn and protrudes into the river.

Such during the war is the case of the Cambridge Backs and, for all I know to the contrary, so far as the wire and the sheds and the asphalt and the pipe and the latrines are concerned, such it may well remain, for, as I have already said, it is nobody's business in this country to remove the mess which it is everybody's business to make.

Marlow Bottom

Or—for another sample—take the case of Marlow Bottom. This is a long winding valley running from Marlow up into the Chilterns. I walked up it on a lovely autumn day, expecting to eat my lunch in solitude amid such quiet beauty as the Chiltern valleys—in Bix Bottom, for instance—can so abundantly provide. To my horror I found not an empty valley but a muddy road running through an avenue of shacks, caravans, villas, bungalows, mock castles, pigsties, disused railway carriages and derelict buses, scattered higgledy-piggledy over the largest possible area of the Chiltern hillsides. Each dingy little abode in this rural setting was distinguished by some dreadful appellation, as, for example, Eretiz, The Nest, The Splendide, Kosy-Kot, Mon Abri, Linga-Longa, or U-an-I, as if to throw into even grimmer relief the dreariness and the shabbiness of the dwellings which facetiousness sought to enhance or pretentiousness to dignify. The thing went on for miles, nor was it until I topped the ridge that lies between Marlow and the Wycombes that I lost sight of these awful places, only to find myself almost immediately in a world of rural factories where ladies' corsets and electric light bulbs competed for the privilege of eating up what was once first-class agricultural land.

Vale of Health

Or take a case near to my heart because near to my home—the Vale of Health in Hampstead. A few hundred yards across the Heath there is a depression forming a small bowl or basin in the sandhills. At the bottom is a lake approached on one side by a stretch of level ground, overhung on the other by a half circle of rising ground. Creeping down the slope and ranged along the borders of the lake are houses. A better spot for the relaxation of the inhabitants of a great city it would be hard to imagine. We are less than five miles here from the centre of London and, if this were the continent, one could imagine citizens coming out with their families on a summer evening to sit at tables on balconies by the lake, to eat and drink, to talk and smoke. There would be secluded walks and arbours where lovers could make love. The terrace would be hung with baskets of flowers and lighted with Chinese lanterns and on state occasions there would be fireworks. Here one could sit after a good dinner, watching the lights reflected in the lake, listening to the orchestra—for, of course, there would be an orchestra—and savouring the life of the great city just beyond the rim of the horizon. One could in a word relax in surroundings whose natural beauty had been improved by the art of man.

But this is not the continent, this is England, with the result that the finest site in North London is neglected. A row of dingy red villas runs along beside the lake. The villas culminate in a pub with a terrace which overlooks the water but it is rarely used, nor is food provided. Men and women stand drinking at the bar indoors, for all the world as if there were no such things as lake and Heath outside the door. There are no flowers, no walks, no arbours, no terrace, no lanterns, no fireworks; only a few old roundabouts, hangovers from the Hampstead Heath Bank Holiday, dismally churning out their mechanical versions of the noises of the jungle.

It is too much, I suppose, to ask that we should create beauty, but why do we so abuse the opportunities that have been given us and so set at nought the beauty that has come down to us? The answer is long and complex and I am not sure that I know it all but part of it is to be found in our conception of the duty of the State, or, rather, in the State's conception of its duty and itself.

Duties of the State. Old Conceptions and New

Looking back over history one notes how all the great civilizations of the past have known and acted upon an important truth. It is that man does not live by bread alone, but also by circuses; that he lives, in other words, not only by work but in play. And I here use the word 'play' to mean not merely the hitting, whacking, pushing and stroking of little round bits of matter at the right time, at the right speeds, and in the appropriate directions by longer and thinner ones in the shape of bats, mallets, rackets, and cues, and the watching of other people hitting, whacking, pushing and stroking; but the erecting, at public expense, of noble works and monuments in which the spirit of the civilization should receive permanent embodiment, so that future ages should marvel at the skill of its craftsmen, at the vision that inspired its artists, and the public spirit which actuated its rulers. In the speech which he delivered at the funeral of those members of the Athenian community who had been killed in the first year of the Peloponnesian War, Pericles speaks of the provision of recreations for the spirit, 'contests and sacrifices all the year round and beauty in our public buildings', as being among the obligations which the civilized State owed to its citizens.

'Play' also includes the staging of public shows and ceremonies in which citizens may take delight when their work is done and feel at one with the community, being imbued with a gaiety and lifted to an exaltation of spirit beyond what they could as individuals compass, and given a sense of the beauty and passion of life keener and more vivid than their unaided vision could realize. Thus the Colosseum in Rome, the Parthenon in Athens, the Hanging Gardens of Babylon, the amphitheatres, the baths, the palaces, the law courts of Roman antiquity are permanent expressions of the greatness of the civilizations that they embellished.

With the coming of Christianity the spirit of the age found its noblest outlet in the construction of cathedrals. (Why is it, by the way, that whenever we are moved to express our admiration for some monument or building, it turns out nine times out of ten to be several hundreds of years old, while the greatest commendation we can make of our towns, villages or inns is to say that they are unspoilt, meaning that they are not as yet spoilt by us?) The shows and ceremonies and festivals which the ancient and medieval State fostered and promoted, the folk dancings and merry-makings and harvest-homes which sprang from the people themselves, were a no less notable expression of the public recognition of the truth that man cannot live by bread alone; that he must play as well as work.

About the end of the eighteenth century there was ushered in by the industrial revolution a new conception of the State and of the functions which it might legitimately assume; a conception that embodied one of the most damnable heresies that has ever militated against the happiness of mankind.

This conception limited the State's function to economics. That it should pay now became the sole criterion that it was legitimate to apply to the activity of the State; pay, that is to say, in returns of hard cash to the State, or pay by contributing to the accumulation of hard cash by private persons. 'Brass', as they called it in the North, became the sole standard of value and the sole ground for State action.

To spend public money on non-economic purposes was to waste it; even expenditure on education and health was defended on the ground that it paid—a man was a better clerk if he knew the multiplication table, a more lucrative workman if he was not constantly going sick. Under the influence of this conception, architecture, music, the theatre and the provision of public shows and ceremonies have all fallen into desuetude. We take it for granted that our State should *not* build pyramids, colosseums, parthenons, cathedrals or palaces; it seems to us wholly in the nature of things that it should *not* provide out of public funds a State theatre or a State opera house, where the best dramatic and musical art of the age could be enlisted for the ennoblement and delight of its citizens.

It was in continuance of this tradition or, rather, it was in continuance of this break with tradition that, when the nineteenth century embarked upon the building of its cities, it should have been guided by no considerations except the narrowly utilitarian and the strictly economic. Hence arose the industrial town of the nineteenth century which—I am quoting from G. M. Trevelyan's *English Social History*—'in the unplanned swamp of its increase lacks form and feature; it is a deadening cage for the human spirit. . . . The pall of smoke and smuts in itself was enough to discourage any effort after beauty or joy in the visible aspect of life. . . . And to make matters worse, there had been practically no town planning of the Victorian cities. The State had permitted the landlord and the speculative builder to lay out modern England as best suited their own private gain, too often without a thought given to amenity or to the public welfare.'

A Vicious Circle

How can we contrive to change this conception of the State's function, so that it shall once again be prepared to admit the existence and the efficacy of spiritual goods and to regard the provision of beauty as well as of bread as falling among its functions? It may be that the establishment of C.E.M.A.[1] bears witness to the beginning of such a change, especially since steps have recently been taken to establish it as a permanent feature of our national life.

Meanwhile we find ourselves enclosed within the circumference of a vicious circle. Until the conception of the duties of the State developed by nineteenth-century capitalism is superseded, it is unlikely that the English will grow up in an environment of beautiful things; until they are accustomed to beauty, they will not recognize it when it is present or miss it when it is absent; unless they acclaim its presence and feel its lack in absence, they will not insist that it should be provided for them and will remain content with the purely economic State or, should the State become benevolent, will be satisfied with a benevolence whose ministrations are limited to the things of the body. We shall find ourselves enclosed within the same circle many times during the ensuing pages nor, short of a fall in the population, do I see how it is to be broken. But of this, more in the last chapter.

[1] Now made permanent as the Arts Council of Great Britain.

4. *The Litter*

We pass here by an easy transition to the fourth feature of the Malvern landscape, the glass, the cigarette cartons, the bits of paper. These, it is obvious, are only the exiguous representatives of what, when peace is once more let loose upon us, will become an inundating flood of litter. In peace-time the top of the Malvern Beacon would have been carpeted with paper—newspaper, brown paper, tissue paper, paper bags—for democracy, when it goes to call upon the country, insists on leaving its visiting card behind it.

And why should it not? Who has taught it that you should not do these things? Plato told us that if you bring up a youth in a beautiful and graceful environment, then his soul will take shape and colour from the environment that it reflects and show forth the pattern of beauty in the form of good taste and good manners. If this is true, so too, it is obvious, is the converse. Reflect for a moment upon the acres of mean streets and undistinguished houses with which unrestricted private enterprise seized by the mania for quick profits covered England in the last century. We can see them by driving in any direction from the centre of London to its outskirts. The predominant note is not even hideousness, but a monotonous dreariness of bricks and mortar unparalleled, one believes and hopes, in the universe. And it stretches for miles and miles and miles of desolation, not a wen, as Cobbett in his day called it, but a vast malignant growth. What a monument to nineteenth-century civilization it is, this teeming desert of mean houses, ugly shops, ugly houses and mean shops repeating themselves endlessly from Woolwich to Wimbledon, from Purley to Highgate, and from Acton to Wood Green. To quote again from G. M. Trevelyan's *English Social History*, 'to millions the divorce from nature was absolute, and so too was the divorce from all dignity and beauty and significance in the wilderness of mean streets in which they were bred whether in the well-to-do suburb or the slum'. Is it any wonder that those brought up amid such surroundings should reflect in their tastes and pursuits the environment which has stamped their souls, that they should like trivial books, empty plays and vulgar films, and that they should be so little able to come to terms with nature that their reaction to natural beauty, when they do come into contact with it, should be to fence and to enclose it, to deluge it with litter, to uproot its flowers and carve its trees, spoiling and ravishing it, until they have effectively destroyed the beauty they could not understand?

You cannot bring up a people in mean streets and ugly houses and ask of them that they should recognize beauty or respect nature. When they do not ignore nature, turning their backs upon the view in order to cluster round the picture postcard shops and the pubs, they will prey upon her and pollute her. And so to the cartons and the glass we must add the piles of tin cans, disused pots and pans and the litter of household refuse which can be seen on the suburban fringes of all our great towns guarding the approaches to the country. We must add, too, the uprooting of wild flowers, the bundles of bluebells tied to the handlebars of bicycles, the rows of daffodils and kingcups and primroses that may be seen in the shops and on the stalls of our big cities and the rare plants dug up to make a suburban garden, or a collector's museum. We must add, too, the destruction of wild life, the rare birds that are persecuted into non-existence by collectors—look, there is a harrier, or a bustard! let us shoot it, or take its eggs and then it will be rarer still!—and the common or garden, everyday birds that are preyed upon by the townsman out on holiday or spending his week in the country and still more by the townsman's evacuee children.

The Bird-Blinding Boys

It was in the summer of 1940 that I was walking along a lane in Monmouthshire. I wish I had the art to describe it, for Monmouth is a comparatively unknown county. The Wye Valley, a stuffy ravine, gathering place of tourists, who have nowhere to walk except up the steep sides or along the bottom of the ravine and very little to do with themselves, everybody knows. To the north are the Black Mountains, beautiful enough with their long ridges and deep valleys, but for some reason not as beautiful as you think and less enjoyable than you expect. The rest of Monmouth is comparatively unknown. To the south there is a ridge of moderate-sized hills looking southwards over the Bristol Channel and intersected on their northern side by a number of cup-like depressions. These are heavily wooded and sparsely populated, the absence of villages being a distinguishing feature of this part of the world. Here and there a solitary poplar of great size stands out, ejaculation marks commenting enigmatically upon the scene, and everywhere there are deep lanes and footpaths. As I was turning the corner of one of these, I came upon three schoolchildren clustered round something that one of them, a boy of about ten, held in his hand. They looked up apprehensively as I approached but went on with what they were doing. This was sticking a needle into the eyes of a young robin. There was a nest of five a couple of weeks old in the bank immediately opposite and each of the nestlings had been treated in the same way. When they had been blinded, the young birds were returned living to the nest. I should have dismissed this as an isolated example of childish sadism, were it not that about the same time a correspondence had broken out in the *New Statesman* in which a number of countryfolk testified amid a stream of shocked and indignant denials from nice-minded townspeople that they had witnessed similar behaviour on the part of children, usually evacuees, in their own district.

I could, of course, cite dozens of examples of more commonplace and familiar outrages, writing of the gates that are left open for the straying of cattle, and the glass that is left scattered for their laming; of the match or the cigarette end that is dropped for the burning of dried grass and the starting of heathland fires; of the sports cars that hurl themselves bombinating at the rear through the quiet village street and of the sweating girls in shorts that enlarge without enhancing their charms; the crowd of hikers singing raucously at night as they pass through the village where everybody is asleep—but these and similar incidents have figured in dozens of books and hundreds of letters to the Press from outraged countrymen. Accordingly, I take as an extreme example of the disastrous effects of the townsman's impact on the country the case of the bird-blinding boys.

THE COUNTRY'S ENEMIES

Some Conclusions

In the light of it, I venture to put forward the following propositions:

(1) This behaviour on the part of the townspeople newly come to the country and knowing nothing of its ways, manners and needs is in some degree inevitable.

(2) The fact that it occurs is not a reason for forbidding the 'townees' to come or for making their coming difficult, any more than the fact that the young jazz addict who beats time audibly with his feet cannot distinguish the difference between Bach and Chopin constitutes a reason for forbidding him to attend concerts of chamber music, since it is only by intercourse with what is good that one recognizes that it is good and learns how to comport oneself when brought into contact with it.

(3) That whether it is, in fact, a reason or not is immaterial, since the number of townspeople going at all times into the country by car, motor bus, train, cycle and on foot, large before the war, is certain, as I pointed out in the first chapter, to grow very much larger.

On Education

It follows that the position of the countryside in regard to manhandling by human beings is like the position of a woman undergoing a difficult pregnancy. It will become worse before it is better. In the long run the only cure is education. People should be taught by the spiritual climate of the society which they breathe how to behave in the country and how to respect it: in other words, they should grow up with good manners and good taste. But here, once again, we come within sight of the vicious circle, since the climate of a society can only induce good manners and good taste in its younger generation, when good taste and good manners distinguish their elders by whom the climate is formed.

These general considerations apply more particularly to the case of teaching. It is urged that we should give children in school specific instructions as to how to behave in the country, instructions about the gates and the glass, the bluebells and the nestlings. I have more to say on this topic in a final chapter. Meanwhile I make two obvious points; first, it is only a community which is itself sensible of the value of these things, a community which knows that man cannot live by guns and butter alone but also by beauty and the spirit, that will consent to set aside time and money for the giving of such instruction; secondly, the instruction will itself be of little use, unless the children are in fairly constant contact with the country to which it relates. I return to this point in the last chapter.

Some Interim Suggestions

Meanwhile we must be content with small things; here, then, are a number of fairly obvious suggestions in regard to litter and wild flowers to be put into operation so soon as the war is over.

First, Local Authorities are endowed with powers for the restraint of litter.[1] The operation of these powers should be made compulsory and not as at present permissive. Penalties should be imposed for litter offences and publicity should be given to them over the radio. The police should take the names of first offenders as they do in the case of motoring offences, and increasing penalties culminating in imprisonment should be imposed for each fresh offence. The same measures might be applied to the ruthless uprooting of wild flowers. Local Authorities already have powers and some have passed by-laws[1] making it an offence to pick or take away the flowers, seeds or roots of certain specified wild flowers; but little use has been made of these powers, nor are steps taken to see that the by-laws are observed. I would suggest that in this case, too, the operation of the law should cease to be optional and should become compulsory; it should, that is to say, be made incumbent upon Local Authorities to protect the flora of their region and to take active steps to bring offenders to book. It should, however, in this connection be pointed out that Local Authorities are themselves on occasion guilty of the very offences which I am pleading that they should restrain, in that they ruthlessly chop down roadside

[1] See Appendix VIII.

herbage throughout the growing season, thus depriving country lanes of much of their charm. It is not necessary when exterminating pernicious weeds to uproot beautiful and harmless plants. Incidentally Local Authorities might well be asked to adopt and extend the admirable policy decided upon in 1938 by the Cornwall County Council which issued instructions to its road men not to cut down foxgloves.

Chapter Three

IN PRAISE OF WALKING

Learning to Walk

It was not until I came as a young man of twenty-three to London, that I took to walking.

I had been brought up for the most part in the country, but if you live in the country you take walking very much for granted, which means, in practice, that you don't take it at all. Tree climbing, yes; mushrooming, yes; birds' nesting and butterfly catching, a hundred times, yes. But none of these is walking and for a country child to go for a walk, a walk and nothing but a walk, for walking's sake is a penance. (I have always believed that children have no souls.) At Oxford I was too busy. The excitement and zest of living left no time, even if the fever of a mind intoxicated by ideas had permitted the serenity which nature demands for her enjoyment. But I hated London directly I saw it and I wanted to walk out of it whenever I could. Walking out of it meant a train to Gerrards Cross or Clandon on a Sunday morning, or, if I were in funds, on a Saturday afternoon. It was chiefly to Bucks that I went in those early days, with chattering parties of Fabians, and, as we tramped through the beechwoods about Chorley Wood, or over the chalk hills near Wendover, we talked of the new world of Socialism which in those days seemed just round the corner—at least, that is what we talked about in theory; in practice, I suppose, like any other party we talked about the other members of the party and of whom we liked and did not like and why. We even pushed on occasion as far as Turville and Fingest and crossed Christmas Common, where is the cream of Bucks walking and the secret heart of the county. As the years went by, however, it was increasingly to Surrey that I went; first, to the Boxhill and Ranmore country; then, as the infection from London spread outwards, southwards to Leith Hill and Friday Street; then farther west to Albury, Blackheath and Pitch Hill and finally, still westward and southward to—as I still go there, it is obvious that I cannot say where—but the sandhills, Leith, Holmbury and Pitch, are behind me and the Weald with its streams and little copses in front. Here is one of the most varied stretches of country in Southern England. For me it is pre-eminently connected with winter walking for it is obvious, is it not, that different kinds of country are for different seasons; you don't eat Christmas pudding in August—not if you are wise.

Winter Walking

And to my mind, the best time for walking is the winter. Many townsmen know little of the joys of winter walking, and only venture into the country in weather that is fine and warm. Winter, they think, is cold and wet. Cold it may be, and why not, pray? For my part, I like the cold, which brisks me up so that I can keep up with anybody on a cold day. But wet it most certainly is not, at least, not especially wet. It rains far more, I am convinced, in July and August than ever it does in December and January.

In the winter I can go across country. There is no undergrowth in the woods; there are no crops in the fields and no bracken on the slopes. One walks free and unencumbered and, broadly speaking, one walks where one likes.

And how much more one sees! In August the country is muffled under a blanket of dull green. The blanket spoils its shape and blurs its contours. (It is sad to think that August, which is the dullest month of the year, is the only month in which most people see the country.) The winds of winter have stripped the blanket away and laid bare the bones and naked structure of the countryside. And how lovely that structure is! I would give all the tender greens of young spring, all the gorgeous colours of the autumn woods' decay, for the bare boughs of an oak with its tracery of little twigs silhouetted against the dark red of an afternoon sky in December. The sun has just set and over against it, glimpsed through the infinitely lovely pattern work of the twigs, there is an evening star. There is a tang in the air; the earth rings hard under the feet; there will be a frost to-night. So home to a coal fire, with lamplight and curtains drawn; the kettle boiling on the hob, and crumpets for tea. What has summer to offer comparable to these winter delights?

A Walk in Surrey

To-day has been just such a day and now, at the end of it, I am enjoying just such a moment. I left London yesterday evening, spent the night with a friend at Guildford and took the bus early in the morning to Smithwood Common.

Smithwood Common is within striking distance of that stretch of country which in the winter I most love, a stretch which, taking Peaslake as a centre, has for its northern boundary the slopes of the North Downs from Merrow in the west to Headley in the east; for its eastern, a line running through Headley southwards to Ockley; for its southern, the Fold country, which is ranged along the borders of Surrey and Sussex; and for its western, a line running northwards through Hascombe Hill to the Cranleigh–Guildford road. It is a very varied stretch, ranging from wooded chalk downs in the north through sandhills covered with heather and pine in the middle, to the country of the Weald in the south.

This last is very lovely and has as yet been scarcely defiled by our times. It is a land of little hills and valleys, so small that one's view changes with every quarter mile; of hazel and chestnut copses through which flow little streams; of big parks running up to the foot of the sandhills in the north and studded with mighty trees. The best time for it is late winter and very early spring, when the primroses and daffodils come as easily and as abundantly as anywhere in the south of England. (I have often found primroses under the lee of Pitch Hill in December.) But the flowers here are at all times incredibly profuse, the hazel copses being carpeted, first with yellow and then, as the primroses give way to bluebells, with blue. Carpeted, I insist, is the exact word; you cannot put your foot down without treading on flowers.

Through this country I walked in the morning, going across country from Smithwood to Ewhurst. This area is not well adapted to winter walking, the streams being swollen to little torrents and the mud being the lush, sticky clay mud of the Weald. But for all that the walk was lovely enough and I was content. I had my bread, cheese and onion in a little beerhouse in Ewhurst and listened to the usual talk of the blackout and the high cost of living. (In parenthesis, it is one of the minor drawbacks of the war that it has still further obliterated the already diminishing gulf which separates town from country talk.)

After lunch I climbed up on to Pitch Hill and then went north-west through the great Hurt Wood. A gloomy tract this, where nothing grows and no bird sings, though occasionally a yaffle laughs. The trees are for the most part dwarf oaks which are said to be enormously old, for this is part of the primeval forest of England; but there are also great belts of pines which fringe the sides of ravines and on a dull day, when the wind soughs through the trees, very sombre they look and very gloomy they sound. But this was a calm afternoon with a clear light in the sky and just a hint of frost in the air, and by the time I came to the stretch of green country which separates the Hurt Wood from Blackheath, I was in a state of considerable exhilaration. This again is a miniature country of little hills covered with copses and valleys threaded by streams, but interestingly different from that of the Weald. There the soil is thick and clayey; here, light with an admixture of sand. As a consequence the vegetation is less lush, the grass less green and the trees smaller. But there are some beautiful hidden valleys running into Blackheath both from the north and from the south sides, and along one of these there runs a brook full of watercress. I descended at tea-time, tired and muddy, upon a friend who lives on the other side of Albury.

The foregoing is for Londoners and it is Londoners' country that it describes. Those who live in the North have a far greater variety of riches from which to choose. The Peak District and Kinderscout, for example, upon which the hand of the keeper lies heavy[1]; the dales of north-west Yorkshire, the less celebrated, but no less lovely moors of East Yorkshire, stretching from Guisborough in the north to Malton in the south; Northumberland and the Cheviot country and, above all, the Lake District. Even I—effete Southerner that I am—know something of these

[1] See ch. vi., pp. 118–121.

joys and have sought in the next two chapters to celebrate some parts of them as they deserve.

Sussex Walking

In these later years, I have increasingly exchanged Surrey for Sussex—though it is a quarter of a century now since friendship first took me to the Amberley country. The stretch of downs running north-westward from Arundel to the Cocking Gap and then north-west by west again to Harting Down and so through the muddled country that lies beyond to the south and west and is bounded by the Portsmouth road, is, to my mind, the finest in the south of England. Barring Dartmoor, it beats Devonshire hollow, and it is lovely and large enough to contain farms which are four miles from the nearest house and an inn which, lost these many years in the folds of the downs, maintains an ever-flowing stream of enchanted beer supplied to it by invisible hands through a magic pipe. But of this, too, more in a later chapter.[1]

The Three Joys of Walking

So much for some places for walking. What of its pleasures? The pleasures of walking are as various as the needs which it fulfils. But of these pleasures most are mutually exclusive, and we do wrong to try to enjoy them together. You must not, for example, expect to enjoy or even notice Nature, if you make one of a chattering party; or to absorb something of Nature's spirit, if you are in the woods with the girl you love; or in deep converse along the roads with a friend. Walking and talking are two good things but, for my part I agree with Hazlitt, they must not be mixed.

Here, then, are the three main joys of walking. First, there is walking alone to heal the ills of the soul; 'I have two doctors, my left leg and my right. . . .' It is thus that G. M. Trevelyan, Master of Trinity College, Cambridge, begins his celebrated essay, *Walking*, bidding us call in the doctors for every disease of the mind and distress of the soul. Walk long enough and far

[1] Ch. x, pp. 208–210.

enough and there is no trouble which at the end of the day will not look different and feel lighter.

Secondly, there is walking for company and walking to know your friend. Go alone for a day's walk with a man or, still better, go for a day's scramble in the mountains, and you will know more of him at the end of it than after a month of Sundays in the town. Nature opens the heart and sweeps away the cobwebs of inhibition; there is a something free and unrestrained about one's intercourse with those with whom one walks in the country, so that converse about little, immediate things—'What was that flower?' 'Where shall we have tea?' 'How many miles before we get there?' 'What is the name of that hill?' 'Did you see that squirrel?'—takes on a new significance and creates a bond of invisible threads between those who hold it. But, I insist, they should be little things. How in my secret soul I have hated and sometimes broken out into articulate resentment against those who think a moor the right place to air their views on Socialism or Town Planning, or who discuss Theology on the seashore. Discussions are artificial things and for the artificiality of indoors; it is a poor compliment to Nature to use her as an arena for the airing of our views; we do better to let her air our brains.

(Two other warnings! If you have been out walking all day with a man, contrive, if you can, a change of company for the evening. Secondly, don't make the mistake of trying to renew at the same level of intercourse in the town the friendship you have made in the country. That way disillusion lies.)

Thirdly, a man walks that he may be impregnated by Nature. I see that I have been betrayed into the use of a gross physical metaphor, yet I know no other that will so accurately convey my meaning. I am one of those who in despite of my reason which, drilled in philosophy, can find no grounds for the belief, are strong, instinctive animists. I believe, that is to say, that there are still in this country of England Nature gods or spirits which, though palpably dying, are not yet dead. The motor, the bungalow and the other emanations of the twentieth century have nearly killed them; nearly, but not quite, and there are still places—in the Rusland valley among the southern foothills of the Lakes, for example, or in the remote downland country south of Kingsclere on the Berkshire–Hampshire border—where they manifestly abide. But even where their presence is less manifest, there is, it seems to me, a something in Nature which enters into and mixes with the spirit of man. In England this something is beneficent and fertilizing. (This is not the case with Nature everywhere, not, I imagine, in the Sahara Desert, or in the Amazon Jungle; one is reminded of that cautionary essay, of Aldous Huxley's, *Wordsworth in the Tropics*.) But if Nature is to fertilize she must be given her chance to do her work. Hence, it is good that a man should be sometimes alone with Nature, with his senses open to country sights and sounds and his mind fallow, which means, of course, that he must be by himself, or at least in the company of one whom he knows so well that there is no need for the passing of words. But, even so, it is better that he should be alone. Besides, he can more easily go across country when alone without being under the necessity of explaining to others why he chose this particular gap in the hedge, or why it is necessary for the women to expose their silk stockings to the embraces of brambles.

Cross Country Walking

For it is across country that you must go, if you would get from Nature all that she can give—and this, I insist, would remain true even if the roads had not been turned into an inferno of noise and stench by the cars. Through a farmyard, over a couple of fields, into a copse, down a lane, through a village, over a stile, into a park, and so through fields again—that is the kind of walk I like best.

Such mixed and varied country is the peculiar glory of southern England. Every hundred yards there is a new scene; every quarter of a mile the country has a new feel and a flavour of its own, and like the courses of a perfectly chosen meal, each feel and each flavour enchances and is enhanced by what went before and comes after. It is by these feels and flavours and essences—it is obvious that I have no language to phrase what I am trying to convey—that the soul is impregnated. One returns to the world of men and things, I will not say a better and a nicer person, but a calmer and a quieter, with a replenished fund of energy to tackle one's tasks and duties, and a new strength of serenity to bear one's crosses and distresses. Moreover, one is purged, purged of the littlenesses and meannesses, which most of us harbour in our souls, so that this grudge you were bearing appears in its true colours, that slight you had resented is seen in its right perspective.

That Pleasure in Nature must not be taken for Granted

A final word of warning. You must not expect all or any of these effects to be had for the asking. As with all things that are of enduring value, the mastery of a subject, the affection of a friend, the appreciation of first-rate work in art and literature, a right relationship with Nature must be worked and striven for, sometimes with sweat, often with boredom, inevitably through periods of disillusionment. For being no longer natural creatures, we do not find it easy to come to terms with Nature. As W. H. Hudson, to my mind the greatest writer on the countryside in the English language, puts it: 'We are not in Nature; we are out of her, having made our own conditions, and our conditions have reacted upon us and made us what we are, artificial creatures. Nature is now something pretty to go and look at occasionally but not too often, nor for too long a time.' And that, I suspect, is true for most of us.

The Literature of Walking

I have now said my piece in commendation of walking, adding my humble tribute to the noble meed of praise by those many English walkers who have delighted to celebrate its joys. Let those who have cared for walking about the countryside as I have done, yet do not know the great literature—an almost exclusively English literature, by the way—that the subject has evoked, read Hazlitt on *Going on a Journey*, Stevenson's essay on *Walking Tours* or, best of all, G. M. Trevelyan's essay, *Walking*— I quoted the opening sentence a few pages back.

In a different vein is the series of books on the English countryside by W. H. Hudson. Hudson walked about England at the beginning of the century mostly through north Hampshire,

Sussex, Wiltshire and Dorset, observing the habits of birds and beasts and staying in the cottages of country folk. In earlier days he travelled with his wife. At this time he travelled on a bicycle, on one bicycle not two, for to Hudson goes the credit of inventing a new mode of married travel. He must, I suppose, have seen enough of his wife in the St. Luke's Road, Bayswater, where at one time they ran a cheap boarding house; but they were too poor to afford separate holidays, too poor, it would seem, even to buy two bicycles. For holidays, therefore, Hudson devised the following plan. Every morning he and his wife would start out together, one on a bicycle, the other on foot. The cyclist would ride three or four miles, dismount, hide the bicycle by the roadside and proceed to walk. In due course the first walker would reach the bicycle, mount, cycle up to and three miles past the second walker, dismount, hide the bicycle and proceed to walk . . . and so on until the end of the day. There are two advantages in this mode of travel for husband and wife; first, each of the pair rides half-way and half the day; second, neither of the pair is in company with the other until the evening comes and the day's journey is done. In the evening, for all I know, Hudson may have devised something else.

That great series of books, *A Shepherd's Life*, *Nature in Downland*, *Afoot in England*, *Adventures among Birds*, *The Book of a Naturalist*, *Hampshire Days*—there are nearly a dozen of them—are the product of a later period when Hudson went on foot and alone.

Walking alone is, as I have said, the best way to see the countryside; it is also the best way to enter into possession of oneself. I cannot, however, but be conscious that it is natural for me, as it is for everybody else, to hold that my way is the best way; I think, in fact, that there is nothing like shoe leather. I must admit, then, to having praised walking in this chapter partly because it is the only way of seeing the country I know—or was, until I took to riding, of which I shall have something to say in the next chapter.[1] Let me, then, confess my consciousness that such praise as I have given to walking might be bestowed by others on cycling, by others again on camping, by yet others on climbing and by some be given merely to lounging. Here are five noble ways of making contact with Nature and

[1] Ch. iv, pp. 73–76.

finding satisfaction for that need for country sights and sounds which in most of us, whether we know it or not, is instinctive.

Importance of Access to the Country

Now who shall say that these pleasures of ours are ignoble? Who will go so far as to assert that in any strict sense of the word they are pleasures at all? I don't mean that they are not pleasant; of course they are pleasant, but to call them 'pleasures' and so to assert their affinity with motoring, or watching football matches, or eating strawberries and cream, or drinking, or making love, as if their pleasantness were the most significant thing about them is, it is obvious, to falsify them. For it is nonsense to say that pleasure is the most important, nonsense even to say that it is the most ostensible element in the benison that descends upon one with one's hot bath, dry clothes, ham and eggs and tea after a day's battling with wind and rain on the moors or the hills. So much I affirm from the evidence of introspection. It is supported by observation. I challenge anybody who was a spectator of the invasion of the country by young people in those fine summers just before the war, who watched the youth hostellers, the ramblers, the cyclists, the scouts, the guides and the campers to deny that what they achieved in escaping from the oppression of the towns was a good thing, good no less for their souls than for their bodies. For the feel of the air upon the skin and of the sun upon the face; the tautening of the muscles of the legs as we climb; the sting of rain upon our cheeks, the mellow glow of an October afternoon as we walk beneath the row of elm trees by the riverside—these things are not of the body alone; they have their influence upon every side of our being.

Walking out of the Towns

Having, as I shall suppose, taken you with me up to this point, I now propose to take advantage of you with the question, what is to be the future of walking?

Walking for the town dweller has, it is obvious, become something of a luxury. It is, for example, something that costs money for, since the country receded from the town, he must pay to reach it. Let us suppose that he is a Londoner deciding to go for a walk. He fixes for his objective a village some twelve miles out of London; it is the sort of place that the townsman in search of rest and recreation naturally inclines to picture to himself as a suitable goal for his week-end walk. In the nineteenth century he would have taken a bus three or four miles out of London and walked the remaining seven or eight over fields, along footpaths and down lanes. Now his way lies along a motor road lined with houses, whose centre is a maelstrom of hurtling cars. If he tries to leave it, he finds himself entangled in a maze of private houses and their gardens, isolated pimples in the rash with which the green face of England has in the neighbourhood of our towns been everywhere infected. When at last he reaches his village, he finds not a self-contained unit with a life of its own which is different from the life of the town, but an extension of his own suburb.

How are we to restore to him the right to walk freely in the country and to preserve to him such country as before the war was still available for walking? The answer is, it is clear, by taking steps to prevent further encroachments by the towns upon the country. What should these steps be?

What we should do. Scott Committee Recommendations

First and most important, we should plan the use of the countryside as a whole and allocate different areas to different purposes. This, in effect, is the burden of the recommendations of the Scott Committee. To quote *The Times*: 'Two notable features of the Report were the lesson enforced in every line of it that planning was essentially a question of balancing the national advantage in deciding the use of any particular piece of land.' What does planning in this connection entail? *The Times* went on to point out that the second notable feature of the recommendations was the Report's insistence 'that the determination of that national advantage was impossible without control and purpose at the centre, that is, a government policy of national development and an adequate apparatus of legal and executive machinery to make the policy a reality'. 'Here' then, we should say 'there must be factories, here residential suburbs, but *there* is the countryside and that, with certain minor exceptions, must be left very much as it is. Also', we must add, 'there must be a comprehensive plan for the country as a whole, to ensure that this result is achieved and such and such must be the machinery for carrying it out.' This demand has been made often enough in the last twenty-five years, since the results of the second industrial revolution made themselves felt. Inevitably, since, as G. M. Trevelyan has put it, 'motor traction created the urgent need for the State to control the development of the whole island, but unhappily the matter was left to chance and the building exploiter.'

For a statement of the demand which is both brief and forcible, I take the following from an article by Mr. Kingsley Martin which was written in June 1945 in connection with a proposal by a Mr. Farr to build a factory in an area, in point of fact, at Takeley in Essex, scheduled by the Dunmow Council for agricultural and residential purposes.

'If Mr. Farr and others who may be less scrupulous than he, were allowed to build factories on scheduled areas, refusing, as Mr. Farr has done, other sites proposed for industrial development by the local councils, then the horror of ribbon development, condemned by every responsible observer, will once again go on unchecked. Mr Farr will build his factory and group of cottages; small shops will then acquire frontages along the same road; then there will be a garage and more cottages, another factory, and so on, all the way from Bishop's Stortford to Dunmow, from Dunmow to Braintree or Chelmsford, and indeed to anywhere else. The result will be such as we already know on many English roads. No one can say whether they are country or town. The fields and woodlands behind the developed front become sterilized country. They lose much of their farming value and their beauty is wasted. The unfortunate dwellers in the cottages have no communal life; they belong to no living tradition; they are far from the amenities of the town and they have none of the alternative advantages of country life. Soon what was once a country road becomes a half-developed speedway; children run from the cottages under the wheels of the passing cars; factory lorries block the way. Soon the road is found to be far too narrow for the new kind of traffic that must pass through it. Then we have to build a new road through another piece of country to bypass the road we have already ruined, till in its turn that too is sporadically developed and the whole countryside becomes a chaos, which is neither town nor country nor suburbia nor industrialized, nor indeed anything but a new slum area, which in time we have to agitate to remove. This sequence of events is to me so familiar, the principle involved so clear that I should be opposed to Mr. Farr's scheme if he had been not a manufacturer of sheet metal but a maker of golden harps for the heavenly choir.'

It is to avert precisely this sequence of events that the Scott Committee formulated its recommendations. These are admirable and if carried into effect would arrest the operation of most of the evil forces that have been at large in England during the last fifty years. At the time of writing, however,[1] there is no indication that they will be carried into effect.[2]

To what would these recommendations if adopted commit us? To a refusal to permit the countryside to be peppered haphazard with buildings; to the prohibition of advertisement hoardings and other disfiguring signs;[3] to the strict control of such building as is permitted in the countryside; to the permitting of building only on those sites where building does not spoil the beauty of a landscape; to the control of the architecture and the elevation of permitted buildings; to the restriction of materials and styles to those appropriate to the district—this means that we should not put up pink slate roofed bungalows in the Cotswolds or pink and concrete houses in the Lakes; to the banning of ribbon development. This last ban entails that, where a considerable number of houses are to be built, they should be grouped together in quadrangles around squares planted with grass and trees[4] and that industries and businesses should not

[1] November 1944.

[2] The most immediately relevant are summarized in Appendix VI.

[3] See Appendix VII. We might even go further and remove from the countryside some at least of the disfiguring buildings of the last fifty years together with all hoardings displaying advertisements.

[4] In ch. ix, anticipating the proposals of the Labour Minister of Health, Mr. Aneurin Bevan, I have ventured to advocate the desirability of flats, see pp. 189–191.

be permitted to establish themselves where they please in the countryside, but only in areas specially earmarked for their reception in pursuance of a general plan designed for the countryside as a whole.

Utopian, impracticable? Possibly; possibly not. Meanwhile, it is clear that, until such a policy is adopted, we shall be forced to go ever further to find the country. Now to go further means to spend more, and what, pray, is the use of being offered by the bounty of modern science a fleet of Green Line motor buses or electric trains to take you rapidly into the country, if you cannot afford the fare? If, then, we care about the goods I have tried so baldly to describe, we must among other things grant increased facilities in the way of cheap fares, more particularly at week-ends to parties of walkers.

Where is the Walker to Walk?

Let us now suppose that cheap fares are available, and that by their aid we have got our potential walker into the country. We proceed to the next question, where is he to walk? Not, it is obvious, on the roads. In addition to the appalling ugliness of the scenery of the main roads, the villas, the advertisement hoardings, the shacks, the garages and the cafés, there is also the stale stench of petrol fumes, the constant chivvying by frightened and infuriated motorists, the risk of sudden death.

Besides roads there are railway tracks and there are footpaths. Of footpaths, more in the next chapter. But in case the mention of railway tracks causes a lifting of the reader's eyebrow, I venture here to point out that the development of modern transport has rendered many single-track railways as obsolete as the stage-coach and the dogcart. They run through lovely scenery, none lovelier than that which borders the track from Guildford to Horsham—I mention it here, only because I walked along it from Baynards to Rudgwick during the week in which this passage is written—and they should be turned into green lanes for walkers. But of these, too, more in the next chapter.

To return to the roads, I have said my say in many other places on the subject of cars, and here I resist the temptation to a renewed outburst of spleen.[1] The best thing, it is obvious, is to prohibit the use of cars on certain roads altogether.

The Escaping Motorist

Many motorists have in recent years shown an increasing tendency to eschew the company of other motorists—the tendency is, I may say, one which I can well understand—and in peace-time there grew up a school of newspaper correspondents whose object was to tell motorists how to do so. Week by week, for example, a man used to write in the *Observer*, giving the motorist careful directions how to leave the Kingston by-pass or the Hog's Back and find his way through deep-cut lanes to Hascome and Ewhurst and Holmbury St. Mary and Capel and Newdigate—even Friday Street used to receive a mention, although since its peace has been destroyed these many years one would have supposed this to be unnecessary. There is scarcely a by-road left in southern England whose praises have not at some time been sung and to which motorists have not been elaborately guided. (With what indignation did I read in 1939 of Dial Green and Balls Cross being commended to the motorists' notice.) And, inevitably, the process defeats its own end. Inevitably, by commending motorists to a particular road because it is quiet, unspoilt and unvisited by other motorists, you cause it to lose all those qualities for which you commend it. You praise it because it takes you to the forgotten heart of the English countryside. And when, as a result of your praise, sufficient numbers of motorists have reached it, the heart stops beating.

The motorist straying off the main roads is driven by a need to escape from modern civilization. He is a man seeking to withdraw himself, in quest, though he may not know it, of a retreat, a retreat bathed in the impalpable fragrance that is distilled by old and traditional things. He finds it, but only for a moment, for, in the act of finding, he transforms it into something other than what he sought. It is a lane, say, leading to a village; yet scarcely has he passed that way, when the lane is widened to accommodate him. Each year the banks are cut

[1] But see outburst and recommendations in ch. iv, pp. 64–71.

back, the hedges trimmed, the edges tidied. Presently the native surface which reproduced the colour and characteristics of the soil disappears beneath a coat of tar, and the transformation from a lane into a road is complete. The motorists' is, indeed, the true anti-Midas touch.

Now there is, I think, no reasonable doubt that this process of introducing motorists to Nature will continue. More and more feverishly will they seek to escape from the sight of one another and more and more, as they escape, will they infest the country lanes. Now lanes, I hold to be admirable in themselves and as a consequence I deduce that they should be allowed to remain lanes. This means that cars should be prohibited from invading them and should, therefore, be restricted to certain roads. The first beginning of an answer to my question, where is the walker to walk, is, then, along the lanes.

The Next Chapter

But it is no more than a beginning. I have glanced at the roads and have mentioned railway tracks and footpaths, but it has been no more than a glance and a mention. On all these topics there is more to say, enough, in fact, to constitute a chapter in its own right. There are also the moors, the mountains, the woods and the coasts. In the north the moors and mountains are dedicated to the slaughter of the grouse; in the south the woods are sacred to the preservation of the pheasant. During the war literally hundreds of thousands of trees have been cut down. The coast is studded with resorts and the wilder parts are dotted with the residences of private owners, who have cornered for their exclusive use those parts of the beach which separate their houses from the sea. There are also the Service departments. All these matters require separate chapters.

Chapter Four

ROADS, RAILWAY TRACKS, AND FOOTPATHS

Casualties on the Roads

The roads, we are gradually coming to realize, are not as safe as could be wished. Here are a few figures. Every year in peace-time some 6,500 persons are killed on the roads of England, that is to say, one every eighty minutes of the night and day, or nearly nineteen every twenty-four hours. The figure for 1938 was 6,596 killed, 226,854 injured. Of the 220,000 persons who are on an average injured every year in road accidents, nearly 60,000 are classed as seriously injured. Many of these are permanantly maimed and remain a burden on public funds or on their relatives. Of those who are killed, five in every eleven are walkers and of the injured one in every three. In the ten years before the war 70,000 people were killed and two and a quarter millions injured on the roads of Great Britain.

Or consider the case of the United States which is interesting since in the United States the roads are not subject to the disabilities with which motorists charge the roads in this country. They are not, that is to say, winding and narrow; on the contrary they are deliberately laid out for the accommodation of motor traffic, so that there is nothing to prevent the cars from going as fast as they please. Here are the figures for 1934. In that year 36,000 were killed, 1,150,000 were injured and 105,000 were permanently injured on the roads of the United States. Here, finally, are the figures for the three other most motor-minded countries in the world for the year September 1935—September 1936:

	Killed	Injured
Germany	8,509	171,019
France	4,415	20,000
Italy	2,320	31,354

In this year in the five countries U.S.A., England, Germany,

France, Italy, the total of killed on the roads amounted to 60,000 and of injured 550,000.

War-time Figures

All these are peace-time figures; now for the war. That these pages may not be overlaid by statistics I confine myself to three sets of war-time figures. First, in April 1943, Mr. Hore-Belisha, ex-Minister of Transport, told us that in the first two years of the war there were 145,000 casualties in the armed forces of the United Kingdom but that in one year of war alone, namely 1942, casualties on the roads in this country totalled 147,540, one-sixth of these casualties being children under fifteen years of age.

In May 1944, Mr. Noel Baker, Parliamentary Secretary of the Ministry of War Transport, gave the House the following figures of casualties from the beginning of the war to date:

War casualties, 370,000 including 140,000 killed. Road casualties in England, Wales and Scotland, 588,000 including 39,000 killed.

Finally, in March 1945, the Ministry of War Transport Committee on Road Safety published a Report relating to War and Road casualties in Great Britain. The following figures relate to *serious* casualties only; they include both deaths and serious injuries from September 1939 to March 1945:

Deaths and *serious* injuries on the roads of Britain, 158,000. Deaths and serious injuries from enemy attacks of all descriptions, 140,000.

I cannot, after all, resist the temptation of appending one final figure which I include for the sake of its picturesqueness. In September 1943, the Education Officer of the L.C.C. estimated in the foreword to a pamphlet *Road Safety and the London Child*, published by the L.C.C., that one out of every twelve boys born in London meets with a road accident before he reaches the age of fourteen. In the circumstances I cannot deny myself the pleasure of repeating that the roads of this country are not as safe as could be wished.

ROADS, RAILWAY TRACKS, AND FOOTPATHS

The Dangerous Pedestrian

When I venture to say in public that most of the casualties on the roads are due to private cars, indignant persons write to motoring papers to point out that on the contrary a large number of accidents are caused by cyclists, pedestrians and even children. These are accidents in which, as the official phrase runs, pedestrians or cyclists 'are concerned'. Pedestrians, in other words, are a danger to the motorist because, when the motorist driving at fifty miles an hour runs the pedestrian down, because the pedestrian being perhaps a little lame or a little old or very young cannot cross the road quickly enough to get out of his way, the motorist is sometimes hurt in the resultant accident. Little children are often regarded as very dangerous in this sense. It is unfortunate that they have come into the world with an ineradicable instinct to play; even more unfortunate that they have not come into the world with a road sense.[1] When they have not got fields or gardens to play in, they will insist on playing in the roads where motorists very naturally run over them. Another accident due to the culpable negligence of the pedestrian! If the pedestrian had stayed at home or had known how to behave the motorist, it is pointed out, would not have run him down. Therefore, it is not the motorist but the pedestrian who is foolish and/or wicked. *'Cet animal est méchant'* said Anatole France of the tiger who when attacked turns on his pursuers, *'il se défend'*!

Finally, the indignant writers end up with an expression of contempt for my ignorance because I do not know that the vast proportion of motoring accidents during the last few years have been due to army or commercial lorries. This in war-time is true for the reason that lorries are many and cars few. In peace-time, however, private cars were responsible for nearly 60 per cent of the total number of casualties and it is with the peace, the post-war peace, that in this book we are concerned.

[1] An omission which the Almighty who, we are told, cares for little children may see fit to rectify.

Increase in the Number of Cars

Now, in peace-time the number of cars will be enormously increased; increased not only in excess of the war-time figure but also well in excess of the peace-time figure. It is hard to believe that only 4·8 per cent of the people of this country were car owners before the war as compared with an American figure of nearly 30 per cent; it is nevertheless true. I ask the reader to imagine that the pre-war percentage figure of English cars has been multiplied by five or six. The prospect conjures up all manner of problems for post-war motorists. How, one wonders, are they so to manage things that they don't all kill one another, or, alternatively, slow one another down to the central London rate of progression of four or five miles an hour, or become wedged together in a solid jam of stationary metal stretching continuously over the roads from John o' Groats to Land's End?

But let the motorist see to his own problems; in this book we are concerned with the walker, that is to say, with the man who wants to see not roads but country and, if he is sensible, will use the train whenever he can to take him there.

Recommendations in Regard to New Roads

Are there any recommendations which from his own point of view the country loving walker can fruitfully make in regard to motor roads? We will suppose that a new road really *is* necessary; or, alternatively, that it is necessary to widen an old one. Are there any elementary safeguards for the preservation not of life but of beauty that suggest themselves? I think that there are. For example, that petrol pumps should be limited in number and tamed in appearance and placed behind the building line instead of in front of it, as so often at present; that, whenever a new road is made, footpaths should, in accordance with the recommendations of the Scott Committee, be laid down when practicable *behind* the hedge on one side or other of the road. That hedgerows and hedge trees should be preserved and that, where a road is widened, the widening should be so carried out that neither trees nor hedgerows are touched. This means that instead of widening both sides and destroying two sets of hedges and trees, widening should take the form of making a new road parallel with the old one, the effect being to leave one hedgerow untouched and to retain the other as a dividing belt running down the middle of the new road[1].

Any Recommendations in regard to the Saving of Lives, of Walkers' Lives?

I have already recommended that motorists should be prohibited from using lanes; I now suggest that certain roads should be reserved for motorists and that walkers should not be permitted to set foot on them. That motorists should kill one another is their affair, nor should they repine. All idols demand their sacrifice and what sacrifice can be more fittingly made on the altar of the speed idol than that of its own devotees? But it is hard that the valuable lives of those who have not yet bowed the knee to the contemporary Baal should be sacrificed. It should, then, be recognized that many motor roads are, like railway tracks, specialized avenues for a particular kind of transport; that they are dangerous—not less dangerous than railway tracks—for other forms of transport, and that walkers and cyclists should not, therefore, set foot or wheel upon them.

Since the roads became maelstroms of metal along which the motors hurl their occupants to destruction and since we are proposing to prohibit the walker from setting foot on many of them, we are thrown back upon our question, where is he to walk?

Well, there is wild country, there are railway tracks, there are bridle tracks and there are footpaths.

Of wild country I shall write in the next two chapters. It is the best country in the world for some moods, but it is not for all and in the south there is very little of it. Let us, then, consider railway tracks, bridle tracks and footpaths.

Railway Track Walking

'Give me the clear blue sky over my head, and the green turf beneath my feet, a winding road before me and a three hours' march to dinner and then to thinking! I laugh, I run, I leap,

[1] See for more detailed recommendations in regard to footpaths Appendix III.

ROADS, RAILWAY TRACKS, AND FOOTPATHS

I sing for joy,' so Hazlitt . . . and as I took the road, it being a
fine morning towards the end of May, the words rang in my
head. But this road was not like that at all. Here was no place
for laughing, leaping, singing for joy and the rest; here were
stench, racket and continual chivvying by irritated motorists.
No track for walkers ran along the side of this road and, directly
one ventured away from the extreme edge of it, one went in
palpable danger of one's life; in fact, even the edge was not
wholly safe, for every now and then a motorist, driven hedgewards
by other cars or driving too near the margin out of pure devil-
ment, bore into me and drove me into the ditch where I lurked
palpitating for a few seconds, cursing the cars under my breath
and, when breath returned to me, congratulating myself on my
escape. Nor, had I wanted to sing, could I have heard my voice
because of the noise; nor smelt the smells of the morning and
the spring because of the petrol fumes. Not less terrible than the
dangers, noises and stenches of this main road were its sights, for
like most of the new main roads of to-day this road was practically hedgeless and treeless; it was lined not by living things,
but by iron or wooden fences, interspersed at intervals by villas,
planted singly or clustering in patches of angry pink. Between
the villas there were pumps and garages. There were also signposts, A.A. notices, builders' boards and estate agents' announce-
ments that such and such tracts of country were to be 'developed' and offered eligible building sites. When the surrounding country could be seen through the gaps in the buildings, it
was raw and mutilated. No, one could not, it was obvious, continue to walk along that road.

Motorists, it may be, do not mind what they see; most of
them, indeed, go too fast to see anything; but how was I, a walker,
to tolerate metal and cement and bricks and hoardings, I, who
had come out to see green and growing things?

By the side of the road at a distance of about a hundred yards
there ran a single railway track: it was almost, but not quite,
disused. Every twenty-four hours two trains still ran along it
each way consisting of a couple of carriages and an engine.
Only the day before I had travelled by one of them and I was
the only passenger on the train. I decided to leave the road and
take to the railway.

ROADS, RAILWAY TRACKS, AND FOOTPATHS

I am fond of walking along railway tracks. They are frequently little canyons running through deep cuttings, the banks of which are ablaze with flowers. (Flowers seem to like railway cuttings; somebody once gave me a good botanical reason for this, but I forget what it was. Presence of smoke, perhaps; or absence of motorists!) Single line tracks, moreover, often traverse deserted and forgotten country—in this respect, by the way, they are like canals[1]—and the sleepers are placed at just the right distance to accommodate the stride of my rather short legs. I have walked miles along that admirable line in North Devon that runs through Parracombe to Lynton and Lynmouth; miles along that magnificent stretch of line from Penrhyndeudraeth to Blaenau Ffestiniog in Merioneth, while the little line that runs west from Pulborough to Midhurst in Sussex is one of my most familiar walking grounds.

I had not walked for more than a mile along this particular track—I think that for obvious reasons I had better not say where it was—when I came to a level crossing where the line was intersected by a lane. Here there was a railwayman, a signalman, who angrily approached and forbade me the track. To walk along a railway line was, he said, trespassing; it was forbidden by law. 'Why?' I asked. 'Because', he said, 'it is dangerous. You must', he added, 'go back to the road.' I looked at the high road visible down the lane, the high road where walking was permitted, the road along which the motors were hurling themselves in a continuous line, hooting and belching at one another in eruptive irritability. For walkers such a road was a death trap. Then I looked at the quiet railway line with its two trains each way every day, where walking was prohibited as dangerous. I stayed on the railway line.

Recommendation in Regard to New Roads and Old Railway Tracks

I mention this incident because it indicates the urgent need for a change in the laws relating to the countryside. In the last fifty years the habits of our community have radically altered; nor are they likely to revert. Yet many of the laws under which we live are adapted to a mode of living which is already obso-

[1] See ch. x, pp. 195, 196.

lete. Thus, walking is permitted on motor roads which are dangerous, forbidden on single track railway lines which are not—you could hear the puffing of the engine of the four-times-daily train at least half a mile away. A double change is required.

First, we ought to recognize that it is as dangerous to walk on certain roads as it is to walk on main-line railway tracks and these roads, as I have already suggested, ought to be segregated for motors only, as railway tracks are segregated for trains. It should be a misdemeanour for a pedestrian to set foot on them. At the time of writing,[1] Mr. Noel Baker, Parliamentary Secretary of the Ministry of War Transport, has announced that immediately after the war a number of motor roads, ninety feet in width, will be laid down and that suitable lengths of them will be reserved for mechanically propelled vehicles. Each road is to cost £100,000 a mile. Well and good! The motorists, I suppose, will pay for most of them; they will drive very fast and they will duly kill one another as they kill one another on the similar roads which have been laid down in America.[2] Part of the cost, however, will fall upon the Local Authorities concerned, which means, I take it, that it will come out of the rates. This in its turn means that part of the cost will fall upon cyclists and pedestrians who, after all, are ratepayers. Again, well and good, on condition that some part of the cost of new footpaths and cycle tracks for the benefit of the walkers and cyclists whom the motorists have displaced should also come out of the rates and fall, therefore, in part upon the motorists. I cannot forbear to point out—I hope the observation will not set the cyclists against me—that, while the cost of the footpaths (which should be laid down *behind* the roadside hedges) is negligible, the cost of cycle tracks will be substantial. I must also record that many, perhaps most cyclists are, in my view mistakenly, opposed to them. In the vexed controversy which the proposal for special cycle tracks is apt to beget I must plead the readers' indulgence for not taking part. I cannot, however, resist the temptation to denounce the infamous proposal made in a recent Ministry of War Transport Report on Road Safety,[3] that cycle tracks

[1] December 1944.   [2] See p. 64 above.   [3] Para. 137.

(asphalt or tarmac?) should be constructed beside the footpaths which run across fields. It is difficult to conceive a proposal better calculated to destroy the special and distinctive pleasure which we take in footpath walking. Out of what blind insensitivity to all the proprieties and amenities was it, one wonders, engendered?

Leaving the vexed issue of cycle tracks and returning to the clear issue of footpaths, I would suggest on the question of finance that a proportion, say two-thirds, of the cost of all new footpaths suggested by the Footpaths' Commission,[1] or the Local Authority and approved by the Ministry of Town and Country Planning, should be met out of the national exchequer, the rest being borne by the Local Authority.

In wild and sparsely populated areas where Local Authorities are poor, it may well be that the whole of the cost of new footpaths should be borne by national funds, should, that is to say, be defrayed by taxation to which the motorist would contribute.

Secondly, a number of single line railway tracks which are rapidly falling into disuse should be set aside for walkers. The metals should be taken up, the grass allowed to grow and the track transformed into a green lane thrown open to the public. An example is the line that runs from Portmadoc through the Aberglaslyn Pass to Beddgelert which used to be known as the Welsh Highlands Light Railway. This fell out of use as a railway some years ago, and the Liverpool Federation of the Ramblers' Association are, at the time of writing, endeavouring to secure that it shall be scheduled as a walkers' footpath. This would entail its purchase and maintenance by the Caernarvon County Council and financial support is required for this purpose.[2] Another track which should be similarly used is the line that runs from Portmadoc through glorious country to Ffestiniog. There is also the line that used to run along the Manifold Valley in Staffordshire, which has been derelict for some years. This has, in fact, been dedicated to public use by the benevolent L.M.S. who just before the war covered it with a tarmac road surface about six feet wide with gates so arranged that

[1] See pp. 84, 85 below and Appendix III.
[2] I am told that of the £2,000 required the Liverpool Federation have at the time of writing (April 1945) secured £900.

only pedestrians could pass through some eight miles or so of the track running from Hulme End southwards. I am all in favour of the gates, but why the tarmac surface? There is, I am told, a strong local movement for converting the track into a motor road. Then, there is the line that used to run from Bewdley through Cleobury Mortimer to Tenbury, with a special branch running from Cleobury Mortimer to Ditton Priors. This last was closed for passenger traffic just before the war, but along the Bewdley to Tenbury line a few trains still run either way. I am fond of small railway lines and no friend to their closers. I hope, therefore, that both will be reopened for passenger traffic; but if either of them is closed for both goods and passenger traffic, I suggest that its track should be reserved as a path for walkers; the country through which both pass is heavenly. We spend enough money on motor roads; it is high time that we spent a little on the walkers whom motors have displaced, which brings me to the question of bridle tracks and footpaths.

Horse Riding

Approaching the subject of bridle tracks, I ought first to speak of the pleasures and pains of horse riding, but, as a rider of only fourteen years' standing, I am too recent a convert and I ride too ill to justify the delivery of the lecture upon which I should like to embark on this absorbing yet humbling topic. Short of religion, there has been nothing in these later years that has made me feel so small as the horse reinforced by the people who ride horses and talk about the horses they ride. What a world it is, the 'horsy' world; how self-centred, how apart, how all alive and kicking and also how self-satisfied with a wholly complacent and not wholly unjustifiable self-satisfaction in its apartness. I see that the lecture is beginning; the better to ward it off, I hurry to substitute an illustrative digression upon one of my own riding experiences.

A Riding Tour

In the spring of 1937 I went, accompanied by a daughter, on a riding tour. We possessed a cob of our own which carried me, and we hired a fierce little pony for my daughter. We rode from Shamley Green near Guildford over Hascombe Hill, then across the Weald to Black Down, over Black Down and so to Fernhurst. After a night at Fernhurst we went southward over Telegraph Hill and Redford and Woolbeding Commons through Iping and Stedham, lovely quiet places, and so on to the downs between Elstead and Cocking. It was high spring and the country through which we passed was a blaze of blossom and flowers. This part of the Weald which runs north and south of the western section of the borderline between Surrey and Sussex is an enchanted corner of England. There are few main roads and the cars have not, therefore, in any appreciable numbers 'got at' it. The villages are small and sufficiently distant from London, sufficiently lacking in 'good class' hotels, to retain a life of their own and some of them, for example Lodsworth and Wisborough Green and Alfold farther north, are very agreeable, though not beautiful. As for the country, its beauty is beyond my powers of description. It is small-scale country and exhibits in a pre-eminent degree those characteristics of rapidly changing view and feature which are distinctively associated with the scenery of southern England. First copse, then dell with stream, then fields and orchard, then farm, then open common—you will see them all within a mile—and you will see, too, what I take to be the special glory of the country in late April and early May, flowers and blossoming trees. These exist in incredible variety and profusion all over this part of the Weald. When at last we came to the downs, the country was no less lovely, but lovely in a different and, to my mind, more commonplace fashion. But everybody knows the Sussex Downs and there is no need for me to say anything about what everybody knows.[1] Indeed, there is no need for me to describe this riding tour at all. I have been led to speak of it by the sheer pleasure of recalling the occasion and writing about what has given me such pleasure to recall. However, to complete the story, we rode along the downs past Linch Down to Cocking and so eastward to Bury Hill, spent a day riding with friends on the downs round Amberley, then turned northward for a night at Wisborough Green and so home again to Shamley Green.

[1] Especially as I say some of it at length in ch. x., pp. 208–210.

Why embark on this digression? Why introduce this little tour? Mainly, I am afraid, because it enables me to deliver another blow at the ribs of our motoring civilization and the kind of travel that it engenders. For the digression enables me to draw and to dwell upon the contrast between the isolation imposed by the car and the sociability, the almost embarrassing sociability, which attends a tour on horseback. Go out in a car, and nobody speaks to you and you speak to nobody; go, as we did, on a riding tour and everybody is your friend. The 'locals' talked to us, cyclists laughed at us, motorists abased themselves before us. When we came to an inn, the place turned itself upside down in an excited endeavour to accommodate the horses and to find them something, even if it were only chicken corn, upon which they could sustain themselves. And everybody praised the pleasures of riding and said what a pity it was that riding had 'gone out', and what a good thing for everybody that it was coming back. The old ladies who, in these parts of Surrey and Sussex, are everywhere to be found dwelling in houses set in great paddocks, which exist solely for the purpose of providing a long drawn-out euthanasia for aged and obese horses, competed for the honour of accommodating our steeds and not only our steeds but ourselves. It is only when riding through the country on a horse that I have been invited to dine and spend the night by complete strangers. One way and another, I cannot remember to have met and talked with so many people hitherto unknown to me as during the five days of our riding through Surrey and Sussex.

Now I do not wish to suggest that there was ever a time when most people spent their lives riding through the countryside and their days in idle chatter with strangers, but I do maintain that, before the motor age, the social texture of men's lives resembled the experience which I enjoyed on my riding tour more closely than it resembles the experience which the average motorist enjoys at the week-end. It has been customary in the past for men to forgather, to drop into casual conversation and to pass the time of day with strangers. All these things happened to me when I was riding, but none of them happens to me when I am motoring; nobody passes the time of day with me, nobody mentions the weather and my fellow motorists regard me with

75

indifference or hostility. More horses, then, means more sociability, more intercourse between man and man, more subjects
for conversation, more—and let us hope—better literature. Just
think of the literature of hunting, of Trumpeton Wood[1] and
Gobblegoose Wood[1] and Bonebreaker.[1] What comparable literature has been evoked by the car?

The second and the more relevant reason for the digression
is its introduction of the topic of bridle paths.

Bridle Paths

Since the roads were made hazardous and hard for the horses'
feet by cars, the rider must diligently scan his map with a view
to making as much of his way as he can contrive by bridle paths.
Surrey and Sussex which are the only counties I know as a
rider are threaded with bridle paths. Take, for instance, the
country round Pitch Hill. Here are a number of old tracks
running through the pine and heather country down to the
Weald. Some of them are said to be smugglers' tracks, a legend
to which their sunken character gives countenance, for in this
part of the country the banks often rise to a height of a dozen
feet or more above the level of the track, so that unless you are
on the top of the bank you can see nothing passing along the
track. Others are said to be old drovers' roads; hence the
thick hedges and high banks, so that a couple of drovers could
manage a large herd without much chance of the cattle or
horses straying. The tracks continue into the Weald, run through
comparatively unvisited country round about Dunsfold, Alfold,
and Plaistow into Sussex and so onward to the downs. Partly
because they are unfrequented, partly because they run through
unspoilt country, that is to say, country not yet spoilt by us,
they commend themselves to the rider. (It is obvious that I cannot let the reader into the secret of these tracks, but just to indicate the kind of thing I mean, let him take the track that starts
from Farley Green just south of Albury and runs over Winter-
fold Heath past Hurtwood House down over the ridge and

---

[1] All in Trollope, *Phineas Redux*, *Ayala's Angel* and *Phineas Finn*, in case the
reader does not know. I do not speak of Jorrocks whom, inevitably, he
does know.

onwards past Wyphurst; or the track running from Field Place near Dunsfold south-westward along by a stream to Ramsnest south of Chiddingfold.) They are the first objectives for which, as he plans his way across country, the rider looks on the map, only, however, too often to be disappointed. For many bridle tracks have been allowed to become choked with undergrowth; or the hedges on each side have become inextricably interlaced with festoons of brambles; or the bridle path is waterlogged, so that the horses are up to their knees in mud; or a farmer has stretched a line of barbed wire across it. There is nothing for it but to turn back, back to the road and the motors. But all this, you will say, is unimportant, for riders after all are few, motorists many and this book anyway is devoted primarily to the cause of the walker. I agree, nor would I have mentioned the bridle paths, were it not that what is true of them is true, too, of the footpaths to which the bridle paths lead by a natural transition.

Disuse of Footpaths

All good walkers look for footpaths. It is fun to find them on the map and they are pleasant to follow when they are found. They take you over hills and through fields; they thread copses and cross streams. They take you away from the roads whither the motors cannot follow you, away from the smell of petrol, the sight of hoardings, houses, pumps and poles and the sound of gears and horns, and substitute the smell of flowers in spring and dead leaves in autumn, the sight of green things, of birds and cattle and occasionally, if you are lucky, of a stray wild creature, a squirrel, a stoat, a hedgehog or even a fox, the songs of birds, the hum of insects or the rustle of leaves under your feet. In short, you get from them precisely what you have gone into the country to find and for a time have surcease from modern civilization. How important, then, for the walker that paths should be many and accessible. In fact they grow fewer and more difficult of access. For this there are a number of reasons. For years past footpaths have been falling into disuse; their main function in the past has been to lead from village to village or from village to road. In the past roads were often boggy and muddy and the footpaths besides being shorter were at least not much dirtier. The roads were first macadamized and then tarmacked, with the result that it was often quicker to go by the road even when the road was longer. Then came cars to take the farmer and his wife to the market town, and presently motor buses to take the labourer and his wife to the village, the pub, and the railway. Throughout this period, a period of over a hundred years, the countryside was being steadily drained of its inhabitants. The result is that many footpaths have become derelict. It is a curious experience to mark out a footpath walk on a map, to arrive at the chosen spot, to look for the path and then to find that it is not there.

Walking in East Anglia

I have noticed this disappearance of footpaths more frequently perhaps in East Anglia than in any other part of the country. The East Anglian is not in general a good countryside for walking. There is not enough detail in the immediate foreground and as a result little feeling of intimacy. The scene changes but slowly and there is not, therefore, enough sense of variety. Walking in East Anglia is in fact a little like walking on the Continent. For cycling and even motoring the eastern counties are superb; the scenery changes rapidly enough to occupy the eye and the lovely skylines especially in Essex make the employment of the eye a delight. The eastern sky, huger, nobler and somehow more eventful, can be seen on a bicycle as well as, perhaps better than it can be seen on foot. You top the rise and see before you an apparently endless expanse of unemphatic, undulating country. There is no distinction, no focal point, no climax, just another rise in the far distance beyond which you know there will spread another similar expanse. All this, agreeable enough to cyclist and motorist, is apt to be depressing to the slow-going walker. Moreover, I like to see more trees about the place and, with the best intention in the world, I have never been able to form a taste for muddy estuaries, marshes and sand dunes. Yet there are such lovely pictures of them and they have evoked so much and such splendid poetry that there must clearly here be something that I miss. After a time I even find them depressing. I can well remember, for example, a walk I once took in the marshes at the back of Southend. I got out at Pitsea Station and followed a muddy path running along an embankment beside a wide ditch. It poured with rain, the war had just started and the military, staring suspiciously at me, were all over the place. I made my way along what presently became a muddy creek past East Haven, Slatey House, Tree Farm and Westwick to the Welcome Inn by the coastguard station opposite Shellhaven Point. On my way back I found myself to my consternation mixed up with the remoter outcroppings of Canvey Island. Lord, what a horror!

I can remember, too, how depressed I was by the experience of trying to make my way wholly by footpaths from Althorne Station to Bradwell. That is a queer part of Essex; it seems to stretch interminably—Bradwell Juxta Mare is eleven miles from the nearest station; it is quite featureless, yet lacks the grandeur of true Fenland country, and it is very sparsely populated. The footpaths marked on the map simply were not there; there were not always even gaps in the hedge to show where the footpaths once had been and in that uncharted waste of flat and featureless fields I got lost. I felt, I remember, as if the land of England falling away as it does on its eastern side into the sea, had no longer the strength to hold itself up—look at those poor, crumbling cliffs south of Dunwich—and was already beginning to assume some of the characteristics of the element that lay in wait to engulf it, its featurelessness, its flatness, its vast expanse. While I am on this distressful topic of the disintegrating body of eastern England, where the sands run out and the spirit of the land ebbs away into the sea, I would like to put it on record that I have never met anybody who has visited that curious country, not thirty miles from London, between the Thames and the Medway where are Cliffe Marshes with their abundant clamorous birds and a railway line featuring stations, shameless under such names as Uralite Halt, Beluncle and Sharnal Street.[1] It is a strange, forgotten district and here, too, the footpaths have fallen into disuse.

[1] I suppose that since 1932, when the Southern Railway developed All Hallows-by-the-Sea as a 'resort', numbers of people must have gone this way by train *en route* for the Isle of Grain.

The Shortcomings of Local Authorities

A further reason for the dereliction of footpaths is to be found in the apathy of Local Authorities. The maintenance of footpaths is a charge which, in theory, devolves upon the Highway Authority, usually a committee of the Local Authority. But why *should* it spend money on footpaths? Nobody, after all, pays to use footpaths, but motorists pay a swingeing tax for the use of the roads. Let us, then—the argument runs naturally enough—give the motorists their money's worth and, incidentally, attract more of them to the town. Meanwhile bridle ways and footpaths are left to look after themselves. As a consequence some footpaths become waterlogged, others are choked by nettles and brambles, while others again are closed by farmers and landlords who break down stiles not already ruinous and block up the gaps with barbed wire.

Effects of the War

These things were happening for years before the war, but the war has raised the mortality of footpaths to appalling dimensions. Their war-time enemies have been two. First, there are the farmers. Any farmer across whose fields a diagonal footpath runs has been entitled to plough it up subject to two conditions; first, he must obtain the authorization of the County War Agricultural Committee; secondly, he must provide facilities for an alternative route and set up direction posts to point it out at each end of the ploughed-up path.[1]

The Ramblers' Association, of which I have the honour to be a Vice-President, was uneasy at this innovation, pointing out that an alternative route was in any event longer, and that in practice its adoption frequently meant going round by the road; that there were 147,000 casualties on the roads in a single year of the war; that in particular the roads are death traps to children who are great users of footpaths; that the country in war-time was crowded with evacuees, a circumstance which brought

[1] There is no obligation to provide alternative routes where field paths were ploughed up, in regard to which the right of ploughing existed *before the war*.

the paths into greater demand than they had been for many years; that country people were short of petrol and that the short cut across the fields had in consequence assumed a new importance; that a walk along a country footpath through a corn field on a summer's evening rests the nerves of the tired man and eases the soul of the distressed man—with much more to the same effect. Also, we asked, who is going to see that the paths are restored at the end of the war?

Officials of the Ministry of Agriculture were sympathetic and did their best to meet us. In particular, they agreed to compile lists of the paths that had been closed, and to take steps to see that Local Authorities enforced their restoration at the end of the war.

Unfortunately, most of this was beside the point, which was that the great majority of the paths which had been ploughed or stopped up by farmers were never notified to the War Agricultural Committees at all. The farmers, in fact, have during the war simply taken the law into their own hands, a circumstance which has imposed upon all of us who care to walk in the country the duty of reporting to the Ministry of Agriculture or to the relevant War Agricultural Committee every case that comes to our notice in which a path has been ploughed up without authorization and without the provision of an alternative right of way.

The other war-time enemies of footpaths are the War departments which, in their eagerness to protect England from its inhabitants, have enclosed within palings and barbed wire great areas of the countryside and in their extreme nervousness at the thought of being approached and observed closed all avenues leading to the invested areas; closed, therefore, the footpaths. There is no reasoning with military authorities; while the war was on, their word was law. But after the war? The Requisitioned Lands and War Works Act[1] gives a Minister acting under the advice of a Commission power to decide upon the future use of the land which Government departments have requisitioned for their various purposes during the war. Much of this land is crossed by footpaths. The argument that to restore the land to its pre-war use will be difficult and costly is bound to

[1] See ch. ii, pp. 31, 32, and Appendix IX.

be with deadly effect—cost, as I have already pointed out,[1] is the only consideration that is taken into account by those who form the policies of modern States—and few will be found to urge the value to the community of footpaths which the people used before the war but have lost during it. Footpaths are humble things and not much thought of by members of Government departments and commissions in their official capacities, though Civil Servants may be seen all over Surrey, Kent, Hertfordshire and Buckinghamshire, particularly Buckinghamshire, striding determinedly along them at week-ends.

The Making Respectable of Footpaths

There is yet a further cause of degeneration in footpaths. Some footpaths which have not been allowed to fall into disuse, which have neither been ploughed up nor closed, are tidied up and made respectable.

This 'making respectable' of footpaths is in its way as bad as their neglect. To make a footpath respectable is to turn it into a corridor which runs between two private properties, with a wall or a thick hedge on each side of it and asphalt or concrete under foot. Like prisoners at exercise, the ramblers file dutifully between the unending fences of wood and iron. To walk between wooden walls or wire fences may be well enough as exercise, but it is fatal to the sense of carefreeness which most of us seek on a day's solitary walking in the country. Even where there are no fences there are regiments of boards—boards telling you that you will be prosecuted if you leave the path, boards insisting austerely on the privacy of the meadows on each side of you, boards threatening you with what will happen to you, if you venture to sit down on those meadows or let your dog off its lead. Many footpaths are little more than cautionary corridors for wicked walkers.

Footpaths having been officially recognized and made respectable, a public official will proceed to set upon them the seal of his approval in the shape of asphalt. Now I loathe walking on asphalt, especially when I might have been walking on good English mud. If anybody desires evidence in support of these

[1] See ch. ii, pp. 40, 41.

strictures, let him go to Headley Church in Surrey and take note of the series of paths which radiate from it. One is asphalted, another is fenced with barbed wire, a third passes between wooden walls, a fourth bristles with boards. Nothing could more effectively inhibit the goods which footpath walking can bestow, the absence of restraint, the feeling of the countryside stretching away on either side of you, the sense of return to a less hurried, more leisurely and gracious age.

The Virtues of Footpaths

When it comes to recommendations, I do not know that we can improve on those contained in the Report of the Scott Committee[1]. This admirable Report bases itself on the assumption that more footpaths are needed not only for utilitarian but for recreational purposes. Its authors see that the purpose of a footpath is not only to meet a need by enabling you to pass as quickly as possible from A to B; it may be also to give you delight and to confer benefit in the course of your passage. Indeed, the value of footpaths to walkers is to be found not so much in the places to which they take him as in the experience which they confer upon him in the taking. There is nothing at the end of any footpath better than may be found beside it, though there would be no walking did men believe it at the time; yet even so what a walker finds at the end of a good country path, where there is no anger, no fret, such a large fireplace and everything different from London, is altogether better than what he will have left behind him in the town.

Recommendations of the Scott Committee

All this the Scott Committee—although it does not always put it quite like this—seems to me to recognize. It concludes very properly that not fewer but more footpaths are needed and recognizes that much of the damage done by trespassers, the breaking down of hedges, the leaving open of gates and so on is the result either of the absence of footpaths or of their growing faintness, due to disuse. Its recommendation is that the supervision and upkeep of footpaths should be a statutory obligation on Local Authori-

[1] For a summary of these see Appendix III.

ties, although it does not, as I should like to do, propose to transfer the responsibility for the care and upkeep of footpaths in certain selected areas to a National Authority, presumably the Ministry of Town and Country Planning. The ground for recommending this transference of responsibility to a National Authority is the same as that which is urged[1] in favour of the national administration of potential National Park districts.

There are certain areas, for example, on Dartmoor, in the New Forest, in Radnor Forest, in the Black Mountains or in Swaledale, where the existence of footpaths is as important to visitors as it is to those living in the locality—perhaps, for the reasons given above, it is today more important. It is a good principle that what is of national interest and national use should be paid for out of national and not out of local funds; apart altogether from the fact that the sparsely populated areas through which run the footpaths which are of interest to those who care for beauty in whatever part of England it may be found, precisely because they *are* sparsely populated areas, are represented by Local Authorities who are too poor to afford expenditure on footpath upkeep.

Proposed Appointment of a Footpaths' Commission

The most important recommendation of the Scott Committee is the appointment of a small Footpaths' Commission which would travel up and down the country with the objects, first, of adjudicating in the case of disputed footpaths and determining whether they are public rights of way or not and, secondly, of recommending the laying down of new footpaths where required, on the ground that an ample provision of field paths is indispensable to what the Committee calls healthy outdoor recreation.

The importance of the first of these two proposed functions of the Commission arises from the enormous complexity of the present law relating to rights of way—I honestly believe that Sir Lawrence Chubb, the celebrated Secretary of the Commons, Footpaths and Open Spaces Preservation Committee is the only man in the country who thoroughly understands it, an

[1] See ch. v, pp. 109, 110.

impeachment which he would be the first to deny—coupled with the fact that its obscure provisions operate strongly in favour of the owner who wishes to dispute the existence of a right of way passing through his land or, if such does in fact exist, wishes to obstruct or to close it. In such cases it is necessary to hold a public inquiry at which a number of witnesses are required to appear and to affirm that over a period of twenty years the footpath has, to their knowledge, habitually been used as a right of way.[1] In some cases, where the path runs through private property the prescribed period is forty years.

During the years between the wars when the countryside was increasingly subject especially at week-ends to invasion from the towns, many landowners and farmers closed footpaths out of hand, not wishing their land to be traversed by hordes of hikers. The question would then arise by what means, short of putting the case to the test by a mass trespass—and in many parts of the country, especially in the North, rambling clubs have ventured upon this heroic course making it a point of honour to walk at least once every year over all the disputed footpaths in a prescribed area—the footpath could be restored to public use. The only method available was that of a public inquiry at which witnesses were summoned to appear and to testify.

Closing of an Oxfordshire Footpath

I remember one such case in South Oxfordshire near Mapledurham where for several years I rented a house. Past the end of the drive there ran a bridle track which became a footpath, passed through a gap into a copse and finally joined the road. If one wanted to go eastwards this footpath saved a good mile since, if you did not use the footpath, there was nothing for it but to go for a quarter of a mile in the other direction, traverse the arc of a circle and then join the road half a mile further back. When we had lived at Mapledurham a couple of years, the owner closed the footpath at the point at which it entered the copse by erecting a locked gate across the gap, the top of the gate

---

[1] The evidence of tenants and employees is in many cases expressly excluded, although it often happens that all the normal users of the path fall into one or other of these categories.

being surmounted by barbed wire fencing. We protested and as a result the owner substituted a stile for the gate, a stile reserved for our especial use as tenants of the estate, at the same time putting up a notice saying that the path was private and was not to be used by the public. Nobody, however, really believed that it *was* private. What was to be done? An energetic and public-spirited old lady living a few miles off took the case in hand and made a tour of the countryside in the endeavour to collect witnesses. The difficulties were immense. There was no village nearer than three miles; the few houses on the estate had all changed hands several times during the last twenty years—all, that is to say, except one. This was occupied by an old couple who would not hear of going to Court and giving evidence against 'his lordship'. As for the path it had, they said, always been used for as long as they could remember, but, they reminded us, they had been 'his lordship's' tenants for as long as they could remember. How, then, could they be expected to go into court and testify against his interests?

A tradesman living in the village also remembered the public use of the path. 'But who was he that he should go into court against the great house? He would certainly lose his connection.' After prolonged effort, involving much cycling from village to village and voluminous correspondence, the public-spirited lady succeeded in finding one old man who was prepared to go into court and testify. But he was very deaf, so deaf that she could never feel wholly assured that he knew what it was all about; or that, if he did, his evidence would be on the right side. He was, moreover, literally the only one and it was far from certain that, if an inquiry were held, one person's evidence would be regarded as sufficient to establish a right of way. The case was accordingly dropped. And that is how under the existing law we establish, or rather fail to establish, the fact that a public path which for whatever reason a farmer or landlord chooses to close is in fact public.

Functions of the Footpaths' Commission

Hence, the necessity for an alteration in the law. I suggest that the relevant Local Authority should be asked to make a survey of all rights of way existing, or alleged to exist, in its area. To assist it, the services of Rambling Clubs and school-children could be enlisted—this incidentally has been done in the preparation of the Land Utilization Maps of the Ordnance Survey. Paths included in the survey and proposed, therefore, as public rights of way to which no objection was laid should automatically become established as rights of way and regi-stered as such. All disputed cases would be adjudicated upon by the Footpaths' Commission and settled out of hand. An order from the Ministry of Town and Country Planning should suffice to make the settlement effective. Once established, the path should be listed as a right of way upon a central register kept for the purpose by the Ministry. Further, the relevant Local Authority should keep a copy of all the paths scheduled in its area.

The Commission should at the same time include within its functions the restoration to the public of all paths which have been closed by the military or ploughed up with or without the authorization of War Agricultural Committees. The cost of restoration and of making good whatever damage has been done should be borne out of the same public funds as defrayed the expenses involved in the original closing of the path.

What is here said of footpaths applies also to the investigation and restoration where necessary of bridle ways, drove ways and green lanes. When restored, they should be maintained, their maintenance entailing an obligation on the local or national authority, as the case may be, to keep stiles and bridges in a usable condition and to prevent the bridle ways from becoming so boggy or overgrown with brambles, as to be impassable.

The Establishment of New Paths

The Commission should also consider the provision of new paths. Three classes of case suggest themselves. First, when new roads are made or when old narrow roads are widened, the Scott Committee has suggested that footpaths should also be provided. These might, as already suggested, run on the 'field side of existing hedges'—I am quoting from the Scott Com-mittee report—'fenced off from the remainder of the fields where necessary as advised by the agricultural authority'. In other cases paths might be laid down going in the general direction of the road but not necessarily following its actual line. Secondly, new footpaths are required to connect areas to which the public already have access, for example, some National Trust properties, their provision being obviously a matter of national and not of local concern.

Third—and most important of the three—is the provision of long distance footpaths so planned that ramblers can walk for several days without being tempted to trespass or forced on to main roads. Such provision is of paramount importance in the future, if England is to remain a land in which walking can still be indulged in for pleasure and it will, of course, involve the creation of new public rights of way.

Where should such long distance tracks run? The most popular suggestion is for a Pennine Way. This proposal which is specially connected with the name of Tom Stephenson is for a walk starting from the Peak District and running northwards over the spine of the Pennines to the Roman Wall. The proposed route runs from the head of Edale in Derbyshire, over Kinder Scout to the Derwent Valley and Bleaklow; past Greenfield and Blackstone Edge, across the Calder Valley and the fringe of the Brontë country, to cross the Aire Gap near Skipton and reach the head of Airedale at Malham. Then over Penyghent to Ribblesdale, Wensleydale and Swaledale, across the Pennines to Teesdale, following the Tees by High Force and Cauldron Snout; thence along the valley of the Maize Beck to High Cup Nick. Climbing Cross Fell on the way to Alston, and following parts of the Maiden Way and the Roman Wall, the proposed route skirts the Cheviots and ends at Wooler in Northumberland. Routes to be followed by other suggested ways are dictated partly by the lie of the land, partly by the exigencies of accommodation. Many Youth Hostels, more particularly in the South, are so situated that it is possible to walk from one to another in a day's march, so that a party on a walking tour can by this method spend every night in a different Hostel. Bearing these considerations in mind, the Ramblers' Association have put forward the following proposals for long distance footpath routes:

1. Along the Chiltern escarpment to the Thames, continuing along the Ridgeway in Berkshire, and over the Marlborough Downs to Avebury in Wiltshire. Then over Silbury Hill and Rybury Camp across the Vale of Pewsey, along the northern edge of Salisbury Plain to near Warminster, and on through Dorset by Milborne Port to Cerne Abbas. Finally, the path would take a due westerly direction by Lewesdon Hill and Lamberts Castle, and come down to the sea at Seaton Bay.

2. The line of the Pilgrims' Way from Canterbury to Winchester.

3. Following the edge of the South Downs from Beachy Head north-westwards and on to Salisbury Plain.

4. Along the line of Offa's Dyke on the Welsh Marches.

The Ramblers' Association also advocates that rights of way should be established along the banks of rivers and canals, where these do not already exist.

I cannot sufficiently stress the importance of the provision of footpaths both short and long, if the enjoyment of the goods celebrated in this book is to be preserved for posterity. Without them walking will become a lost pleasure. No other subject here dealt with, not even that of National Parks, is of greater importance.

Chapter Five

THE MOUNTAINS AND THE MOORS

I. The Lake District and National Parks

'The fundamental joyous refreshment that one gets from wild scenery touches the deepest springs of mental and spiritual life.'—PROFESSOR TANSLEY.

Early Indifference to the Lakes

I am not among those whose eyes open readily to the perception of visual beauty and the mountains knocked long and often before they forced the doors of my sealed sense.

The first time I came to the Lakes was in the Long Vac in 1912, as a member of an undergraduate reading party. I went to Carlisle, stayed with a friend on a farm near Maryport, and thence via Maryport and Cockermouth passed along the shores of Bassenthwaite to Keswick. I mention the fact because this mode of approach, a curious one, has never been used since. I was quite unversed in mountains—I don't believe I had hitherto seen anything higher than the Wrekin—and, so far as I can remember, I took no notice of them at all. We stayed at Grange in Borrowdale, worked at our books and went into Keswick for a fair. I spent most of my free time prowling along the road between Grange and Barrow House on the lookout for one of the Keswick girls, who had promised at the fair to come out to Grange and meet me—prowling, need I say, in vain. Once only did we go—or rather, once only did I go, for the others stayed behind—on to the hills in the company of a Nonconformist minister on holiday; a young man, all rucksack, compass, map and hobnail boots, who seemed to entertain an affectionately personal enmity for the mountains—'You great brute!' he would say, shaking his fist genially at Great End. Under his guidance I went up the Styhead *en route* for Scafell Pike—I might as well, I must have thought, go up the highest peak of the lot

ΡΕΙΑΣ

right away and then I shall have got the thing over and done with—but the mist came down and after wandering about on the slopes of the 'great brute' we subsided ignominiously into Wasdale. Next day we walked back over Styhead to Grange. I do not remember having walked again on to the mountains—I used to go for my walks through the late September woods along the River Derwent between Grange village and Castle Crag—but for all that they had done their work with me, little as I knew it at the time.

The second time, I went to Barrow House to a Fabian Summer School and fell in love. It was August 1914 and the war had just broken out. I played tennis on a sodden lawn, made speeches on every conceivable variety of topic, saved, as I fondly but falsely believed, the loved girl's life by going in after her when she had got out of her depth in Derwent Water Lake and, except for one expedition to the top of Windy Gap— I talked all the time and was too indifferent to go on to Great Gable—took no more notice of the mountains than of the war. Yet there was, I remember, one walk in the late evening taken by the pair of us, inevitably to the top of the Lodore Falls, where I permitted myself to conclude that 'really it was rather lovely'.

The Magic Works

The third time was the summer of 1920 and now at last the magic began to work. Again I was at a Summer School, this time in a hotel in Keswick of all places. The manager of the hotel had recently been a lion tamer and in respect of his treatment of his guests appeared to have imperfectly comprehended the fact that his occupation had changed. I was by this time running into good physical form, went up most of the stock 'tops' and on one occasion ran (with Kingsley Martin) all the way from the top of Eel Crag along Sail, Scar Crags and Causey Pike down into Newlands, down, in point of fact, into the beck which runs beside the Holiday Fellowship Hostel to bathe and so to tea in the Hostel. When the Summer School at the ex-lion tamer's came to an end, a few of us moved on to Buttermere and from Syke House Farm I climbed for the first time on to the Dale Head group, Hindscarth and Robinson, went on to the Grassmoor Fells, Whiteless Pike and Wandope, ranged over the plateau of Grassmoor and on a memorable day walked the ridge on the far side of the Lake over High Crag, High Stile, the Saddle and Buttermere Red Pike. From here, too, I got my first sight of Crummock and walking up Scale Force and later on to Mellbreak was moved by its beauty to begin my only novel—a very bad one and a sad tribute to the Lake.

The Lake Hunt

The fourth and the fifth and the sixth visit, and so on probably into the 'teens, was spent with the Trevelyan Lake Hunt. This is too remarkable an affair, too complex in its origins, glorious in its history and august in its traditions to be squeezed into a chapter on the Lakes, so I confine myself to a bald account of the proceedings as they were in my time.

Some twenty to twenty-five men gathered for three days at Whitsun under Mrs. Honey's roof at Seatoller House. In the morning at eight-thirty three of us, the hares, went off on to a given area of mountains, with red scarves over our shoulders. The boundaries of the area ran roughly from Grey Knotts along the ridge from Brandreth to Great Gable; then over Kirk Fell to Looking Stead; across Ennerdale to Scarth Gap and the Hay Stacks and so round by Fleetwith Pike to the disused railway running down to the top of the Honister. The hounds, the remaining twenty of us, started an hour later. The game was simple; the hares had to remain uncaught until five o'clock. The game, I say, sounds simple, but it was one of the most exciting I have ever played. When the hounds were heard baying on his track, a hare would hurl himself unthinkingly over edges from which in a quieter mood he would shrink as precipices. I can remember following G. M. Trevelyan, now Master of Trinity College, in a mist down the western slopes of Great Gable over a wilderness of rocks and screes the very aspect of which now fills me with alarm; I can remember a hard-pressed hare identifying himself with a party of tourists going up Great Gable; I can remember running in company with another hound off the Hay Stacks down Wharnscale Bottom after a hare who led us by a short head all the way to Buttermere where, finding a boat conveniently moored, he jumped into it and rowed jeeringly on to the Lake leaving the disconsolate hounds on the bank.

I can remember . . . but if I remember all the episodes of the hunt I shall go on to the end of the chapter.

In the evening there was a Gargantuan meal—at midday we ate exiguous sandwiches eked out by slices of cold, very heavy, Christmas pudding—in which rounds of beef and legs of mutton competed for a place on the table with chickens and geese, and we finished up by singing unaccompanied hunt songs, squeezed like sardines in the comfortable little parlour at the far end of Seatoller House.

Lunching at Sawrey

It was, I think, at my first hunt in 1921 that I was woken up in the middle of the night by a hail of small stones on the window pane. I got up to let in Kenneth Spence, who, arriving characteristically at midnight from Norway, had walked to Seatoller from Keswick to find the house locked up. At the end of that—or was it the next?—hunt, Spence and I walked over Esk Hause into Eskdale, threading our way through that muddled wilderness that surrounds Eel and Stoney Tarns and bathing in Eel—or was it Stoney? It was my first experience of the southward looking dales and, as next day I took the toy railway that ran from Boot to Ravenglass on the coast, I swore that Eskdale was the loveliest valley of them all, a view which I still hold.

Spence, who stayed behind in Eskdale, had fallen complete victim to the spell and took a house at Sawrey where he lived for the next twelve years, became a Lakeland character and founded the Friends of the Lake District, a body designed to protect the Lakes from pylons, roads over the passes, charabancs, speedboats, bungalows, tea huts on Helvellyn, hotels on Great Gable, shacks, shanties, concrete, tin, brass, barbed wire, gramophones, beach pyjamas and whatever else in the way of progress there may be.

On the morning of the fourth day, the hunt being now over, it became a custom for half a dozen of us to go to lunch with Spence. We would walk up Greenup Gill over High White Stones, the navel of the Lake District, and so on to the Langdales, whence we would run from Harrison Stickle all the way down to the Dungeon Ghyll Hotel, where a couple of cars would be waiting to take us to Sawrey. Whether it was the milder, lusher but no less lovely scenery of the southern dales, the masses of wild cherry blossom—for these occasions took place at Whitsun when the Lakes are at their best—the elegiac beauty of Esthwaite glimpsed through the trees, or the gigantic lunch beginning at about two-thirty after cocktails and Norwegian smoked herring and ending with port some two hours later—or whether it was the effect of all these things together, I do not know, but Sawrey came to wear for me a Capuan aspect and the journey from the rigours of the Seatoller Hunt to its warmer airs, softer company and luxurious living, to be likened to the passage of Hannibal's Army into winter quarters after the crossing of the Alps and the victories in Italy. How deliciously relaxed one felt, so that the late afternoon's walk on to Claife Heights, whence is one of the best views of the Lakeland peaks and the bathe in Claife Tarn seemed almost too great an exertion for the Capuan languors of the enfeebled body.

The Eastern Hills

From Sawrey House I explored ranges of the Lakes till then unknown to me. We would take the car up to the top of the Kirkstone Pass, climb Kilnshaw Chimney and so down into Ambleside; or we would go to Troutbeck, ascend and walk along the ridge from Yoke, Ill Bell and Froswick to Thornthwaite Beacon and High Street. We even penetrated into Kentmere and Mardale, before Mardale was submerged to make a Mancunian drink. Yet, even so, I have never had more than a superficial knowledge of these eastern hills and could wish that I knew them better than I do. I doubt now whether I shall. It is not merely that I grow old and tired and with difficulty heave my fattening form to the top of its one poor peak a day; this is bad enough, but worse is that I grow giddy.

Let there be the smoothest and safest of green slopes without a hint of difficulty or danger, then, provided that there be empty space on either side of me with nothing for my eye to rest on to break the drop, I become the victim of sensations indescribable but appalling. I shut my eyes, grovel and crawl like a beast on the ground, and presently rush down forbidding and even dangerous slopes in a frantic endeavour to get away from that terrifying emptiness.

The Lakeland Foothills

And so in these later years I have come to gravitate—it is the exact word—towards the hills and valleys of the south-west, where the Lakeland mountains dwindle through lovely complexities of tangled foothills to the sea. Here are richer and more varied flowers, wilder and more numerous bird life than anywhere in England that I know. So I came to unknown Rusland, loveliest of hidden Lakeland valleys with its great view of the mountains, saw the slopes of Winster covered with their April daffodils, walked up Miterdale, penetrated to Devoke Water and explored the lower reaches of the Duddon. And when the increasing invasion of the Lakes has sent me scuttling in search of solitude, I have made my way up the River Bleng to the heart of Copeland Forest and going over Caw Fell and Iron Crag found myself in the Kinniside country, where a man may walk a whole day in August and not only not meet a soul but—a more healing thing still—know in his heart that he won't meet a soul. And Lank Rigg anyway is a fine hill and not to be despised by those for whom 'the Lakes' means only 'the tops'.

This chapter has fallen between the stools of guide book and personal reminiscence. I could continue in the same vein, telling for instance how Rydal on a summer evening is my favourite lake, the scramble over Bowfell and Crinkle Crags my favourite ridge walk, Lingcove Beck my favourite stream and Eskdale my favourite valley—but this, I see, I have already told, and what anyway is a mere catalogue of likes and dislikes?

THE MOUNTAINS AND THE MOORS

Reasons for the Spell of the Lakes

Let me, then, try as briefly as I can to analyse the reasons for the hold which the mountains came so gradually to exert upon me. At first I don't think I liked them; brought up in the south of England, I instinctively inherited the eighteenth-century view of wild and mountainous scenery. It is little more than two hundred years ago that Defoe was writing of a tract 'the wildest, most barren and frightful of any that I have travelled over in England, or even in Wales itself. . . . But 'tis of no advantage to represent horror as the Character of the Country, in the middle of all the frightful appearances to right and left; here are some very pleasant, populous and manufacturing towns.' Once I agreed.

It is difficult to put on record the reasons for your likings, and when liking deepens into love, the difficulty becomes insuperable. At first the attraction was largely physical, the joy of the tautened muscle and the stretched limb and the exhilaration of running down a slope. The Lakeland mountains are the best for scrambling that may be found anywhere. They are friendly and, provided that you don't go out of your way to affront them, tweaking their noses and pulling their eyebrows, as climbers do, they will let you have your way with them and do pretty much as you like. In Switzerland a man not knowing the mountains behaves like a fool who ventures out without a party or even, it may be, without a guide, since lacking party and guide, he may well get into trouble; but in the Lakes neither guide nor party is necessary, and unless a man does behave like a fool he won't get into trouble.

Later, aesthetic factors came to predominate. There was the factor of size and shape. It is rarely in Switzerland that from the valleys the mountains can be seen as a whole and, when they can, those vast, unmanageable hulks of rock are too big to take in. The Lakeland mountains are sizable. You can see them and take in their lovely and ever changing shapes at a glance. (Parenthetically with what interest did I see a Swiss guide point at midday from the bottom of the Styhead to a ledge halfway up Gable: 'A good place', he said, 'to pitch a tent for the night'; with what incredulity did he receive my announcement

98

that we would be there in an hour, and with what amusement did I see him verify it!) There is the factor of light which is in large part the factor of mist. When the mist comes down, I am filled with an indefinable depression. I am afraid of getting lost, but the losing of my body is less formidable than the apprehensions of my lowered spirit. Then the mist breaks, and through a shifting veil one sees the valley, Ennerdale say, below. It is one of the great moments of one's life and, however often it is repeated, the magic of it holds. There is the factor of contrast, the barrenness of the hills enhances the lushness of the valleys and to descend from the former into the latter is to be enfolded by an atmosphere of warmth and welcome which is never purely physical, for always it includes a sense of homecoming. There are Lakeland farmhouses and, once, there was rum butter; there are the becks, the tarns, the skylines, the ever changing shapes of the hills—but, not knowing how to express or convey the emotions which the Lakes have aroused in me, I see that I am falling back on repetition and will have done.

Passage to other Districts

Just as my praise of walking might, had the necessary knowledge and experience been mine, have been given to cycling or to camping or even—though the bitter-sweet delights, painful pleasures and agreeable distresses which go to the making of the rock climber's complication of emotions may well have been intended for the enjoyment only of spiritual masochists—to rock climbing, so my praise of the Lakes might have gone to Snowdonia or the Cheviots or the Peak District or the Yorkshire Dales or to Dartmoor or Exmoor or even the New Forest, had I known them and loved them equally well. I do know them— indeed, I have lived for considerable periods both in Snowdonia and the New Forest—but not with the same particularity, nor do I love them so well.

The Highlands

There is, also, of course, the question of the Highlands. These demand a chapter to themselves but I do not know them well enough to write it.[1] They provide, however, it is obvious, sites not for one but for a number of National Parks. As I write there comes news of the gift of the Kintail estate in Western Ross to the National Trust for Scotland. This would make the nucleus of an ideal National Park, comprising as it does 14,000 acres of untouched mountain and moorland with fine views of Glenshiel and Loch Duich and including a great miscellany of peaks all of them over 3,000 feet high. Along its southern borders runs that lovely road to Kyle of Lochalsh which so many of us have followed to Skye, a road which solves the problem of access for motorist and cyclist. If this estate were made into a National Park, accommodation would, of course, have to be provided, since the whole area has been deliberately laid waste to facilitate the amusements of the deer stalkers.[2] But the question of accommodation arises in connection with any proposed National Park and will be discussed below.

I mention the Kintail estate here because, together with Glencoe and Ardgartan, this new gift to the National Trust for Scotland enables us to comfort ourselves with the assurance that some part at least of the Highland scenery, some of the loveliest in the world, will be made permanently available for the enjoyment of us all. A number of so-called Forestry Parks have recently been proposed, notably in the Cairngorms and the Galloway Hills. These, provided that he is made free of them, the walker will welcome, but he will be well advised not to accept them as substitutes for National Parks proper, if only because they are too small to qualify by the standards generally accepted for National Parks. For example, the smallest of the areas proposed by John Dower in his Report on National Parks,[3] published in May 1945, is 64,000 acres this being the area of a park running along the coastline. But the area of the proposed Forestry Parks is considerably less. The consideration of smallness of size is an objection which also may be brought against the Kintail estate, if it is regarded as a separate National Park in its own right. Here with apologies for platitudes and the general insuffi-

---

[1] A friend has stepped in with a statement on the Highlands which is a valuable supplement to the meagre treatment in the text. It is printed as an Appendix to this chapter (pp. 110–113).

[2] See Postscript to Appendix II, pp. 247–252.   [3] See Appendix I.

ciency of my treatment, I leave the Highlands to be dealt with in the Appendix[1] printed at the end of this chapter and return to the Lakes.

The Cumberland Coast

There are two considerations which commend the Lake District as the most eligible of all the possible texts which I might have chosen for the sermon which I wish to preach. First, it is small and very compact; not more than twenty-five miles as the crow flies from east to west or twenty-eight from north to south. Secondly, partly for this reason, partly because of the distinctive characteristics of its scenery, it is peculiarly defenceless against the forces and influences of our time. Take, for example, the case of motor roads.

Along the coast of Cumberland lie a string of towns which in peace-time constituted a severely distressed area. Whitehaven, Maryport and Workington suffered in pre-war days from some of the highest unemployment figures in the country. In Maryport, I believe, at one time over 70 per cent of those registered as insured persons were living on the dole.

One of the reasons for their distress was the inaccessibility of these places; they lay in a back-water cut off from the main stream of our national life. From the north you reached them from Carlisle via Cockermouth, and the journey was slow. Coming from the south, you branched off from the main line at Carnforth and took the train to Barrow. From Barrow the line winds in and out along the edge of a highly indented coast. The coast of this part of Lancashire—Furness, it is or used to be called—reminds one of the teeth of an irregular saw. Bits of it stick far out into the sea. I think of them—I expect I am wrong, and that if I knew them better I should be disillusioned as usual—as romantic; they are at least remote and unvisited. A W.E.A. tutor who took a class in these parts told me strange stories about the people. It appears that in these further parts they still sing; for all I know, they may even dance.

And if you think that this chatter about remoteness and romance is a private whimsy of my own, read that astonishing

[1] See pp. 110–113. See also the Postscript to Appendix II.

novel, *The Lonely Plough*, by Constance Holme. The author has the feeling of and for this part of the world in her bones; has it so strongly as to lull and overcome my prejudice against lush and romantic books, so that I read her with the same kind of fascinated appreciation that one brings to the Brontës or Hardy. Her account of the breaking in of the sea and the flooding of the low lands of the Duddon estuary is one of the most exciting things that comparatively unknown English literature has to offer.

As you approach Millom, the line runs round the curve of an enormous loop so that you first see the town right in front of you and then find yourself making a long detour of a dozen miles or more to reach it. The line goes a long way inland in order to find a bridge over the Duddon whose estuary was too wide to seem worth bridging to the engineers of those more leisurely days in which the Cumberland coast line was constructed. If you are not in a hurry, this journey is delightful, in fact, it is one of the most romantic railway journeys in England. On your left is the sea; on your right are the rivers and mountains, assuming every conceivable variety of lovely shape as the line twists and turns to let you get a new view of them. On a fine day they look blue and insubstantial, seeming to float rather than to be. They look in fact like the backcloth of a stage scene which might at any moment be lifted to reveal a reality behind. (All this, I suppose, is due to some trick of the light. Those who know the west coast of Scotland will know at once what I am talking about, but I have not the poetic insight to say more than that the effect here is perceptibly the same as excites visitors to the west coast of Scotland, but is less marked. The point is that you feel that the veil that separates the seen from the unseen world is thinning and that at any moment it might part to reveal a glimpse of a different order of reality. I am told that on the south-west coast of Ireland the veil is thinner still. On the list of the many places which I have contracted with myself to visit after the war, the south-west coast of Ireland comes first.[1]) The foreground of this coastal railway scenery is also attractive; the vegetation is surprisingly lush and

[1] Since the above was written I have visited it, and what I have been told is true.

south-westward looking places like Grange and Arnside have that almost tropical appearance which you find at Port Meirion on the Merionethshire coast, or even more strikingly at Parknasilla on the south-west coast of Kerry. But most people are in a hurry; so are you, if you have come up from London and have grown impatient over this last long stretch to Seascale, where you are only too glad to get off the train and take Mr. Irvine's car to Wasdale. So, too, are the products of industry and nothing will alter the fact that from Barrow to Whitehaven is a journey which takes nearly three hours. Hence arises the demand for a quicker approach to these places. The journey could, of course, be shortened; for example, by a bridge over the Duddon estuary to cut out the Millom loop. But that would be a costly and elaborate undertaking.

What alternatives are there? One is to approach them from the east. Now, to approach them from the east means driving a good road through the hills and passes of the Lake District, a project which the Cumberland County Council have had under consideration for years.

Roads Through the Lake District

The making of such a road would, it is said, give employment to many hundreds of men over a period of many years. More important still, it would open up the towns on the coast to through traffic from the east and so bring them back into the main stream of our industrial life.

Another proposal is for a road over the Styhead pass. Such are the resources of modern engineering that the thing could, alas, be done. That some contrivance has been devised or some increment of power obtained which will enable human beings to move faster, fly higher, kill more of their fellows or alter more rapidly the position of matter in space than before is in the contemporary world regarded as a sufficient reason for making use of it. Nobody ever asks whether the use of the contrivance, the employment of the power, will make us happier, wiser or better. Hence, the fact that men now have the power to drive a road over Styhead seems to many a sufficient reason for doing it. Why, after all, should it not be done? Why should the solitudes of Wasdale *not* be made available to the motorist? Why should old ladies *not* be carried in state and vehicles propelled by petrol through the proud and lonely fastnesses of the mountains, proud and lonely no longer when the car has humbled and peopled them? Why not, indeed? I do not know what answer I can make to this question, except to invoke again the values which I have sought to indicate in earlier pages.

The Values Involved

For what is involved here is assuredly a question of values. Is it better that all the wild and lonely places that are left in England should be made accessible to all and in the process cease to be wild and lonely; or, is it good that some places should be set apart, where a man may be assured of quiet and solitude and in face of the grandeur of nature know the ways of the spirit and enter into the possession of his soul? And if it be thought that this is too rarefied a phraseology to describe the effects of a ramble in the hills, I will be more humdrum and express the view that it is right and proper that all people and especially young people should be assured of the opportunities of occasional escape from the trivial safety of our mechanical peacetime civilization; that the chance of adventure, even it may be of danger, should be given to them so that they may feel the awe and the mystery of the world. Such feelings come to men more easily in the mountain solitudes, especially when they have known fatigue and exposed themselves to risk, than anywhere in nature save, perhaps, in the desert or upon the sea. Our young men have been driven increasingly to resort to the mountains of Norway and Switzerland to enjoy these experiences, since a visit to the Highlands costs too much and, when you get there, there is nowhere to stay, while the Lakes and Snowdonia have become too accessible and too many are already in occupation. For these 'too many', the small area of our mountain scenery is being made comfortable and with comfort comes vulgarity. To enjoy vulgarity in comfort is, no doubt, very well; it is the only form of enjoyment of which many, perhaps most of us, are capable. But, let it not be doubted, the roads over the passes, the cars and the soft, fat hotels upon which the enjoyment and the comfort of the many depend, destroy for the few those rarer and more difficult goods which it is so hard to describe and so easy to forget. (I say 'the few', yet I would include all those who by their own sweat and labour have climbed the passes and made their way into the secret places of the hills and these are, in truth, many and grow more.)

We have already experienced the effects of new roads in the Lake District. There is the road over the Honister Pass, on the top of which motorists may be seen in their overcoated hundreds picnicking by the roadside with their backs to the view and their faces to the cars, inhaling the incense of petrol as they worship at the shrine of the mechanical god. By that road Buttermere has been laid open and one of the loveliest of the quiet places of the Lakes ravished. Again, there is the road over Hard Knott and Wrynose where motor-cycles snort and stink in the emulation of ignoble competitions. A road over the Styhead would destroy the loneliness and mystery of Wasdale as surely as a stone shivers a piece of glass, just as a through road over Black Sail pass to the Cumberland coast would vulgarize Ennerdale. There is, too, a terrifying proposal to enlarge and modernize the little road that runs through the solitudes of Loweswater, mildest and most meditative of the Lakes. Two small stretches of this road were in fact 'improved' (awkward corners were rounded off and the road was grossly widened) in 1937, but the undertaking lapsed with the war. The widening of this road was part of a larger scheme for a good, wide road running all the way from Cockermouth to Buttermere to link up with the road over the Honister. This proposal raised strong local opposition and has been temporarily stopped.

The Other Enemies

The district has other enemies, legions of them. There are the villas built of concrete and pink, southern slates. I have heard of factories—there is already one on the shores of Windermere—and of a proposal for a hydro-electric station at the lower end of Wasdale. The electricity companies would send pylons stalking over the hills, the Forestry Commission would blanket them with trees. And continuously the motorists are demanding more roads and wider roads that they may travel the more easily to more hotels and smarter hotels. Squalid camps spring up in Borrowdale; gramophones are heard upon the waters of Derwentwater, and young women grill their bodies like steaks upon its shores. All the apparatus of the seaside resort plus the Butlin Camp plus the smart hotel rolled into one great ball of entertainment are clamouring for the right to exploit the beauty of the Lakes for their profit. They will succeed, unless we can turn the Lake District into a National Park.

What National Parks Mean

What does the expression National Park mean? An established and respectable body, the Standing Committee on National Parks which is composed of members of organizations representing ramblers, cyclists, campers and naturalists and also of the Councils for the Preservation of Rural England and Wales who convene the meetings of the Committee, after considering the matter for some ten years has recently[1] produced a definition of a National Park. National Parks are defined as follows: 'Regions of our finest landscape brought into full public service—preserved in their natural beauty, continued in their farming use and kept or made accessible (in so far as they are not cultivated) for open-air recreation and public enjoyment and particularly for cross-country walking.' This contains the heart of the matter; it brings out in particular the important point that the main principle which the concept of the National Park embodies is a negative one. The principle is, in fact, the principle of 'let alone'. The principle of 'let alone' means that an area such as the Lake District should be left in its natural state, left, that is to say, just as it is; that no steps should be taken to open it up, or make it easier for people to get there, or to make it easier for people who *have got there* to sit about in it or be carried about in it or to be entertained in it.

Applied in practice, the principle means no villas, no wide concrete roads, no road houses, no elaborate pubs or smart

[1] December 1944.

hotels, no pylons, no sprucing and smartening up, no iron railings, no privet bushes, no advertisement hoardings. Local industries which do not disfigure the countryside, e.g. sheep farming in the Lake District and on the South Downs, pig and pony keeping and timber cutting in the New Forest, should be maintained, even encouraged; quarrying and mining should be prevented and, where they already go on, stopped. (Who does not know those mounds of slate and shale that disfigure the surroundings of Blaenau Ffestiniog, or the white scar which the china clay works have left upon the purple face of Dartmoor? It is the dispensation of a merciful Providence that nobody has yet found anything in the way of iron, coal, oil or clay in the Lake District; let us pray to God that they never will.)

Parks of Different Types

Within the context of the general principle of 'let alone' there can, it is obvious, be National Parks of different types. The treatment given to a comparatively cultivated countryside, for example, to parts of the Sussex Downs, would be different from that which commends itself in the case of wild country. And while I am on the subject of National Parks of different types, I propose to put in a plea for Rutlandshire. Rutlandshire is easy to find though tantalizingly difficult to stay in; however hard you try, you always find yourself slipping off it into some other county, into Lincolnshire, or Leicestershire or Northamptonshire. The county is very largely composed of great estates. These cannot, it is obvious, be maintained indefinitely and, so soon as their owners give up the unequal struggle, their lands will be sold and broken up for building. Now the landscape of Rutland consists of beautiful, rolling country. It is the archetype and quintessence of the country which we delight to see in sporting prints. It has not yet been spoilt, but it soon will be. The towns of Rutland, Uppingham and Oakham, are both as pleasant as can be. This is the moment for the State to step in and institute a special scheme for the county as a whole, the main purpose of which would be to ensure that any development which might be permitted should be strictly controlled. I am tempted to apply the term National Park to such an area as Rutlandshire. I refrain on the ground that the treatment which it requires differs in radical particulars from that which is suitable for the Lake District; for example, no special facilities are required for access and accommodation. But I refrain only on the understanding that abstention from scheduling an area as a National Park is not to be regarded as tantamount to a concession that it should be left to the mercies of unrestricted development.

The principle of National Parks would, I should have thought, commend itself to this generation, since very little has to be done in them and the expenditure on their upkeep is, therefore, negligible. The initial cost of turning a mountainous region like Snowdonia or the Peak into a National Park would be practically nil. Where some development value presumably exists, as I fear may be the case in the Lake District, in the North Yorkshire dales or on the Pembrokeshire and Cornish coasts, the burden would not fall upon the rates but upon the administering authority.

As to accommodation, it should be a charge upon the administering authority to ensure that places to sleep in and feed in should be available. They should be simple and unpretentious and should not aim at making a profit. For young people, the Youth Hostels constitute an admirable model; for older people, who need more comfort and places to read in and rest in, the Hostels and Houses of the Holiday Fellowship and the Co-operative Holidays Association might be taken over and extended. I say 'taken over', yet the administering authority would be well advised to turn over the whole business of accommodation and catering to these admirable bodies, reinforced by members of the Youth Hostels Association and the Workers' Travel Association, who have been engaged on this sort of work for years and know pretty well by now what to do and what not to do. As to the administering authority, it should be national and not local; should, in fact, be a National Committee set up by and responsible to the Ministry of Town and Country Planning.

THE MOUNTAINS AND THE MOORS

Administration by a National not a Local Authority

This last is of fundamental importance. At present the wild areas in this country are under the control of Local Authorities, the assumption being that they are of concern only to those who live in the area. The assumption of course dates back to the days of restricted transport when men travelled rarely and with difficulty outside their own areas. Now it does not occur to the Local Authorities who administer the wild areas to treat them as if they were national assets to be preserved for national use, nor, indeed, is the average Local Authority qualified to do so. Just because an area *is* wild, it is thinly populated and the Local Authority therefore is poor. Therefore, it is usually without the means to operate such legislation as may exist for the protection of the countryside, legislation which is almost always permissive, hardly ever compulsory,[1] nor can it afford to exercise such powers as it may possess to prevent the area under its control from being developed and ruined. On the contrary, just because it *is* poor, it seeks inevitably to attract the largest possible number of tourists to its area. It further desires them to be as rich as possible and it proposes, so far as lies within its power, to give them the kind of entertainment that they enjoy at Bournemouth or Blackpool. Thus, Keswick clamours for a great by-passing motor road and plans its Winter Garden.

Local Authorities are, after all, mainly composed of those townspeople who are tradesmen in the town. How can they not wish to make of the area under their control a vast pleasure ground, run on ordinary commercial lines and designed to attract the largest possible number of people who will spend their money in and about the town on the pleasures and the goods that it pays members of the Local Authority to offer and to sell? The main objection to walkers is after all that they are such bad consumers. Are they at the cinema, at the dance hall, or at the roundabouts? They are not. Are they at the dirt track, or 'the dogs'? They are not. Are they riding in buses or charabancs, or dancing to gramophones? They are not. For the most part they consume nothing but shoe leather and occasional

[1] See Appendix VI.

pints. Their amusements are confined to the ninepenny Pelican or Penguin they carry in their packs. In extreme cases they are content with a green thought in a green shade and consume nothing at all. Who, then, who has money to make and things to sell wants walkers?

In the case of the Lake District the difficulties that arise from Local Authority administration are complicated by the fact that the district as a whole falls within the area of three separate County Councils, Cumberland, Westmorland, and Lancashire, of eight Rural and three Urban District Councils, and of eleven separate planning authorities who do not always see eye to eye. It is largely because of their disagreements that they have been unable or unwilling to take concerted action. For this reason, it is essential that the controlling authority for a National Park should be not a local body concerned only with local interests, but a national body which, regarding the area as an asset to the nation as a whole, regards itself as responsible for the preservation of the nation's heritage.

Appendix to Chapter V on the Highlands of Scotland

By Philip Cleave

These present problems differ somewhat from those of the other areas discussed. There is the matter of size. Confronted by a map of the Highlands the walker rejoices, but feels a little overawed. In that vast expanse there is, he might think, scope enough for a lifetime of experience and of effort. And he would be right. But the systematic depopulation of large areas in order to reserve their use for a select few, followed by decades of economic neglect, has raised problems of access, accommodation and transport which are likely severely to restrict his movements. The dangers which menace the Highlands are pressing, but the threat of hordes of people swarming over the country and disfiguring it with unplanned agglomerations of brick and tin is fortunately not one of them. The remoteness of all the finest regions from centres of population will serve to limit the amount of new building undertaken. Nor, given the large scale of the country, are new roads, properly sited and of minimum width, likely unduly to mar the scene; indeed, some increased transport facilities will in any event be necessary. Along a magnificent coast sea transport can be improved without damage to amenities; busy little harbours are not necessarily less sightly than derelict ones.

Water-power schemes, conifer plantations, the depredations of service departments—these and 'sporting rights' are the chief dangers from which the Highlands must be protected. As usual, the very choicest spots are those selected for attack. The best solution is to schedule the whole area west and north of a line running from Loch Long through Glen Falloch, Loch Tay, Pitlochry, Glen Shee, Braemar, Inverness, Dingwall and Lairg to the Kyle of Tongue as a National Park. When this suggestion is made, it is objected that the plan is too ambitious to be practical politics and that we should seek rather to form a number of smaller parks. What, it may be asked, has already been done in this direction?

Glencoe with its superb surrounding mountains has been acquired by the Scottish National Trust, not, unhappily, before a broad new speed-road had been blasted through the glen. The Trust has also secured control of the area round Loch Duich and the Five Sisters in Kintail. All that is needed to make this magnificent mingling of sea, loch and mountains accessible is some modest accommodation. Since the inn at Shiel Bridge was closed, there is nowhere to stay. The Trust holds many other properties such as waterfalls and historic buildings. It is reasonable to expect their number to grow and to include such places as the Trossachs and Loch Lomondside, regions outside the area principally considered here.

Of the areas calling for protection, priority goes to Ben Nevis and his neighbours, the Aonachs and Glen Nevis, buttressed on the south by the peaks of Mamore Forest. All this area is technically deer forest, but prior to 1939 the shooting had been unlet for several seasons. Britain's highest mountain with its lovely glen should be saved from the assault of railway and refreshment booth, and from any extension of the hideous pipelines which disfigure the slopes above Inverlochy.

Next come the Cairngorms, the largest expanse of peaks over four thousand feet and the wildest and most inaccessible mountain group in the Highlands. This was the first region actually proposed as a National Park for Scotland. It is eminently suitable, but the proposal will be fiercely resisted, as the whole stretch is deer forest and in the thirty miles from Aviemore to Braemar by the Lairig Ghru there is no accommodation. An offer by Scottish mountaineers to repair a ruined hut for use as a shelter in emergency was refused by the owner.

Of all the beauties of Scotland, glen scenery is perhaps the most characteristic. Undoubtedly the finest glens lie west of the Caledonian Canal—the finest mountains and, many hold, the finest coast scenery also—and Glens Affric and Cannich, at least, should receive protection, particularly as they are the objects of recurring water-power schemes, if, indeed, such protection is not in these cases already too late.

In the islands, the Cuillin Hills of Skye and the mountainous northern part of Arran are intrinsically and by virtue of compactness pre-eminently suitable for Parks.

There are other areas no less suitable than necessary.[1] Of particular interest is the unique district stretching across the borders of Ross and Sutherland from Ullapool to north of Loch Assynt, where the great detached mountains of Coigach and Suilven, Canisp and Quinag rear their spiky backs like dinosaurs from a moorland sprinkled with hundreds of lochs great and small. The reader may ask what object is served by 'protecting' wild mountains that nobody wants to spoil anyway. The answer is that many of the finest mountains lie in deer forests, and the walker is sternly warned off. Moreover, lest he ignore the warnings, more practical steps are taken. At least one inn has been closed in Scotland. This was no accident in the ordinary course of business but part of a deliberate policy which has included obstructing roads, the breaking up of their surfaces, the erection of menacing notices which are often illegal—although, under the Scottish Trespass Acts, it is actually an offence to camp on private land without the owner's consent—forbidding tenants to succour the

---

[1] A full list of National Parks proposed for Scotland is given in Appendix I.

wanderer under threat of penalty or dismissal, and closing inns by the simple process of opposing the renewal of their licences. (The licensing authorities and the deer forest interests are frequently identical.) Access thus involves walking prohibitive distances. In a National Park access would be a right, transport could be discreetly improved and modest and seemly hostels and small inns established.

A Postscript on 'access' in Scotland, by Edwin Royce, is printed at the end of Appendix II.

Chapter Six

THE MOUNTAINS AND THE MOORS

II. Access and the Peak

The Peak Country

I am not an enthusiast for the Peak District. It is wild; it is even grand, but the grandeur partakes of the savage rather than of the beautiful. All the ingredients which make the north of England so attractive to the southerner are present; hills and rocks, heather-clad moorlands, swift rushing streams of clear water, wide views; above all, the sense of space and remoteness. For this is a big country; it is austere, almost scornful in its disdain for the adventitious prettinesses of flower and coppice and hedgerow. It can be formidable, too; to be lost in a mist on Kinder Scout and put to the necessity of dropping into and climbing out of the deep peat ditches with which the top of that gloomy plateau is seamed and scarred is no joke, while the outcropping rocks of blackened gritstone, grim enough at all times, when the mist comes down and the rain falls look very forbidding indeed. Just beyond Haworth—you need not tell me that this is not in the Peak District; it is enough for my purpose that the geological formation is the same and the aspect of the country is, therefore, the same—are the moors, described in *Wuthering Heights*—Withins Heights, the place is called on the map. Here is a derelict farmhouse, commanding great views over heather-clad slopes of moorland to the distant green of the valley of the Aire with the skyline of remoter moors, Rumbalds and Ilkley rising to the north beyond. Last time I visited Withins there was a storm. The thunder rumbled, the lightning flashed and all those miles of country were half hidden behind a veil of streaming rain. Nowhere in England or in Wales, I thought, had I seen so wild and savage a scene. Certainly not in the Lakes, not in the Cheviots, not even in the Dales—nowhere in fact but in the Peak district, looking north-eastwards from the edge of Kinder on to Bleaklow under a sky darkening for snow. Perhaps because I like the adventitious prettiness, like at least to know that it is not too far off and is there for the visiting when I want it, I have never taken this country to my heart as I have the Lakes.

Nor do I feel for it the affection which I have for the Yorkshire Dales or the Cleveland Hills and the moors of East Yorkshire, though these latter are in many ways like the Peak District, particularly the country round Lilla Cross at the back of Ravenscar. (Yet whether it is the felt proximity of the sea, or the exhilaration of the east coast air, or the many valleys, Whisperdale, Silver Dale, High Dale and so on, which thrust their green fingers into the moor, I have never here had the same feeling of unfriendliness and indifference, as if I were an alien creature travelling across a remote and hostile environment, that sometimes oppresses me in the Peak District.

In all this I am, it is clear, speaking only for myself and I bid myself beware of the temptation to treat my private tastes and fancies, dictated by who knows what accidental associations, into canons of aesthetic judgment. Also I am speaking only of the northern area of what is called the Peak District. I have said nothing of the green and friendlier country which stretches on the south nearly to Bakewell; of Hope Valley and Cave Dale, of Bretton Clough and Middleton Dale, of Miller's Dale and Monsal Dale, of Grindleford and the valley of the Derwent. There are high moors between these Dales, but the greenness, the curving contours and the wide views to the high escarpments which lie on their boundaries, Axe Edge to the west, Curbar, Baslow and Stanage to the east and Rushup and Grindsbrook to the north, give an impression of grandeur without unfriendliness. Here week-end after week-end come men and women from Sheffield and Derby, from the Derbyshire coalfields and the Staffordshire potteries.

But the Manchester men with whom I have chiefly gone in company make for the grimmer country to the north, which evokes an affection amounting at times to a fanatical zeal as week-end after week-end they tramp vast distances over the moors.

And how well they know it! To go with one of them over

Bleaklow or the Stanage Moors is to tap a knowledge of the countryside which only a great personal love could have inspired. How, too, they champion it against the Lakes, against the Dales, against even Scotland itself.

Perhaps they champion it the more eagerly for the disability under which it and they labour, for upon all this country lies a curse, the curse of the keeper.

Crocodile in the Peak

I shall not easily forget the first time I saw the curse in operation. I had gone out from Manchester early on a Sunday morning in April for my first view of the Peak District. I found the Central Station alive with ramblers, all dressed up for a day's walk on the Derbyshire moors, complete with rucksacks, hobnail boots and shorts.

My walk started from Hayfield and we found ourselves almost at once on a path leading on to the moor. It was a gorgeous path commanding wide views over miles of moorland country and finally descending steeply by Jacob's Ladder to Edale. It was, of course, unfenced and on either side of it there stretched for mile upon mile the empty spaces of the moor. The walk, nevertheless, was a disappointment, for we were not unaccompanied. Straggling along the path both in front and behind there must have been hundreds of walkers; indeed, so close were we packed that we looked for all the world like a girls' school taking the air in 'crocodile' on a Sunday afternoon.

Why did we keep so religiously to the path as though we were ants on a run? Because to leave it was to brave an encounter with the keepers, and being for the most part law-abiding folk, we were prepared to be penned, cribbed, cabined, and confined rather than transgress the rights of private property. Yet so confined, we were deprived of the healing power of solitude, deprived of the exhilaration of emptiness and vastness, deprived of the sense of spaciousness which are the great gifts of the moors by which we were surrounded, but which we were denied.

In this whole area of uncultivated moorland which lies between Manchester and Sheffield, an area of over 230 square miles, there are only twelve public footpaths which are more than two miles long; of the 150,000-odd acres involved, only 1,212 acres are open to the public; 109,000 acres are in private ownership, while 39,000 are owned by Local Authorities who mysteriously debar the citizens whom they are supposed to represent from access to the land of which they as citizens are part owners. The Peak itself, a bare plateau of some thirteen square miles, is uncrossed by a single right of way. Bleaklow, thirty-seven square miles in extent, which is only sixteen miles from Manchester and sixteen from Sheffield, boasts not a single footpath. For Bleaklow, in common with most of the rest of this country, is preserved for the shooting of grouse. Upon it, the hand of the keeper lies heavy; walkers are frowned at by notice boards and everywhere trespassers are prosecuted. Hence to leave the path was to risk an encounter with a keeper, with the certainty of being cursed and the possibility of being prosecuted. Let us see what it means to encounter a keeper.

Encounters with a Keeper

I am with a party—it is, in fact, a club—of ramblers from Manchester and we are ascending Kinder Scout by Kinder Downfall, where a fairly substantial stream makes its way in a series of leaps down a gorge. It is a hot day in June and, as the party includes several inexperienced walkers, it takes us a couple of hours to reach the top. We sit down and rest; we are, in point of fact, having our lunch and enjoying the view which to the north extends over many miles of moorland, when we hear ourselves hailed by a voice. We turn round and see a man approaching with gun, stick, dog and threatening aspect.

'Off with you,' he says. 'You know you are not allowed here.'

I am for expostulating; for explaining that we are doing no damage, that we are peaceable and ordinary citizens who have left the prison of the towns in order to enjoy the air of the countryside and to look at the view, that we have only just finished fighting—this, by the way, was in 1920—to preserve, or so we had been told, the freedom of the land of our forefathers, and that as free men we are jolly well going to enjoy it and that he ought to be ashamed of himself—hired lackey of the rich, that he is—for trying to stop us, and so on with more to the same effect. In case my eloquence and arguments produced no result—I don't suppose for a moment they would have had any—I should have led the keeper a dance (I could run in those days) in and out of the ditches which criss-cross the top of Kinder Scout.

However, I was not the leader of the party and the leader said none of these things. He was a docile chap—most ramblers, by the way, are; they come from the class that has for centuries been used to obeying rather than to issuing orders—and all he said was, 'But we have only just got up to the top of Kinder and the ladies are tired and want to rest. Can't we, please, stay for another ten minutes before we go down again?' This had no effect. We must get up, the keeper said, and get off at once. If we did not, he would find means to make us and, as if to make good his word, he marched forward and stood over us, threatening us until such time as we had hurriedly put together the remains of our lunch, after which with our tails between our legs we allowed ourselves to be hustled off the plateau, the keeper, still complete with dog, stick and gun, shepherding us until we were well down into the valley.

I am again walking over the Derbyshire moors, this time over Froggatt Edge, a long frowning escarpment of gritstone rock, rising some six hundred feet from the valley and constituting the edge of a wide-spreading moorland plateau. Seen from below, it looks like the cutting edge of a rather dissipated saw. We had come up to it from the country round Chatsworth, enjoying the contrast between the purple heather on the moor in front and the green parkland that we had left behind. Over the edge we went and out on to the moors beyond. These were studded, wherever a track left the road, with notices asserting their uncompromising privacy and warning all-comers that they would be prosecuted and fined, should they venture to set foot upon them. But you cannot placard a tract of country stretching perhaps a dozen miles along the whole range of its edge, and we presently found a track diverging from the road on to the moorland proper, which was unprotected by any notice. We had scarcely walked for more than a couple of minutes along this track when the inevitable keeper made his appearance. For a hundred yards or so he stalked us, and then, popping up abruptly from behind a wall, demanded to know what we thought we were doing. Did we, he asked, know that this was private property? If so, how came we to be there? If not, how had we avoided seeing the notices? Anyway, whether we knew it or not, private it was, and we must immediately return to the road. This time I was with one friend and as we were both young and fairly fleet we could have defied the keeper, running off over the plateau and challenging him to follow us. However, we did not run or challenge, for it so happened that on that very afternoon I was to address a Winnats Pass demonstration in favour of access to mountains and moorlands and I wished to interrogate the keeper, thereby obtaining ammunition for my speech and heaping fuel on the flames of just indignation.

I asked him, accordingly, whether he spent the whole day and every day upon the moors trying to keep other people off them, whether he was proud of his job, whether he liked it, and how much he was paid to do it; whether he thought it was creditable in him to spend his life playing dog in the manger by frightening away from the moors which bored him the hundreds of people whom the moors would have delighted, and so on. Under this rain of questions the keeper was for the most part inarticulate, or abusive when he contrived to be articulate. In so far, however, as he supplied me with any coherent account of his activities, it ran more or less as follows—or rather, since this is a convenient place to summarize the reasons which are adduced in favour of preserving the moors inviolate from the feet of walkers, and since the keeper made such a poor job of his apologia that I should be ashamed not to put a better case before my readers, even though it be a wicked one, assuming him to have marshalled and properly presented such pitiful arguments as you will sometimes find in articles in papers such as *The Field* or *Country Life*, it *should* have run more or less as follows.

Arguments of Landowners

He would have said, in the first place, that complaints on the score of the monopolizing of the moors by sportsmen and land-owners are without foundation, that, in short, the walkers' fuss is a fuss about nothing. 'Those who delight in long walks know well enough by experience that, for example, in the wilder parts of Scotland, Wales and the Lake District and the dales, they are free to wander where they like, provided always that they show a due consideration for the convenience and rights of other people.'[1] Secondly, let us suppose that the walker were given free access to the moors, and that the original 'Access to Mountains' Bill[2] had become law. In five years' time, he would have continued, 'game birds would be practically extinct', and the practice of shooting them would have, therefore, to be abandoned. 'You cannot have both ramblers and grouse,' as a candid landowner bluntly asserted in a B.B.C. talk on The Future of the Moors in 1939.

Why can you not have both ramblers and grouse? It is not altogether clear. It seems, however, that sportsmen are very fond of grouse. I don't mean merely that they are fond of their dead bodies when they appear cooked on the table; they are fond also of their live bodies when they fly over the moors. They have an affection for their targets and don't like them to be disturbed. Now the grouse, it is said, *would* be disturbed by the trampling feet of many walkers. I have heard speakers lash themselves into a fine frenzy of noble indignation on the score of these outraged feelings of the grouse. We are asked, for example, to picture the plight of the young grouse, parted by the wicked walker from his parents. With what unction have I been invited to consider his condition as, startled by the heedless walker, he flies lonely and disconsolate over the moor, until, after hours of wandering, he drops with fatigue and dies from hunger and exposure. The mildest of these oratorical flights pictures the grouse growing up nervous, wasted creatures, because of the walkers' invasion of their haunts. Grouse, subject to interruption by walkers, do not, it is said, grow plump; on the contrary, they grow wary, restless and neurotic.[3]

And therefore? Therefore they are not such good targets for the guns of 'sportsmen'; they are not so easy to shoot. (A fact of some importance, this, when the 'sportsman' is only a stock-broker on holiday.)

[1] *The Times*, 15 April 1924. [2] See p. 126 below. [3] See for an elucidation of these sentiments that remarkable and intriguing work, *The Twelfth*, by J. K. Stanford.

It is, indeed, difficult, as one listens to these arguments based upon a tender compassion for the feelings of the grouse, to realize that they are being put forward by those whose sole concern is to ensure that the birds shall be easy to kill. Stripped of hypocrisy, the argument runs as follows: 'We desire that there shall be as many grouse as possible, that they shall be as plump as possible and that they shall be as unsuspecting as possible, in order that our bag may be as large as possible.'

The wary vigilance so lavishly employed in excluding walkers owes much of its inspiration to the desire for a large bag. The craze for record bags is of comparatively recent origin. A 'sportsman' does not now go forth upon the moors and shoot a stray grouse when he sees it. He lurks, in company with other 'sportsmen' complete with loaders, behind a wall of butts, while hired men drive frightened birds in serried masses upon their guns. As a result enormous numbers of birds are killed. In one of these holocausts on the Abbeystead Moors near Lancaster, as many as 2,929 grouse were shot by eight guns in a single day. . . . And in order to facilitate this slaughter of birds during a few weeks each year, the public are not only excluded throughout the whole of the year from hundreds of square miles of moorland adjacent to thickly populated areas, but are regaled with arguments designed to show that the exclusion is dictated out of consideration for the welfare of the distressed victims, arguments which testify to the intelligence of those who propound no less than they insult the intelligence of those who are expected to be taken in by them.

Meeting at the Winnats

To return to my meeting at the Winnats. For many years past there has been in the North an insistent demand that the moors should be open to the public for air and exercise, and every year protest meetings have been held attended by thousands of ramblers. It was one of these meetings that I was to address. But the word 'meeting' is misleading. It conjures up a stuffy, overcrowded hall where beneath the glare of electric lights the practitioners of the art of oratory perform before the audience their words are designed to excite. Or it suggests men sitting round a table in a back room agitating themselves over the collection of subscriptions or the insertion of amendments in minutes. They look out of a dirty window over a backyard on to a wall streaked with drain pipes. . . .

The gathering at the Winnats meeting is a very different affair. Here is a cup-like depression in the middle of the hills; on each side the ground rises gently at first and then more steeply, until you come to the escarpment of the moor. The bottom of the depression is a green grass slope where, unless it is wet, you can sit and read your book or lie on your back and look up at the sky; or, if you are so minded, listen to the oratory. For by some trick of acoustics the orator is audible, and even if there are 8,000 of you—the number which the Ramblers' Association regularly prides itself on amassing; for my part, I would divide the number by half—you can hear almost everything the speaker says without the assistance of loud speakers.

But before we come to what the speaker says, let us forget him for a moment and look at you; for you are very picturesque. You have come from Manchester, Salford, Sheffield and Rotherham, most of you by train and on foot, although there must be nearly a thousand bicycles; there are also trailers, motor bikes and motor-cars. There are several horsedrawn traps; there are even a couple of donkeys. Having got yourself to the Winnats, you are standing, sitting or lying all over the sward, eating your lunch, playing games, making love, even, some of you, listening to me as I stand on my commanding knob of ground exhorting you. But you are not listening too seriously, for, in spite of a sprinkling of stalwarts, most of you are young men and women out for the day.

Speech at the Winnats

What am I saying to you? Pretty much what I have said in this chapter. I am asking you how this land from which you have been driven came into the occupation of its present owners. In order to answer the question, I am exhorting you to make a cursory acquaintance with the history of England during the last two or three hundred years. You will learn how land came into the possession of its present owners by no better right than the right of the power to take it. Your history will tell you of the enclosure of the common lands, of the filching of footpaths and the closing of bridle ways. You will read how Enclosure Acts and Game Laws enabled a few men to usurp the rights of common people to the land of England, and in the name of property to withhold from them the enjoyment of their natural heritage.

Meanwhile the practice of the industrial revolution assisted by the theory of *laissez-faire* was covering the north of England with a chain of industrial cities, whose ugliness and squalor were unequalled in Europe, but which incidentally contrived to fill the pockets of these same landowners with wealth beyond the dreams of avarice. Thus, while one part of the face of England was being maimed and blackened to enrich the few, these same few were establishing a monopoly of the other part, which, while carefully preserving from spoliation, they no less carefully withheld from the enjoyment of all but their own class.

I shall remind you how widespread is this evil. 'You', I am saying, 'know only the Peak district but I, who have been walking about the country for many years, know that the Bowland and Bleasdale Fells on the borders of Lancashire and Yorkshire, the Wharfedale and Nidderdale Moors and Whernside in the West Riding, the heather country round Goathland and Grosmont inland from Whitby in the North Riding and the Berwyn moors in North Wales are similarly infested. Upon all of them the hand of the keeper lies heavy.

'And then there are the Highlands where there are not only the grouse moors but three and a half million acres of deer forest. That the Highlands might remain inviolate, they were de-populated; that they should remain inaccessible to tourists, inns were closed or converted into shooting lodges, while the landlords forbade cottagers and crofters to provide accommodation for visitors. Some years before the war a "Come to Scotland" campaign was being widely advertised in the south of England. We were shown glorious pictures of the Highlands and told that this was the finest country in the world. So, indeed, it is. But the campaign was, none the less, deceitful, for all the time that we were being urged to come to Scotland, you might have seen in many Highland glens, notices of which the following is a typical example.

' "Visitors are strongly advised to keep to the path after 12th August so as not to disturb the deer. The modern rifle carries far and makes little noise. The soft-nosed bullet inflicts a very nasty wound."

'A wit has remarked that the manufacture and erection of such notices is the chief industry of the Highlands.'

From this and similar cases I should ask my audience to draw the conclusion that, if you want to wander at large over moors and mountains and know the joy and uplifting of the spirit that they can bring, you will be well advised to go abroad and spend your money in Norway or Switzerland or the Tyrol, where the rich either do not shoot or do not regard their selfish pleasure as a justification for inhibiting the pleasures of other people. I should reinforce my conclusion by repeating a remark of Professor Trevelyan to the effect that it is fortunate the Alps are not controlled by the British since, if they were, 'they would long ago have been closed on account of the *chamois*'.

I should end my speech by admonishing you that you must not look to the moor owners for concessions. They will fight for the exclusive right to the surface of the moors as hard as they have fought for their right to the minerals which lie below the surface. Sport closes men's eyes; closes them to social obligation no less than it closes them to beauty. As Sir George Stapledon has put it, 'Sport has blinded men's eyes to the other uses to which highly esteemed sporting land could be put. In so far as the masses of the people in this country are concerned, the glorious general scenery provided by our uplands might as well be on the moon or in Mars for the amount of pleasure and health it actually dispenses.' And so, coming to my peroration, I should tell you that, if you want the moors to be free, you must free them for yourselves.

The Mass Trespass

Admonitions of this kind are sometimes taken too literally. It was in 1932, soon after one of these Winnats meetings—not, I am glad to say, after a meeting addressed by me—that a celebrated mass trespass on Kinder was carried out. A number of young men from Sheffield advertised the fact that on a certain Sunday they proposed to assert their right to walk over Kinder Scout. On the day named some four hundred of them duly walked up from Hayfield to find a considerable body of gamekeepers reinforced by policemen waiting for them on the top of the plateau. Something in the nature of a pitched battle took place, as the young men tried to force their way across. I have been told that after the battle was over and the forces had returned to Hayfield, the police fraternized with the trespassers and gave the impression that, in their view, the whole thing had passed off very well. It was, then, with a feeling of shocked surprise that half a dozen young men found themselves served with a summons to appear before the next Derby Assizes on a charge of illegal assembly calculated to lead to a breach of the peace and in one case of illegal assault. The witnesses for the ramblers could not afford the fare to Derby and the evidence was given almost exclusively by the police, with the result that, although they were all first offenders, the defendants were given sentences of imprisonment ranging from two to six months—seventeen months between the six of them. The most outstanding feature of the trial was perhaps the composition of the Grand Jury. It was as follows: two brigadier generals, three colonels, two majors, three captains, two aldermen and eleven country gentlemen!

But this was certainly not the kind of thing to which I conceived myself to be exhorting my audience when I bade them free the moors for themselves.

History of the Access Agitation

What I had in mind was an Act of Parliament giving people the right to walk on uncultivated mountain and moorland above a certain height, irrespective of the sporting rights of the owners. Our endeavour should, I thought, be concentrated on securing the passage into law of such an Act. It had not been difficult to get such a Bill introduced into Parliament; a number of M.P.s were known to be friendly. As democrats, however, we believed that in order to ensure its passage it would be necessary first to create a public opinion, which would not only demand it but would be of sufficient weight to render the demand effective. Hence the meetings, hence too, the considerable propaganda upon which the Ramblers' Association and other bodies have been engaged for many years past.

For the agitation has a long history behind it. As far back as 1888, Mr. J. Bryce, afterwards Lord Bryce, introduced the first Access to Mountains Bill into the House of Commons. It was a simple Bill which provided that no owner or occupier of uncultivated mountain or moorland should be entitled to exclude any person from walking or being on such land for the purpose of recreation or artistic study, or to molest him in so walking or being. The Bill was very naturally rejected—after all, in those days many M.P.s were still sportsmen—and was again rejected on a number of subsequent occasions on which it was again introduced.

Mr. Creech Jones's Bill and the 1938 Act

In 1938, however, largely as a result of years of propaganda, a Bill was introduced into Parliament by Mr. Creech Jones, designed not to give access, but to set up certain machinery under which application might be made for access in particular cases and in certain circumstances granted. After a good deal of negotiation behind the scenes, which evoked vigorous protests from the Ramblers' Association on the ground that the Bill not only failed to meet their needs, but in respect of certain of its clauses went back on promises that had been given to and agreements that had been made with them, the Bill, under the name of the Access to Mountains Act, found its way on to the Statute Book in 1939. The provisions of the Act may be summarized as follows:[1]

'A Local Authority, a landowner or an organization such as the Ramblers' Association may apply to the Minister of Agriculture for an Order granting access to a specified area. The applicant must bear the costs of advertising the application as directed by the Minister; of providing a map of the area on the

[1] I give the summary in the words of Mr. John Bolland who is far more expert in these matters than I am.

scale of six inches to the mile; of receiving objections and of forwarding them to the Minister. The applicant must also meet the expenses of a public inquiry, should the Minister decide to hold one. Should the Order be granted, the applicant will also be required to erect and maintain notice boards in stipulated positions, and to send copies of the notice to the police and the Local Authorities in the area. After all this trouble and expense has been incurred, the Minister may subsequently revoke or amend the Order.

'Where he considers it desirable, the Minister may grant an Order giving access subject to limitations for specified periods. If the public disregard the limitations, the Minister may invoke the Trespass Clause[1] whereby a person may be fined for merely being on the land. Even when access is granted it is only for the period between one hour before sunrise and one hour after sunset. So if a rambler goes on the land during the daytime, when the Trespass Clause is in operation, he can be fined £2 for merely being there. If he goes there in the dark he can only be sued for damage, or, if it can be proved, for being in pursuit of game.'

The Act places an intolerable burden upon applicants. Its approach to the problem is piecemeal. (Scotland, for example, where the demand for access first arose, is not included in it.) It is overloaded with petty restrictions. It involves applicants in considerable expense, the expense of the inquiry, the expense of printing notices and sending them to the police, the expense of providing and erecting notice boards, expenses which ramblers, who are usually poor people, cannot afford; and it entails considerable acquaintance with legal forms and procedures on the part of those proposing to make application, involving and including the giving of evidence before a public inquiry. It is significant that though the Act has been on the Statute Book for six years, no application for access has up to the time of writing[2] been made, and the cumbrous machinery of the Act has not, therefore, yet been brought into operation. In spite of arduous efforts and prolonged negotiations, the public has not, in fact, secured access to a single square inch of uncultivated land.

In addition to all this, the Act contains one provision to which

[1] See next page.　　　[2] June, 1945.

ramblers have taken special exception, the provision relating to trespass.

The Trespass Clause

There is a hoary controversy as to whether you can be prosecuted for trespassing or not. The legal position, as most of us have always understood it, is, so far as England and Wales are concerned, that you cannot be prosecuted unless it can be shown that you have done damage. If you are found trespassing all that the affronted owner can do is to order you to proceed by the shortest route to the nearest highway. It cannot, therefore, be assumed that he is entitled to send you back the way you came—it may not be the shortest—and it may well be that to continue in the direction in which you are proceeding when he found you, that is to say, to continue to 'trespass' is, in fact, to go by the shortest way to the nearest highway.

What constitutes damage? It is, of course, very difficult to say. Hence the uncertainty of the law. It may well be the case that to bruise one or more blades of grass with your feet, as you walk across a field, is to damage them. . . .

However that may be, most ramblers adhere strongly to the view that, unless unmistakable damage can be shown, they can only be warned off. Some still hold, on what authority I do not know, that if they offer the token sum of sixpence and if the offer be accepted, this sixpence will cover whatever damage they may be conceived to have caused. In actual practice, provided he goes away when he is told to, a man never does get summonsed for trespass and ramblers are reasonably well content with this very English arrangement. It should be added that, if the land is frequented by game, the trespasser must be able to show that he is not in pursuit of it.

Now consider the new Access to Mountains Act. Let us suppose that to area A access has been granted as the result of an application, granted, that is to say, during the daylight hours out of every twenty-four. But the permission is not for access to the whole of area A; in the middle there is a small area A^1, to which the grant of access does not apply. Or, again, let us suppose that access has been granted to area A not at all times, but only during certain months when, for example, the birds are not laying, or not during all the daylight hours, but only during some of them. Now, if you are found on A during the forbidden months or during the forbidden daylight hours, you are liable to be fined two pounds for just being there.

But if you are found on A^1 or on B, B being a neighbouring area to which no right of access has been given, or if you are found on A in the dark, that is to say, found during the period to which the access provisions do not apply, the ordinary law of trespass comes into operation and damage has to be shown.

In this way the Act makes the position of walkers who wittingly or unwittingly commit a trespass worse than it was before the passage into law of an Act which had originally been drawn up in response to public demand with the express object of ensuring that walkers should be given certain rights. The Ramblers' Association, the organized body which exists to further the demands and protect the interests of ramblers, has at the time of writing decided (very rightly, in my view) not to operate this Act.

The Issue

What is wanted is surely something very simple, namely, an Act on the lines of Lord Bryce's original bill. The issue here is also, as it seems to me, very simple. What is at stake is a question of values.

On the one hand, are a few well-to-do people who wish to enjoy the sport of grouse shooting undisturbed; on the other, are the close-penned populations of great industrial towns hitherto deprived of their heritage of natural beauty. The 'sportsmen' are not always—indeed, they are not usually—the owners of the property; often they are Americans who have hired an English moor in the belief that by so doing they will commend themselves to English society by adopting the habits of English aristocrats. It is not claimed that it would be impossible to shoot grouse if citizens were allowed to ramble on the moors, merely that it would not be so easy or the grouse, perhaps, so numerous. Would this, after all, be such an unmitigated disaster? Would the disaster be so serious as to justify us in depriving citizens at large of the beauty and the benefit of wild scenery?

It may be added that the considerations mentioned elsewhere in this book, more particularly in Chapters I and XI,[1] show that the need of the townsman will grow greater and not less, as the suburbs extend and the roads grow more hazardous.

[1] See pp. 19, 20, and pp. 218, 219.

Chapter Seven

TREES AND FORESTS

The Loppers

Along the road at the bottom of my Hampstead garden runs a row of noble trees. Last autumn their enemies descended upon them and assaulted them, hewing, hacking and lopping them out of all recognition. Now they stand like a row of corpses in a German atrocity picture, holding their mutilated arms in dumb protest to the skies. What is more, I can, for the first time, see the ugly houses for which they were so merciful a screen.

Now 'they' are at it again. Every spring, about February or March, there begins a great pruning and lopping of the London trees. It is ruthlessly, often abominably, done. Granted that for some obscure reason of arboriculture it is necessary from time to time to cut large pieces from fine trees, some attention might, one would think, be paid to the shape of the trees selected for treatment, some regard to the amenities of the landscape. No such considerations appear to weigh with the guardians of our London parks and heaths. There is, or rather there was, a particularly fine group of elms on Hampstead Heath, not a hundred yards from my house. They were old trees, shapely and spacious, showing a network of delicate tracery against the winter sky; to-day their beauty is gone. Instead there is a ragged outline of melancholy stumps with their truncated limbs jutting bleakly from the outraged trunks.

A large and lovely willow stood at the meeting of two roads overshadowing a trough of water, from which horses used to drink on their way up the hill. Two years ago, it was cut down. Many willows have been cut down—in fact, the number of old willows in Hampstead must have been diminished by over half in the last twelve years.

TREES AND FORESTS

That Trees Are Dangerous

The official explanation in this and in every other case is that the trees are dangerous, by which is meant that in a gale of abnormal strength they are liable to lose a branch or so. In this sense of the word every tree, not only in Hampstead, but throughout the length and breadth of the country, is dangerous. If people insist on standing under trees in hurricanes, they must expect what they get. In this sense chimney pots are dangerous because they may be blown down, or roofs are dangerous because in a gale they may shed their tiles; but nobody regards these facts as constituting a sufficient reason for removing people's roofs and chimney pots.

Why, then, one wonders, should a similar excuse be allowed to justify the destruction of what little beauty remains to our London suburbs? Or we are told that a branch might fall on a passing car—trees, it would seem, are dangerous, but cars are not. I do not know how many people are killed in England every year by trees, but the number, I imagine, is well under a hundred. I do, however, know that in the second year of the war cars were responsible for the deaths of nearly 10,000 and the mutilation of some 350,000 persons on English roads. (The number of cars in peace-time is, of course, very much larger, though the casualties are smaller). Yet trees forsooth are dangerous; cars are not!

The Rage Against Trees

What, one wonders, is the reason for this rage against trees? Is it perhaps because they are beautiful? This seems at first an intolerable suggestion. Yet there have been times when I have been hard put to it to find another. A few years ago a group of pine trees, immediately to the west of The Spaniards and close to the famous Constable clumps on Hampstead Heath, were cut down. They were old, celebrated and beautiful but, so far as I could ascertain, gave no other cause for offence.

Here there were and could be none of the usual excuses for cutting down noble trees, as, for example, that they might blow down and destroy ignoble houses, or that some fool had built

ΔΡΥΑΣ

a house behind them in order that he might then complain that they were darkening his rooms, or impeding the view from his windows, and must, therefore, be removed. There are no ignoble houses within reach and nobody's view was being impeded. The trees, no doubt, were rotten, but what of it? Who was, or was likely to be harmed by them? There is no answer and so, I repeat my question, 'Why this rage against trees?'

Partly, no doubt, it is official zeal; partly, the pleasure that the operation gives. We all like cutting and hacking something about and we are all, therefore, glad of an excuse for a bit of destruction, not less glad if we are urban municipal employees with time heavy on our hands. But the real reason, I suspect, lies deeper. Urban man has lost the power of taking natural things naturally. A piece of untouched country puts him out of countenance, making him feel small and trivial and vulgar; and, to put himself at ease, he must contrive, somehow, to set his mark upon it. And so he goes to work 'improving' and 'developing', laying down paths and putting up fences, pruning and clipping and draining and smartening and tidying, making ornamental and useful the haphazard uselessness of natural beauty. So he justifies himself in his own eyes and, having made his mark, is appeased.

Our Heritage of Trees

Let us turn from town to country. Let me say again, as I have said before, that the English countryside is one of the most beautiful, to my prejudiced mind, the most beautiful in the world. But this beauty is, in large part, a man-made thing, a blend—one of the happiest—of God's work and of man's. It was in the eighteenth century that men first set deliberately to work to beautify England. For this work of beautification the seventeenth-century diarist, Evelyn for whom trees were a passion, was in part responsible, in part, Capability Brown. The result of their work was that unique English feature, the hedgerow tree, which gives texture and warmth to a pattern which, lovely enough in outline, might else have seemed colourless and cold.

The avenue, too, came in the eighteenth century to a new splendour and a new use. It can be seen at its noblest at such a house as Savernake, but all over the country the avenues of the great houses had their charming, domestic counterparts in which lime and chestnut and plane tree were planted to shade the approaches to village, church and farmhouse. The Cotswold country is particularly rich in them. Or take a walk along the banks of the Thames, from Mapledurham to Goring or farther west to Moulsford. Your enjoyment will be that which one feels for a work of art. Every hill is crowned with its clump of trees in which oaks, beeches and pines are mingled in exactly the right proportions. A line of enormous elms stands in a meadow at just the right distance to give perspective to a line of poplars by the river bank. Rare trees are dotted here and there among the more familiar English varieties, so that the colours of their leaves in spring and autumn may gratify the onlooker with just the right degree of contrast.

Down vistas cut through the trees the flat faces of Queen Anne houses are intermittently visible, the roofs and windows exquisitely proportioned, the bricks of so mellow a red that they seem to glow, as if suffused by a light from within. Across the river a single poplar set in a meadow points its green finger at the sky.

Or take the Rookery, that lovely estate known to hundreds of Londoners, just beyond Westcott in Surrey. The house where Malthus lived lies at the foot of a green hill topped by a row of beeches. They form the perfect background for the little valley through whose rich watermeadows runs the Pip Brook. How well some of us, taking the train from London Sunday after Sunday to Boxhill or Dorking Stations, know that valley, linking as it does two lovely stretches of country, Ranmore Common in the Down country to the north and Leith Hill with its pines and heather to the south.

The Victorian Climax

It was, I suppose, some fifty years ago that the fruits of this loving labour of the eighteenth century reached maturity. The trees had grown to their full stature; the grass floors of the avenues were soft and velvety; the houses richly mellow. The motor was as yet unknown, and the depredations of the builder were confined to the towns. Our grandfathers knew England at its best. One could find it in one's heart to blame them for neglect, in that they did nothing to perpetuate or protect the beauty they so justly admired. One could, that is to say, if it were not for one's consciousness of one's own guilt; for while the eighteenth century beautified the countryside and the nineteenth century neglected it, it has been left to the twentieth to ruin it.

For example, in this matter of trees. Admittedly we still plant trees; but what kind of trees?

The Conifers

The answer is larch and spruce and pine and fir, especially pine and fir, serried lines of conifers with which we regiment the sweet irregularity of our woodlands. A hundred and fifty years ago the trees of Southern England were the oak, the ash, the beech and the elm. To these we looked for our wooden walls, while the pine was the ornamental luxury of the eighteenth-century gentleman's garden. In the nineteenth century came a use for pines as pit-props, and after 'the great war' that ended in Waterloo, the inevitable crowds of unemployed soldiers were set to work to plant them. Meanwhile wooden ships were superseded and the commercial value of the oak and the ash declined. With what result? In 1930 in England south of the Thames the pines outnumbered all the other trees put together, while the oak and the ash bid fair within the next fifty years to subside into the occasional ornaments of gardens and parks.

Nowhere are these changes to be seen more clearly than in the New Forest. Under the influence of that efficient and, from the pit-prop point of view, expert body, the Forestry Commission, vast areas of once enchanted woodland are surrendered to the commercial utility of the alien, self-seeding conifers. The pines blight everything that comes within their malign influence. Flowers wither away, cattle pastures dry up, the birds take flight. Those who have known the Forest woodlands either in the leafage of early spring or in their autumn gold or glittering in their winter constellations of coral-red holly berries, will admit that the destruction of their beauty would be a national calamity. Yet within a hundred years, if the present policy continues, destroyed it will assuredly be, and the old greenland enchantment will yield to garden suburbs in the woods, nurseries for fir-tree pit-props, and poultry farms managed by maiden ladies.

For those who are interested in statistics, I append the figures of the planting programme of the Forestry Commission for a typical year just before the war:

SOFT WOODS

Scotch and Corsican pines	15,000,000
European and Japanese larch	6,000,000
Norway and Sitka Spruce	23,000,000
Douglas Fir	1,400,000

HARD WOODS

Beech	2,000,000
Oak	800,000
Ash	560,000

The soft woods were 45½ million, the hard woods 3½ million.

Especially lamentable is the case of the elm, the most distinctive and, to my mind, the loveliest of all the trees of the English landscape. Some, planted a hundred and fifty or two hundred years ago, have fallen from old age. Others have been attacked by the disease which has recently raged among English trees, among elms particularly, and have either succumbed to it or been cut down as unsafe. Hundreds have been blown down in gales and hurricanes. But not all these causes added together have been so deadly as the builder and the 'developer'.

It is one of the most distressing sights I know to see a noble tree cut down to make room for an ignoble house. Yet it is a sight which could have been seen daily at any point within a distance of twenty miles from the centre of London at any time during the last fifteen years. West Ewell, for example, was famous for its elms, which were many and stately. It has now few elms, but many houses. It is unlikely that it will be famous for its houses.

The Forestry Commission

The exigencies of the times in which we live are, no doubt, largely to blame for this substitution of soft woods for hard. Soft woods grow more quickly, give rapid profits and a quick turn-over. We cannot be left again to depend for the bulk of our timber—and, let us remember, timber means paper—upon imports from abroad, notably from Canada and Sweden. Before the war our imports of timber cost us more than £63,000,000 a year; yet only about 4 per cent of our total consumption was being met by home production. Hence the Forestry Commission does right to prepare a vastly increased planting programme, to extend its nursery areas ånd to have accumulated, as we are told, some 300,000,000 young trees in various stages of growth for purposes of replanting.

All this is true, yet it is not the whole truth. The whole truth reintroduces a theme which I have already announced,[1] that we live in an age in which utility and profit are the only recognized motives for Government action and in which beauty is not valued except for its commercial possibilities. The Commission is a Government department and must pay its way; it cannot, then, afford not to rely almost exclusively upon soft woods.

'But why', it may be asked, 'should it not rely upon them?' Why all this 'to do' about trees and especially about hard-wood trees; why, in fact, such an indignant fuss about lopping and pruning and cutting down, about the planting of soft woods, about the destruction of elms and beeches? The question raises large issues. Let me try very briefly to answer it.

In Defence of Trees

The answer turns, in the last resort, upon the kind of life we think desirable for men and women, turns, in fact upon our conception of the good life. One of the elements in the good life is, I insist, contact with Nature. Nature is the mother of our race; we have evolved as part of a natural process and our ancestors lived for millennia in natural conditions. As a result, there

[1] See ch. ii, pp. 39, 40.

lies deep-seated within us a natural love of country sights and sounds and smells and an instinctive need for occasional moments of quiet alone with Nature. The smell of fallen leaves or new-mown hay, the tang of a mountain brook, the feel of lush meadow grass against the face, the texture of the bole of an oak, or the sight of its first young leaves showing yellow-green against the April sky, these things touch in us an ancestral chord that stretches back to our savage, perhaps to our sub-human, past.

Most of us who live in great cities are unaware of this need, just as we are unaware of the need of religion. It exists none the less, and to the extent to which it is not met, we live maimed and thwarted lives. A man is a richer, a fuller, and a more many-sided being; he touches life at more points, getting more out of it if only because he brings more to it, provided he be not wholly cut off from these ancestral sources of our being. Yet most of us do not know these things and, because we do not, we heed-lessly overrun Nature and destroy its beauty.

A Vision of the Future

In a hundred years' time, if present tendencies are not checked, there will be neither town nor country in Southern England, but only a vast suburb sprawling shapelessly from Watford to the coast. What will the inhabitants of that suburb do? I will assume that we have abolished war, overcome our economic difficulties and superseded alternating booms and slumps and that, under some form of national ownership, men and women are assured of comfort and a competence on a few hours' machine-minding a day. In what sort of England will they be living?

If present tendencies continue, one can foresee an England in which whatever land is left over from cultivation is covered with a network of golf courses, tennis courts or whatever kind of ground the popular game of the future demands. Our coasts will be ringed with a continuous string of resorts at which dance bands will discourse the wailing of crooners to tired sportsmen and their overnourished wives; our roads will be covered with a stationary mass of metal stretching from John o' Groats to Land's End, consisting of cars wedged together in a solid and inextricable jam; a deluge of news, warranted not to arouse thought and carefully chewed so as not to excite comment will descend upon the defenceless heads of the community through all the devices of television and telephotony that the science of the future may have been able to perfect. Finally, men will be driven to make life hard and dangerous again in despair of tolerating the burden of amusing themselves for eighteen or nineteen hours out of every twenty-four.

This jaundiced vision is of a future in which man, having conquered Nature, finds that in the process he has lost his own soul. For man cannot live by movies and radio alone, but by the spirit of God as it manifests itself in the visible scene that He has set before us in hills and valleys and rivers, in the air and the sky, in fields and flowers, in meadows and woods, and in great trees ranged in an avenue along a road or standing brooding and solitary in the fields. This exhortation to keep our trees is, then, in its last analysis a plea to preserve the conditions which are necessary to our full human development as beings having minds and spirits as well as bodies and appetites.

Now the first thing a farmer does to-day when he buys and occupies his bit of land, is to cut down the trees; the first thing an estate agency does when it buys some land with a view to 'developing' it, is to cut down the trees; the first thing a government does when it goes to war, is to cut down the trees. Of this last I do not complain—before all things we had to beat the Nazis—but the Government owes it to the people, now that the war is over, not only to repair the devastation it itself has made, but to pass legislation preventing the further destruction of natural beauty.

What, then, is to be done? I have already conceded that more trees are wanted and that the Forestry Commission does right to plant them. This being granted, the adequate safeguarding of the values I have been trying so inadequately to convey depends upon the right answer to two questions; first, what sort of trees are we to plant; secondly, where are they to be planted?

Kinds of Trees

As regards the first question, I hope I have already said enough to indicate the importance of hard-wood trees. That these take longer to come to maturity and that they have, therefore, less commercial value cannot be denied. They have some value, of course; they shelter farmhouses, prevent soil erosion, afford shade and can be used for purposes for which soft woods are useless. Men still make wooden vehicles, oak settles, log huts, garden seats, and for these hard woods are better. There is an increased demand for chestnuts for fencing, while elms are used for benches. Nevertheless, hard woods have outlived many of their commercial uses or, rather, many of these uses can now be more economically served by pines and spruces. In spite of this fact, hard woods should, I urge, continue to be planted, if England is to remain beautiful; not so often as they used to be, perhaps, nor in such numbers as the soft woods—that would be too much to hope—but in numbers in excess of the beggarly seven per cent of the total planted by the Forestry Commission between the two wars. 'If England is to remain beautiful'. The words slipped out before I had noticed them, slipped out so easily, because I had unconsciously taken it for granted that beauty is important and that those who dwell in our country desire that it should remain beautiful, beautiful in and for itself because beauty is a good, and not merely as a magnet for tourists.

Negotiations with the Forestry Commission

But my countrymen, or those of them who govern the destinies of the countryside, do not share these views with the result that when one is negotiating with private owners, laying considerations before public bodies or preparing memoranda to send to government departments, the aesthetic is the one argument that, if one is wise, one will not permit oneself to use. It carries no weight. Having discovered this, you find yourself inventing specious utilitarian pretexts in support of a course that commends itself to you on other grounds. You spend a wealth of ingenuity explaining that the proposals against which you are protesting will not pay, when what you mean is that they will destroy what is beautiful. In this matter of trees, for example! The Forestry Commission, who, now that there are few land-lords who can afford to plant, fewer still who can plant in the conviction that their great-grandchildren will enjoy the fruits of their labours, are chiefly responsible for deciding where trees shall be planted, how many and of what kinds, insist on choosing for their plantable areas some of the loveliest tracts of wild country remaining in England. They have chosen, for example, the Lake District. To the south of the Whinlatter Pass there is already a great belt of firs, while the lower end of Ennerdale is dotted with row after row of scrubby little spruces—thank God, these horrid little trees are not prospering—looking for all the world like the occasional hairs on a badly shaved chin. The Forestry Commission have appropriated part of Eskdale—though they have not here as yet completed their planting pro-gramme—and parts of Dunnerdale, and it was only after pro-longed negotiations that the central knot of the Lakeland hills was permanently secured against their depredations.

In the course of our negotiations with this body, in the articles that we wrote, in the speeches we delivered, we had to make use of any argument that hypocrisy could invent or ingenuity suggest, in the hope of demonstrating that the Lakeland valleys and hills were not really the best places in which to plant pines. No, we insisted, they really were not! There were the Herdwick sheep for instance; they constituted the staple local industry, and it would never do to take away part of the area over which they grazed; moreover, the ground might be poisoned for their grazing by reason of the proximity of the pines. The pines, we said again, would not do well in these parts—look at Ennerdale. The soil was unsuitable for them; it was not sandy enough. Or, we would point out, with all these tourists about the possibility of forest fires from the dropped match or cigarette end so lightly thrown away were very high, and so on and so on. . . . The upshot of all this was—wouldn't it be better for the Forestry Commission to carry on their activities elsewhere?

The case that we did not dare to put was very different. It runs as follows. 'The Lake District is the loveliest thing in England. If you muffle the clean, clear edges of the fells with a blanket of alien firs, you will certainly destroy some part of this loveliness. Beauty is important. It is, indeed, one of the most important things that is vouchsafed to us here on earth and it must, therefore, be carefully guarded. Therefore, we beg of you, refrain.' But these arguments we did not use, since, to have done so, would have dubbed us novices inexpert in negotiation and because of our inexpertness relying on considerations which, however important to us, carried no weight with those to whom they were addressed. In so far as aesthetic considerations were touched upon, they were considered by the authorities with whom we were negotiating to tell strongly in favour of conifer planting. The pines, the firs and the spruces would, the Chairman of the Commission thought, look very fine ranged in rows up and down the mountainsides. Had we not been to Switzerland? But these, we said, were not Swiss mountains but English fells. The Chairman of the Commission could not see the point of the difference. 'What, after all,' he asked, 'is the matter with pines?' Really, I'm blest if I can tell him. I can say, as I have said before, that pines poison the ground and that there grow in their shade no flowers, no grass and very little undergrowth; that they offer no attractions to birds and that pine woods are, therefore, silent; that they offer very little attraction to animals and that pine woods are, therefore, very largely empty. (I make the Chairman a present of W. H. Hudson's essay 'Life in a Pine Wood', published in *The Book of a Naturalist*, in evidence of the fact that they are not quite empty.) That pines are planted in regulation rows, often protected by barbed wire and look alien and artificial; finally, lest he should think that these are private whimsies of my own, I can quote him an extract from a poem entitled The Old Mansion by the poet Southey, which, by the way, to make the extract topical, was in Cumberland:

> . . . *Plague, I say,*
> *On their new-fangled whimsies! We shall have*
> *A modern shrubbery here stuck full of firs*
> *And your pert poplar trees.*

But the Chairman of the Commission is or was an Australian, or it may have been a New Zealander, and I doubt if he would have understood.

The Forestry Commission Replies

Moreover, to all these arguments the Chairman of the Forestry Commission has an effective reply. 'I have', he says in effect, 'a very extensive planting programme arranged for the immediate future. I don't mind letting you into the details of this plan. Roughly it will involve an increase of one million acres in Britain's forests and woodlands at a cost of fourteen million pounds during the first ten years after the war, and a further one and a half million acres during the second decade after the war. Now that is a very big increase indeed; it is, in fact, nearly double the area 1,239,000 acres which we already hold, of which we have as yet planted less than 500,000. What is more, I have acquired vast quantities of seeds (of course, for soft woods, Norway spruces, Scots pines, Sitka spruces and Douglas firs) from Norway and the U.S.A., not to speak of the 300 million young trees in my nurseries up and down the country which are in various stages of growth. These, it is obvious, cannot be wasted; they must be planted somewhere. It is, then, incumbent upon you and those who like you are kicking up all this fuss about blanketing the Lakeland fells to suggest alternative sites. So, please be practical and tell me where else to go.'

The question, I submit, is not a fair one. I am not an expert and I have neither the knowledge nor the experience to justify the making of recommendations. Besides, I do not know enough about other areas which might suggest themselves as suitable waste land.

That the Forestry Commission should be Incorporated in the Ministry of Agriculture

The right answer is the one suggested many times in this book, namely, that we should, as the Scott Committee has recommended, set up an authority charged with the duty of taking a synoptic view of the country as a whole. In the light of this view, and having regard to the competing demands of industry, housing and agriculture, the authority should determine how much of the country and what parts of it should be reserved for the growing of the various things that we need. I emphasize 'the growing of things' as opposed to making things in factories and housing the people who make and need them. And the point of the emphasis on 'growing' is that it enables me to say and the reader to see that the Forestry Commission, instead of being a semi-independent government department, should become part of the Ministry of Agriculture which is concerned, unlike the restricted Forestry Commission, with the growing of *all* the various things that the country needs. Grass and crops and vegetables and trees—all these are things that grow as opposed to things that are made; all these, then, should be under the control of a single department, which would be in a position to allocate our natural resources according to the comparative urgencies of our different demands. The need to bring the Forestry Commission under the control of the Ministry of Agriculture is sharpened by three new advances in technique which have been made during the last decade. The first is the caterpillar tractor which can draw ploughs up steep slopes of tussocky grass which no team of horses could manage; as a consequence, we can now plough up land which was beyond our reach in the days of horse-drawn ploughs. The second is our mastery of a new technique for improving grassland by ploughing and sowing it with improved strains of grass. As a result, we can now sow with valuable grass land hitherto neglected or regarded as fit only for rough grazing. The third is our discovery of how to drain boggy peat soil, so that we can break up the peat pan that underlies it and form water channels to drain the land, in the knowledge that we can then plant trees on the upturned furrows. By the time the land has settled down again the trees will be established. The first and second of these advances mean that land hitherto regarded as useless is now attractive to the Ministry of Agriculture for crop growing and grass seeding. The third advance means that it is attractive to the Forestry Commission for tree planting; indeed, thousands of acres of spruce are to-day being planted on land which the Forestry Commission has hitherto been unable to use.

We shall be confronted, then, after the war with the prospect of an undignified though all too familiar struggle between Government departments for the right to take over wild and waste land. This struggle can only be avoided if the work of the

Forestry Commission is correlated with and dovetailed into our programme and policy for agriculture as a whole. With this end in view the Forestry Commission should become a department of the Ministry of Agriculture.[1]

If the foregoing considerations be granted, it looks as if a double allocation is required; first, an allocation of land as between industry, housing and agriculture, the word 'agriculture' being here interpreted in the widest sense; secondly, within the sphere of agriculture so widely interpreted, an allocation between agriculture in the strict sense and forestry. The first allocation depends upon a plan for the country as a whole. Such a plan would be markedly facilitated by the nationalization of the land. The second allocation demands that the Forestry Commission would become a department of the Ministry of Agriculture.

I hope I have now excused myself from answering the question, where should the Forestry Commission go to find the land required for its planting programme, by passing it on to an enlarged Ministry of Agriculture. Let me, however, put in a plea for the utilization of some of the waste land of the Highlands especially in Sutherland and more particularly north of Loch Shin; also for the country west of Otterburn where there is a huge expanse of moorland round the headwaters of the Tarset Burn stretching up to Oh Me Edge, and for some of the Cheviot country on the Border. Along the Border, there is a big stretch of wild country—I wish I had space to write about it here. It is very fine, but it does not run naturally into lines and shapes which have significant beauty as the hills of the Lake District are significant, and its value is not, therefore, so easily destroyed by the planting of trees. Another stretch which I commend to the Commission's notice is the wide desolate landscape east of the Pennines and immediately south of the road over

---

[1] I am glad to note (January 1945) that since the above was written, it has in fact been decided to transfer the Forestry Commission to the Ministry of Agriculture, of which it will in the future become a department. The few M.P.s who now sit on the Commission will cease to do so and it will become, what it should always have been, a Commission consisting of technical experts only. Among its duties will be the giving of advice to private owners on the planting and treatment of their trees. To those who take and adopt it certain remissions of taxation will be granted.

Stainmoor. The district is called Bowes Moor, a wild, almost ugly stretch of bare flat grassland, intersected with peaty streams flowing along featureless shallow troughs, extending southwards almost to the headwaters of the Arkle Beck. The Pennine slopes bounding it are desolate without being grand. Conifers might even improve this area!

Chapter Eight

THE COAST

Observations on August, September and the Sea

I am not a great lover of coast walking. This is partly because I have little feeling for the sea; partly because I like richness of detail and variety of vegetation.

As to the sea, I am, I suppose, afraid of it. In August the seaside is well enough partly because the country in August is very ill. August, as I have already remarked, is the dullest month of the year and by the end of it the harvest has in the south been mostly gathered. The leaves are all of the same tint, the birds have stopped singing, the flowers are comparatively few and colourless. Above all, there is a feeling of tiredness abroad, a sense of anti-climax as of a race run, a development ended. By September, the heavy dews have begun, the evenings are perceptibly drawing in; there is a sparkle in the air, a stirring of change, even of challenge, a sense of new beginnings. For the autumn rather than the spring is pre-eminently the time for new undertakings; people are coming back, projects are forming, sessions and terms beginning and one is filled with a sense of vigour which causes everything to seem possible.

But this is August and we turn for the moment to the coast and the sea. For my part, I do not go *on* the sea, if I can help it. It is, I know, a treacherous element and I can never wholly forget, as I sit precariously in the fishing boat, the thinness of the planks of wood that lie between me and it. But the sea is very pleasant for bathing, especially when you are bathing solitary and nude in a deserted cove. There is no business with huts and bathing attendants, no putting on and off of dank bathing costumes, no trouble over sand. You go in off a rock and swim along a channel, or across the cove to another rock. The water is clear and you can see the bottom, while always between you and the open sea there lies a comforting barrier of rocks and reefs so that, if by any chance there were a current, they would mercifully interpose themselves and arrest your drift seaward. Afterwards you lie on the floor of the cove, naked to the sun. . . . All this, I say, is very pleasant. Yet I would not exaggerate its attractiveness.

In respect of this comparative lukewarmness of feeling for the sea I am, I gather, at one with most of my countrymen, though not with most of my *contemporary* countrymen. 'As yet,' G. M. Trevelyan tells us in his *English Social History*, writing of the late seventeenth century, 'as yet the seaside had no votaries: doctors had not yet discovered the health-giving qualities of its air; no one wanted to bathe in the waters of the ocean or to rhapsodize over its appearance from the shore. The sea was "the Englishman's common", his way to market, his fishpond, his battleground, his heritage. But as yet no one sought either the seaside or the mountains for the refreshment they could give to the spirit of man.'

In the eighteenth century King George III gave a vogue to Weymouth and in the early nineteenth the Prince Regent to Brighton, but as late as the beginning of the nineteenth Mr. Woodhouse is recommending lodgings at Cromer to his daughter, Isabella, on the ground that, 'by what I understand, you might have had lodgings there quite away from the sea—a quarter of a mile off—very comfortable'.

Observations on Coast Walking

The other reason for my lukewarmness in regard to coast walking is the comparative bareness of coasts. The fields are few and infertile and the crops poor. Even the September blackberries tend to be dry and stunted. Except where the sea birds gather, there are few birds and apart from the occasional rabbit, no beasts. I tire of the view; on one side always the sea; on the other a hedge maybe or a field or a wall, but rarely an expanse. Finally, when it comes to walking, you can walk only in three instead of four directions which is, I suppose, one of the reasons why walking by the sea side always seems limited.

I hasten to make handsome avowal of the fact that these opinions of mine on coast and sea may well be evidence only of my own limitations and to add that they are very far from

ΠΟΣΕΙΔΩ

being shared by my contemporaries. Nor always by myself; I consider that to walk from one green, smoothsided cliff top to another crossing on the way a ravine filled with heather and brambles, or to follow a cliff footpath until perhaps, as on the East coast it so often does, it finishes over the cliff edge, is very fine walking. You are exhilarated; you feel that you can go for ever without stopping; yet you feel also that nothing could be more agreeable than to stop on that next rise, to lie down on the heather, read a book and look at the sea, or just look at the sea.

The Cornish, Devonshire, and South Coasts

I am writing this after a day's walk along the Pembrokeshire coast. I used once to go to Cornwall for coast scenery; indeed, I was partly brought up on the Lizard Peninsula and know the stretch from Poldu in the north down through Mullion and Kynance to Landewednack at the Lizard, as only a boy can know the cliffs on which he spends his holidays. That was before the motor age thronged the Cornish coast with people. Since then, I have been much up and down the west and south coasts of England looking for a stretch where a man can sit and gaze at the sea in solitude.

The south coast along the greater part of its length is already 'done for'. West Wittering still stands at the end of its solitary marsh—what a job by the way we had to save it—and there used to be a stretch by Lymington, but this, I am told, is already beset by villa and bungalow. Of the Dorset coast I have more to say below, but there is a good stretch from Seatown running into Devon by Branscombe. The west coast, of course, is in better case, but before the war it had even here become difficult to find what one wanted. There is, or rather there was, an unspoiled stretch of the Devonshire coast near the North Devon–Cornwall border, but this was a unique survival. I suspect the War Departments have since 'got at it', in which event it will be unspoiled no longer.

Let us suppose that after a long search you have found a place which seems to you fairly solitary. There are no pier, parade, shops, or hotels; but there is a small inn at which you can stay overlooking the sea. You arrive there, we will suppose, late in the evening. Not a soul is to be seen and you go to bed congratulating yourself on having at last found solitude by the sea. The impression persists during breakfast; by ten o'clock at latest it is shattered. The place, it turns out, is approached by a road—inevitably, now you come to think of it, since that is the way you came last night—and this road is your undoing. For presently the cars begin to arrive and from ten to six the place, being a cul-de-sac, is an inferno of petrol fumes and throbbing engines. The cars decant their contents of whining children, nagging mothers and bored fathers. The children play, the women sit and knit and litter the beach and cliffs with the *débris* of meals, and father reads the paper on the rocks. The fact that the road is only a glorified lane makes matters worse; for as there is nowhere for the cars to park and no adequate space for them to turn round in, the sounds of the milling cars can be heard throughout the day over long stretches of the cliff in either direction. Through these or similar experiences, I have been first attracted, then disillusioned and finally routed at Noss Mayo on the South Devon coast, at Lee Bay on the north, where a charming old mill stands on the shore and, most ignominiously of all, at Welcombe on the North Cornwall–Devon border where the cliffs are wild and high, the scenery superb and the distance from the nearest station—Bude is eight miles direct, and ten by road, Bideford eighteen—would, one might have supposed, have ensured a comparative absence of molestation. For all these places, charming from dusk to dawn, charming, for all I know, in winter—but I have never seen them then; who, after all, wants to be on the coast in winter?—are during most hours of daylight in the spring, summer and autumn ruined for the seeker after solitude by the invading cars.

The Pembrokeshire Coast

These reflections bring me back in thought as they have done in fact to the coast of Pembrokeshire. This is not so grand as the coast of Cornwall, nor are its cliffs distinguished by outlines of rugged granite or enriched by the glowing colours of serpentine. The rock here is slate or limestone interspersed with green and red sandstone, so that in places it resembles a Cubist design and cuts up the cliffs into striated blocks, dun in colour, occasionally veined with marble or splashed with lichen. The cliff face consists of soft friable shale which crumbles easily and makes the cliffs difficult for climbers. Nevertheless, they *are* cliffs; the coast is highly indented and the coastline is, therefore, very long; there are coves, fine views over the Atlantic and an enormous variety of bird life. This last, I suppose, is the peculiar glory of the Pembrokeshire coast. There are stretches of cliff which are alive with birds; one outstanding pinnacle of rock, the Stack Rock, in particular being so thickly covered, that one could not throw a stone on to it without hitting one of the perching guillemots, supposing, of course, that they stayed there to be hit. Westward from the Stack Rock are the Linney burrows and thence a tract of coast stretching out to Angle Point, as remote and solitary as anything in England or Wales—at least it used to be so.[1]

A Walk along the Coast

Suppose that, as I did in the summer of the year 1944, you set out to walk along this coast, starting from Tenby and intending to go round the point at Angle along Milford Haven to Pembroke Dock, a distance of, I suppose, fifty miles of continuous cliff walking.

The first obstacle encountered only a few miles out of Tenby is a camp on a ridge of cliff top. Naked and exposed to the sky can be seen rows and rows of unlovely huts. There are pylons, poles, chimneys and a generating station; there is a waste of asphalt and the whole is enclosed by miles of barbed wire fencing. A more hideous sight it would be difficult to conceive. To avoid it, you must make a detour of several miles inland. When at length, somewhere near Manorbier, you venture again to approach the coast you have an unspoiled stretch of some miles in front of you. Gradually you become attuned to the solitude; you forget your personality, commune with nature, lose yourself in earth, sea and sky and are doing whatever other

[1] I do not know the western coast of Pembrokeshire from Milford Haven to the Cardiganshire border. It is, I believe, comparatively unspoiled.

good things there may be to gladden the heart and grace the path of the solitary walker, when, topping a rise, you draw back with a start of horror. Your first thought is that the cliff opposite has caught a disease, for it is spotted with a rash of pink, deepening on occasion into an angrier red. The rash consists of villas, bungalows, shacks and huts, scattered higgledy-piggledy among the heather and the gorse without shape, order or pattern. The effect is disastrous. You are reminded of a hillside pitted with mine workings; of the surface of a pear which the wasps have 'been at', of a piece of cheese which mice have nibbled, or of the jagged teeth of an old and dissipated saw. There seems to be no particular reason why the outbreak should have occurred just here for the place, Freshwater, has nothing in particular to recommend it above its neighbours. It is neither more nor less beautiful, neither more nor less approachable. In fact, it is extremely unapproachable being at the end of a lane which runs for some miles before it reaches the main road. There are no shops, no streets, no adequate sanitary arrangements; also there is no solitude and no sense of nature; as for beauty, what there was has been largely destroyed. It would, indeed, be impossible to imagine a settlement which combined in a more eminent degree all the disadvantages both of town and of country.

Camber Beach and the Rottingdean Downs

Now, at any point, on any stretch of our coastline this sort of outbreak is liable to occur. Take, for example, Camber Beach near Rye. This was in old days a glorious stretch of sand flanked by low dunes with their coarse grass. To-day, before and behind the dunes a bungaloid growth has sprung up of unspeakable ugliness and vulgarity. Shacks and old tramcars have appeared on the beach. A dozen shabby stalls, built apparently from sugar boxes or petrol tins, pressed in peace-time tea, sweets and aerated waters on your unwilling attention. The dunes where formerly you could picnic or bathe at will are now for the most part shut off by barbed wire entanglements. On a summer's day gramophones and portable wireless sets compete against each other in a horrid cacophony.

Or take the downs behind Rottingdean. These are magnificent, high and bare, with great views over the sea. Twenty years ago, except for an occasional barn, the austerity of their lines was unbroken. To-day their tops are covered by a sprawling bungalow town. The houses which compose this town are arranged in my opinion according to no discernible plan, but are dumped down anywhere, anyhow, according to the caprice of the builder. The one consideration which appears to have influenced him is the desirability of placing every house as far away from the next one as possible, in order that the infection may be spread over as large an area as possible. The houses are built in no recognizable style. They are like brick boxes of assorted shapes and sizes dropped on to the surface of the down; chunks of marzipan set up on end. The houses, again, conform to no scheme of colour; they are of all colours—pink, white, blue, grey and green—according to the taste of the builder or the owner. A particularly unpleasing variation is afforded by concrete houses covered with pebble-dash. But most are an angry and irritable pink.

Now this place, horrible in itself, is rendered ten times more horrible by contrast with that which has been ruined in order that it may be. The South Downs, especially in the east where they run down to the sea, form one of the most beautiful natural ramparts that could well be conceived. They are green, and are covered with soft, springy turf; they are reasonably high and fall naturally into beautiful folds and curves, making lines full of significance against the sky. They have been praised well and often in our literature and they are, or were, well loved. But the greater the value we place upon our downs, the greater the exertions we should make to protect them from spoliation. Their nature renders them an obvious prey, at once easy and attractive to the despoiler. They are bare and high. Consequently a single house placed upon the skyline can ruin the prospect for miles, standing out upon the bare high surface like the excrescence of an ugly tooth. They are green; consequently the pink buildings usually put up in the south of England, instead of merging into the surrounding environment like the traditional grey, stand out strident and staring.

They stand out, these settlements, as typical monuments of

our land, welcoming the visitor to her shores with an earnest of what is to come. For it is they, rather than the white cliffs of Dover or the Seven Sisters, which constitute the most appropriate symbol of what the traveller will find in contemporary England.

Return to the Pembrokeshire Coast and the Tank Corps

To return to Pembrokeshire. Having given Freshwater a wide berth, I rejoined the coast at Barafundle and walked on by the Fish Ponds of Bosherston to the headland of St. Gowans. All this part of the coast is very fine and fine, too, as I remember it, it continues to be for miles ahead. But just at this point where, with the Camp and the Freshwater outbreak well behind me, I was congratulating myself on a long stretch of empty coast, a new enemy appeared in the shape of the Tank Corps. Just as I topped a rise, I came upon a man with a red flag. He told me that the cliffs from that point onward had been taken over by the Tank Corps and that I could not go any further. How far, I asked, did the occupation extend? He named a distance which ran into double figures. I should, it appeared, have had to go inland almost to Pembroke before I could rejoin the coast. This was too much for me and, thoroughly discouraged, I gave up my project of walking further along the Pembrokeshire coast.

I heard afterwards some details of this occupation by tanks. Granted that there must be tanks in this iron age and granted, too, that they must be exercised, the seizure of this particular stretch of coast for the purpose seemed, as I reflected on what I heard, to be open to criticism on three gounds.

First, from the point of view of agriculture, it had involved, I was told, the dispersal and taking over of nearly sixty farms. These had been farmed for generations; the land, for coast land, was rich and particularly well adapted to the growing of early potatoes, the staple local industry. It had been so cut about by the tanks that, even if it were restored to agricultural use, its value would be small for years to come. Meanwhile families who had lived in the same house for generations, old women who had lived there all their lives, had been evicted. Secondly, the occupied part of the coast included some of the most famous bird rocks and bird sanctuaries in the country. These were now closed to ornithologists, let alone to humble bird watchers like myself. Thirdly, though I don't suppose this consideration would have much weight with anybody, this was in fact one of the loveliest and most beautiful stretches of coast in the county. There is not so much left that we can afford to have what little there may be so ruthlessly filched from us.

I thought of the large barren wastes known to me, where the tanks could have had their exercise with equal benefit to themselves and less deprivation to their human servitors; of waste stretches on the Pennines and the Cheviots; of the Breckland in Norfolk; of the sand dunes and mudbanks on the coasts of Essex and Lincolnshire. Granted that there might be some loss of convenience in choosing these areas rather than those actually selected, is the factor of amenity, which resolves itself into the factors of public welfare and enjoyment, never, one wonders, to be considered? Tanks after all are designed, so we are told, to keep England free; free for whom? Free, presumably, for the enjoyment of those Englishmen who love it. It seems illogical, to say the least of it, that in planning the means to this desirable end, we should impair the enjoyment of the end which is invoked as a justification of our action.

War Departments and the Coast

Some devil that enters into War Departments has endowed them with a genius for choosing for their exercises some of the wildest and scenically most valuable tracts of country. One thinks of the northern slopes of Dartmoor—the War Office, by the way, are now infesting large tracts of the southern area as well—of the moors and hills round Trawsfynydd, where the army has been in occupation for years. Vast tracts of the Highlands have been denied to the public by permanent military occupation. There is a widespreading area of first-class farmland on the downs running south and east from Amberley Mount nearly to Findon which early in the war the War Office 'took over', forcibly evicting the farmers and from twenty to thirty families of farmworkers, many of whom had lived there all their lives.

But of all parts of the country there is none that the devil causes to seem more attractive to military eyes than the coast-line. I have spoken of the Pembrokeshire coast because I know it best. I have no doubt, however, that what has happened here has happened along other stretches. I know, for example, that it has happened on the Dorset stretch. Take, for example, that unique coastline of the Isle of Purbeck stretching from Swanage to Osmington, undisfigured before the war by development. I knew the area well and used to stay often at Lulworth. It was one of those parts of England which had acquired distinctive and unmistakable characteristics; it was not that it was more lovely than other coastlines; it was lovely in a different way. Like so much that is charming in England, it was peculiarly vulnerable to the assaults of our age that cares little for charm. In 1916 the War Office started a Gunnery School somewhere between Lulworth Cove and Mupe Bay. It was a modest affair extending over not more than a mile of coast. It aroused strong protest and after the 1914-1918 war a demand was made for its removal. This demand was, as usual, ineffective. To quote Ward Lock's Guide-book, 'The action of the War Office was accepted during the war, but when, after the end of hostilities, it was found that the camp was to be permanent, strong opposition was aroused. It failed, however, to effect its object.' During the next two decades the area of gunnery-infested coast was very considerably extended. I have not been to these parts since the recent war, but this is what a correspondent writes in February 1945:

'During this war I have seen what the combined efforts of the War Deparment, the Ministry of Supply (with deforestation) and the Air Ministry could achieve in the spoliation of that rare peninsula. It was a painful process to stand on the tumulus at Swyre Head and see on the east hand the woodland of Encombe Bowl fall beneath the axe and on the west hand the downs running down to Kimmeridge Bay being turned into a tank-training ground. However, such sights, and others even sadder, were necessary for the war effort, and the hope was cherished that after the war Purbeck would be left to recover in peace, and her exiles to return to their stone farmhouses and cottages.

'But now it appears that another battle has to be fought and if there are some to whom the names of Arish Mell, Worbarrow, Brandy Bay, Flowers Barrow and Steeple are music, I can only hope that they can make their protests heard in time to prevent the War Department from going ahead with its plans to turn that isle of refreshment for the soul into a permanent battle range.'

'A permanent battle range!' Yes, permanent, for, once the War Office has got its teeth into a piece of countryside, it very rarely lets go. As I write[1], comes news of a letter which has been pinned up in the West Lulworth post office, signed by a Lieutenant Pymm, 'for Adjutant, Gunnery Wing, A.F.C. School, Lulworth Camp'. The letter announces the *permanent* closing of certain roads between Stoborough and the coast and says that 'starting on the 30th May 1945, shooting will be taking place daily over the whole of the East Holme Range area'. This edict permanently closes five miles of the loveliest part of the Dorset coast including Mupe Bay, Arish Mell, Worbarrow Bay and the western part of the Purbeck Hills. Must the War Department, one wonders, rage just here? Why not choose the Swannery at Abbotsbury? But perhaps that has already gone. I seem to have heard somewhere that it has.

But now that I have returned to the coast and its enemies I cannot too quickly be done with them. For the subject is a dreary one and has already depressed me to the extent of making me hasten to the welcoming end of this chapter. Nevertheless, there are two matters that must still be mentioned.

The Anti-Social Private House

First, there is the isolated house, perched gaily on a high point on the cliffs and, if built, as it all too often is, of unsuitable materials, ruining the aspect of a whole stretch of coast. As an example take the big house that dominates Mother Ivy's Bay in Cornwall. It is not a bad house in itself, but its erection in just this particular spot is in my view an anti-social act. Not only does it break the beautiful line of cliff tops, its garden running to the very edge of the cliff compels the walker to make a wide detour inland before he can continue his journey. A better example of

[1] July 1945.

anti-social building on the coast could not well be conceived. There are many private owners who, having bought stretches of the coast upon which they have built their anti-social houses, have not scrupled to divert, even in some cases to block, rights of way that run through their land. Their habit is to extend their private gardens to the very edge of the cliff, to surround them with thick hedges so that nobody can see them and then to compel the excluded public to make a detour round their back premises in order to rejoin the interrupted path. But this is not the worst. When a man owns land adjoining the sea, his ownership normally extends to high-water mark. All that part of the beach which lies above high-water mark may be and often is fenced and shut off for the exclusive use of these selfish owners. I have even known them to claim stretches of sand covered at high but uncovered at low tide, so that nobody could at any time walk along any part of the coast between their property and the sea. In this they are probably exceeding their legal rights, since ownership of the 'foreshore', the beach below high-water mark, is normally vested in the Crown. The Crown sometimes leases the 'foreshore' to a Local Authority desirous of controlling the use of the beach by the public, but very rarely to a private owner.[1]

The Seaside Place

This other enemy must, I fear, be expected to be with us for all time; it is at once too firmly established in the public esteem and too far gone in the horrors of its ugliness to be vanquished. The ordinary seaside resort seems to me a terrible place. I exclude from this stricture those that were established before the late nineteenth-century rush to the sea; Margate is an attractive town, parts of Brighton and Hove are beautiful, but the Worthings, the Littlehamptons, the Bognors, even their grander relations, the Bournemouths and the Torquays, how terrible they are! Not the least of their enormities is that they make people pay to enter the sea. The sea is what the seaside is for; the sea is the Englishman's heritage; the sea

[1] See Appendix IV for a Summary of the legal enactments governing the use of the foreshore.

belongs to nobody, certainly not to the Municipality of ——; yet we must pay the Municipality of —— for the privilege of entering it, simply because it happens to lie on the far side of the beach that the Municipality has appropriated. However, I digress. Indeed, this whole section is as unnecessary as it is unwise, since I have no remedy to offer for these places except that they should be painlessly eliminated. So far as I can see, there is no chance whatever of this remedy being adopted, so long as large numbers of people make their livelihood out of keeping them going and even larger numbers provide them with a livelihood by paying for the privilege of visiting them. Perhaps, in time, the ingenious Mr. Butlin[1] and his successors may have taught us how to supersede them; till then we must suffer them.

But though the established seaside places are irremovable and will continue to flourish until our civilization changes its tastes and habits, the long antennae which they proliferate into their hinterlands and along the coasts on either side of them, where in due course they join the antennae of other proliferations, so that the coastline becomes fringed with a scurf of squalor stretching almost continuously from Deal to Portsmouth, need not have occurred in the past and should be prevented from recurring in the future. They could be prevented by restrictive planning, which refused to permit seaside towns to spread beyond a certain point, while some parts of the worst of what has been put up in the past might even be destroyed, the bungalow town of Shoreham, for example, the line of shacks that stretches out from Hunstanton, the horrible outbreak upon the cliffs above Filey. None of these places has any permanence; they are by their very nature ephemeral. It is not, therefore, necessary to pull them down; it is sufficient that when they become uninhabitable, as in five or ten years' time they will do, we should refuse to permit their replacement.

Some Recommendations

Not wishing to burden the text with a detailed list, I have relegated most of these to an appendix.[2] The remedies, I hope,

[1] See ch. xi, pp. 228–232.   [2] See Appendix IV.

are sufficiently clearly indicated by the foregoing description of the disease. They are, moreover, remedies upon which most of us are agreed; they appear in the Scott Report, in the post-war proposals of the Ramblers' Association laid before the Scott Committee and in greater detail in the second Report, dated October 1942, of that admirable body the Coastal Preservation Committee, set up by the Commons, Open Spaces and Foot-paths Preservation Society, the National Trust and the Council for the Preservation of Rural England. The object of all these recommendations is stated very briefly by the Ramblers' Association to be that 'British citizens should be able to walk along their own coast and along their own shores'. To this end there are recommended: (1) The compulsory acquisition by the State of all sea coast not already built upon; (2) The compulsory acquisition of all gardens lying across public footpaths and of such parts of the seashore as are now in private ownership; (3) Public right of access to all coasts and foreshores so acquired; (4) A planned scheme for the coastline as a whole, features of which should be: (a) provision for preserving unbuilt on stretches; (b) the zoning of a belt extending sufficiently far inland to en-sure the preservation of the natural features of the coastal land-scape; (c) the control and proper siting of such additional buildings as may be permitted; (d) the compulsory purchase and subsequent destruction of isolated anti-social houses whose presence destroys the beauty of long stretches of otherwise unspoiled coast; (e) the rescue of coastal stretches from War Departments; (f) administration of the coastline not locally by Local Authorities, but nationally by a special Department of the Ministry of Town and Country Planning or of a Ministry of Amenities, if one should be set up.

Chapter Nine

THE THREE ENGLANDS AND WHAT HAPPENS TO THEM

England may be divided into four different parts. The first consists of the old pre-industrial towns; the second is the England that was brought into being by the industrial revolution; the third is the England of the twentieth century, and the fourth the England which is still country. I have something to say about each.

I. Pre-Industrial England

Visit to War-time Oxford

First, there are the old towns of which, since I know it best and have loved it most, I take Oxford as an example. As I write, there comes vividly to my mind a memory of a visit that I made to Oxford in the fourth winter of the war. The 4.45 from Paddington was packed with people; the compartments were full and the corridor jammed. I was assured that the great majority of those travelling performed this journey daily. They were refugees who ran away for the night from the bombs in London to the families they had parked in Oxford and returned the next morning to their offices in London.

The good old 4.45! How often had I travelled by it before the war; travelled in evening dress to speak at the Union, travelled to dine with a Don, to address an undergraduate society, to meet a girl. . . . With what pleasurable anticipation has Oxford been approached. Oxford which I feel I should never have left and to which I have always hoped, albeit as I grow older with a hope that fades, to return to end my days as an old Don lecturing on philosophy, fussing about his dinner, drinking his port afterwards and steeping himself in the beauty of the place for, to me, Oxford has always been the most beautiful town in England. In those days the 4.45 arrived at 6.5 and was scarcely ever late. Now it was scheduled to arrive at 6.15 and was, I was assured, anything up to three-quarters of an hour late. However, I was not to dine in Magdalen until 7.15 and, even if it were three-quarters of an hour late, I should still be in time. Just outside Maidenhead the engine broke down. We waited for half an hour or so in a siding while another engine was found; it was a very slow one. Time passed, it grew later and later and we finally crawled into Oxford about 7.15. The train disgorged its teeming contents on to the platform. There was a scrum at the exit from which I emerged into darkness and pouring rain. What few taxis there may have been had already been snapped up. I supposed that I had better take a bus and walked to the bottom of the station incline to the point at which the buses usually stop. A long queue had already formed at the bus stop. I joined it. So far as I could see—and it was very dark—the queue was composed almost entirely of men. In this queue I stood for six or seven minutes; it was still raining but there was no bus. Then a disquieting thought occurred; suppose that the bus, when it did come, did not go down the High at all; it might turn down the Corn or go along Walton Street. I turned to the man next to me in the queue and asked him if the bus we were waiting for went up the High. 'The High?' he said, 'don't know. Where's that? This bus goes to the Works.'

'What Works?' I asked.

'Why, the Pressed Steel works, of course.' And then, looking at me curiously, 'You a stranger here?' he asked.

This story is from my own experience, but it was not at first hand but from hearsay—I was told of the incident by the respected wife of the Head of an Oxford College—that I learnt of two ladies discussing in an Oxford bus the many discomforts and difficulties of Oxford life, the queues, the shortages, the crowds; 'And then,' one concluded—or is said to have concluded—'as if all that weren't bad enough, what do they want to go and dump a University down here for?'

ΝΑΙΑΣ

THREE ENGLANDS AND WHAT HAPPENS TO THEM

Oxford in 1904

I give these stories because they seem to me to have a symbolic significance. They symbolize the decline in importance of the University and of all that makes Oxford distinctive and its gradual overshadowing by the town and all that makes Oxford common. Going to Oxford as a schoolboy in 1904, I knew a country town of some 60,000 inhabitants, engaged in the production of marmalade, sausages and undergraduates. All these were of high quality, the first two of uniformly high quality. Trams drawn by two horses cruised noisily up and down the streets; St. Aldates after seven o'clock in the evening was a deserted thoroughfare and the only place known to us for a meal was Buol's, the faintly wicked and raffish Buol's—the Cadena opposite was just starting. North Oxford was still a land in which it was always Sunday afternoon.

There was little as yet save the gas works near the station, the slums in St. Ebbes and the villas of North Oxford to mar the city's beauty. This was an Oxford of which Max Beerbohm could still say, 'a bit of Manchester through which Apollo had passed'. The beauty, indeed, had I had eyes to see it, was still conspicuous. Nor had it much diminished when in 1910 I returned to Oxford as an undergraduate. But it was then, with the coming of the motor age, that the rot set in.

Oxford's Proliferation

I am told that Lord Nuffield has conferred great benefits upon the University, including many handsome endowments for the encouragement of science—under the impression, apparently, that we don't even now possess as much knowledge as, given our existing stock of public wisdom and private virtue, we can conveniently manage. In return he has received many degrees. He has also, I suppose, by bringing in people, increased the wealth of the city's tradesmen. Nevertheless, it is, I think, an open question whether he has not done more to diminish the true values of Oxford, beauty, quietude, meditation, non-utilitarian learning and speculative talk than any other single individual, past or present. He has caused a large industrial suburb to spring

169

up on the outskirts of the city, with the consequence that the city has stretched out its tentacles to join the suburb; he has cut off the central core of Oxford from the surrounding country from which it derived no small part of its distinctive charm, and he has introduced into the streets at the core regiments of working-class folk and their women, who are alike blind to the beauty and ignorant of the traditions of the city to which they have been brought, and by their spiritual, no less than their bodily presence, impede the appreciation of those who value the things that belong distinctively to Oxford, while at the same time diminishing that in them which made them worthy of being valued. In a word, Lord Nuffield will go down to history as the man who enabled Oxford to be spoken of as 'the Latin quarter of Cowley'. It is a distressing epitaph.

Granted that the motor age had to come, granted that cars must be both many and cheap, granted, too, that Lord Nuffield must build them, why must it be Oxford of all places that he should choose for their building, or—to put the question further back—why should an ill-choosing destiny have so ordered matters that it was in Oxford of all places that this creative genius of the motor age should first see the light? Since after all he *is* of the new age, is it an unreasonable demand to make of destiny that it should have begotten him upon one of the places distinctive of that age for the wider scope and better exhibition of his talents? Are there no Midlands? Is there no Corby, no Kettering, no Luton, no Retford? Why must it have been Oxford, one of the few places in England where there was beauty still to spoil? Since, as I ventured to point out when viewing the lorries drawn up on the Cambridge Backs, our age cannot create beauty, it should be the more scrupulous to preserve the beauty which has come down to it. It is not, and destiny might have seen fit to be jealous on beauty's behalf.

The Morris Works are only one, though perhaps the most important, of the influences which between the two wars were turning Oxford into a large industrial town. To the north, the east, the south and the west, it was stretching out during the inter-war years long pink arms. North Oxford extended itself to infinity so that what in my schooldays was the end of the bus route is now less, much less, than half-way along it. There are streets of small shops and pink-roofed houses running on to Headington and Shotover, while buildings creep up to the bottom of Cumnor Hill. For the North Oxford schoolboy, country walks in every direction except due south were within reach—how intensely, by the way, I hated them! As an undergraduate, I could still go for an afternoon's walk up to Cumnor or through Hinksey to Boar's Hill—even if I came back by bus —without too many miles of new suburban streets to traverse on the way out. Or there was that heavenly walk from Cumnor village down the Long Leys to Bablock Hythe. I would do that walk to Bablock and back again on a summer afternoon and evening. Once I spent the night at the Bablock Hythe inn—it was small and simple then—just across the water. (It was the first time I had ever gone to the country for a night alone. I was steeped in the literature of walking and expected to enjoy profound spiritual experiences. In fact, I was lonely, bored and a little scared. It was one of the first occasions on which I discovered the difference between literature and life.)

Walking from Oxford in the 'Thirties

The point that I am making is that until the early 'twenties, all this country was still reasonably accessible from a not yet overgrown Oxford.

When, years afterwards in the late 'thirties, I visited my daughter, who was an undergraduette, I used, in spite of her reluctance, to take her out for walks, walks which, I insisted, must be in the country.

The planning of these walks was an elaborate affair. If you really wanted to walk in the country you had, I discovered, to take a bus for some miles out of the town, taking care to look up your bus time-table for another bus to bring you back again. I came to the conclusion that the best plan was to make for some private estate, where the chance of being harassed by gamekeepers was outweighed by the probability of country sights and solitude. The nearest that I could find was Wytham Woods, so we used to take a bus along the road running west from Carfax, get off about a couple of miles beyond the station, turn up right on to the hills above Wytham, walk there for an hour or so on the wooded ridge with its fine views over the river and so down again to the plain at Godstow. I was challenged once or twice by keepers and once by a shooting party, but I had discovered that the woods where the encounters took place belonged to some Oxford college, and by temporarily adding myself to the roll of the college staff—I forget now, alas, both the college and the subject I professed—was allowed to go my way in peace. (These little subterfuges I consider to be wholly allowable. One does not trespass because one wants to, but because only too often in the neighbourhood of towns to trespass is the only method of getting away from people and into the country. Since I grew too dignified to cheek and too old to run away from keepers, I have come to dislike trespassing. The fear of being found and the altercation when one is found are alike inimical to the mood of quiet serenity in which one is most receptive to country influences. The pool cannot reflect the sky when it is troubled. Hence, whatever petty shifts and chicaneries may be necessary to get one quickly away from towns and people and to give one leisure to go about the country with the minimum of disturbance to the spirit are, I repeat, allowable.) From Godstow we used to walk to Wolvercot whence we caught another bus back to Oxford. But what a business! And to think that Oxford should have been allowed so to grow and swell that such a business should be necessary to get out of it and into it again. Of course there is still the lovely central core, the walks through the parks and Mesopotamia— yet when you get to Marston, you find another outbreak of sporadic building; there are Addison's Walk, Christchurch Meadows and the rest, and very lovely they are, especially in spring and summer. In spring and summer, indeed, they suffice, but in autumn and winter one wants to walk further afield and to sense the sights and sounds of country proper. For the country of the central core is in spite of its loveliness country preserved, rather than country proper.

Such is the condition to which Oxford has been reduced that those who want to walk for a couple of hours where, though country is never reached, there is yet sight of trees and grass and flowers and water, the sound of birds, tree-fringed skylines, grassy slopes on which to sit and lie about and some surcease from the company of one's fellows, will be better advised to live in Hampstead than in Oxford; for in Hampstead the Heath is at their front door. Admittedly it *is* only the Heath, but it is as good as the Oxford Parks and is not much more effectively insulated from the country. Granted a little more endowment for scientific research, whatever small advantage may remain with the Oxford Parks will vanish altogether.

Such, then, are the two bad things that we have done to Oxford. First, we have surrounded the lovely central core which we inherited with concentric rings of ugliness and squalor; the inner ring of ugliness and squalor deposited by the nineteenth century and the Edwardian age, the ring of gas works, banks, slums, yellow brick and North Oxford Gothic; the outer ring of smart, garish suburbs, complete with petrol pumps, factories, and cinemas laid down by the twentieth century. Secondly, as a result we have allowed Oxford to be invaded by armies of people who are alien to her traditions and care nothing for her beauty.

The War Comes

The last chapter has still to be told. With the war Oxford became a dumping ground for colleges, *crèches*, schools, schools of art, training schools for officers, ladies' finishing schools, government departments, civil service offices, airmen, soldiers, cadets, refugees and evacuees and the women and children of refugees and evacuees, not to speak of the annual influx of conferences, week-end schools and summer schools. Somewhere buried beneath all this *débris*, the heart of the University still beat, but it was buried deep and beat but faintly, so that the still small voice of its beauty could scarcely be heard amid the hullabaloo. But this chapter, the chapter of Oxford in war-time, I cannot bring myself to write.

Now what we have done to Oxford, we have done in greater or less degree to most of the lovely old towns that have come down to us from the past; to Winchester and Salisbury and Exeter and York and Stratford and Worcester and Tewkesbury. All in their degree have been vulgarized and cheapened. These cities retain a central core of loveliness surrounded by hideous outskirts. The central core was built long ago; the outskirts are of the nineteenth and the twentieth centuries. And inevitably, to reach the centre you must pass through the outskirts which grow continuously more extensive. Moreover, Oxford is very far from being the only victim of industry. These lovely old towns seem indeed to have a sinister fascination for industrialists. The story of Beauty and the Beast repeats itself but with a difference; in the story the Beast is transfigured by the contact with Beauty; in modern England the transformation is of Beauty by the Beast.

The Case of Durham

Take, for example, the case of Durham, which is being discussed as I write.[1] Everybody agrees that one of the noblest views in England is the view of Durham as you approach it from the south by train. By some freak the city escaped being blighted by the industrial revolution and though it is a place of extremes, of noble buildings and mean streets, of squalid homes and picturesque thoroughfares, yet the predominant impression that it makes is one of great beauty. For dominating all are the Castle and the Cathedral, built more than eight hundred years ago, two lovely and impressive buildings.

As I write, however, this beauty, the beauty of one of the few non-industrial towns in the North of England, is threatened. The North Eastern Electricity Supply Company proposes to build a power station in Durham. The power station will involve the erection of three cooling towers, each 250 feet high, while two chimneys, 350 feet high, will rear themselves to dwarf the central tower of the Cathedral which is only 218 feet. Meanwhile Thomas Sharp has drawn up and the *Architectural Press* has published on behalf of Durham City a plan for Durham entitled *Cathedral City*, which, if carried into effect, would retain and, indeed, enhance the beauty of the old city. New groups of public buildings, including law courts, a youth centre, a theatre, a library, a museum and an art gallery would be put up; an industrial estate for light and medium industries would be planned sufficiently near the city for the fear of unemployment

[1] July 1945.

174

to be removed from its citizens, a system of external bypass roads would displace and replace the slums, while such new private dwellings as were permitted would deliberately aim at creating a sense of neighbourhood and avoiding the segregation of classes. Now this plan and the proposed power station exclude one another. To quote from an admirable article by Mr. McCarthy which appeared in the *News Chronicle*: 'If the proposed power station is built this plan for the Durham of the future is gravely imperilled. Its site is a quarter of a mile from the only reasonably extensive area of the city available for future housing and only half a mile from existing houses. These houses will suffer from smoke and fumes from the plant. The electricity company, who argue that they can find no other suitable site, have promised to install an expensive dust-precipitating machine, but still there must be a great bulk of wastage to fall on the city. In addition dust will come from the coal being transferred from the railway to the conveyor, and steam and spray will come from the cooling towers. And, architecturally, the city will be ruined. That view which Ruskin described as "one of the seven wonders of the world" will be destroyed. From almost every part of the city the eye will be caught and held by the soaring chimneys and massive cooling towers of the power station.'

On the other side of the argument is one consideration and one only—the power station will employ three hundred men.

By the time this book has appeared the issue will have been decided.[1] I mention it here because it throws into high relief the alternatives by which our age is confronted. We are bidden to choose between beauty and electricity; the choice, of course, is not necessitated, for the electricity might just as well be generated elsewhere. But it is in these sharply defined terms that the 'forces of progress' will present the issue and, so presenting it, decide it by default. For, unless the immediate future breaks

[1] Later (August 1945). It is now understood that owing to widespread opposition the proposal is to be dropped, and we are told that the site, originally announced as 'the only available site', is not suitable. In Lincoln, on the other hand, where the City Council turned down a similar proposal, on the ground that enormous cooling towers would disfigure the city, they have now (August 1945) reversed their decision and the cooling towers are to be erected. Here and there, now and then, the tide of ugliness is beaten back; but on the whole it advances.

utterly with the past, the issue in these cases is already decided; electricity, which means power and profit, wins every time, while beauty no man regards.

Other Pre-Industrial Towns

Few indeed are the towns surviving from pre-industrial England which we have not yet spoiled. There is Bath and there is King's Lynn and there is Ludlow, each of them so lovely that one can hardly bear to visit them for fear that something should have happened in the interval since one's last visit to impair their loveliness. There are also a few small towns, scarcely larger than big villages, such as Chipping Campden and Burford in the Cotswolds, such as Brackley on the Northamptonshire–Buckinghamshire border, such as Uppingham in Rutland or Midhurst in Sussex—yet even Midhurst has its many nineteenth-century villas.

There are also a number of predominantly Georgian towns and villages, such as Abingdon and Blandford and Farnham and Stamford, large parts of which are comparatively unspoiled. Pre-eminent among them is Bewdley on the Severn which, having lost its trade about 1790, has been crystallized in a state of arrested development around its own loveliness for the last one hundred and fifty years. Mercifully, there are no archaeological remains, no antiquarian curiosities, no buildings of outstanding interest to attract tourists. Bewdley is just a neighbourly old place, which happens to be beautiful;[1] so is Coggeshall in Essex and Ottery St. Mary in South Devonshire, with its rows of friendly brick-fronted houses, deep-set windows and old gardens with their lawns running back behind. But the English towns that neither the nineteenth nor the twentieth century has spoiled are comparatively few.

Recommendations in Regard to Pre-Industrial Towns

What is one to say about this neglected heritage of lovely old towns? What recommendations can one make for the preserving

[1] An excellent plan for Bewdley has been prepared by that indefatigable champion of landscape beauty, Clough Williams Ellis.

of Oxford and Winchester and the rest? Very little that has not been said often enough already. It can all be comprised in the single principle of 'let alone', which I have already invoked in connection with National Parks. The principle means simply that the distinctive character of Chipping Campden and Ludlow should not be destroyed by new industrial development or residential fringes. This principle covers the ground; if one could hope that it would be observed, there would be no more to say. Since, as things are, any such hope must of necessity be dim, I venture to add one or two observations designed to brighten it.

Nearly all our towns are, I suggest, too large and a check should in any event be placed on their continued growth. Oxford, Winchester, Salisbury and towns of their type should not be permitted to grow at all. I cannot deny myself the pleasure of adding that considerable areas which have sprung up during the last fifty years should be pulled down. But this, of course, is a purely imaginative fantasy. Nothing that is ugly is in this country ever pulled down, just as no mess is ever cleared up. If England is ever again to be beautiful we shall have to wait until the population grows smaller. A sizable population might permit itself the enjoyment of beauty. It might even permit itself the pleasure of destroying Cowley!

If the question of development be pressed—for England is, I suppose, doomed to grow even more populous for a time —let us consider the question of the type of town which could be permitted to grow larger without harm either to itself or to the country round about it. Towns selected for development should, I suggest, conform to the following conditions: (1) They should be already ugly and, therefore, comparatively unspoilable; (2) They should be served by a good railway system; (3) Alternatively or additionally they should be served by a good road system; (4) They should not yet be fully developed; (5) They should be situated in comparatively dull country. A number of old railway towns, such as Crewe or Doncaster, fall within this category; to the same type belong Stafford, Retford and Nuneaton. In a different category are places which have expanded very rapidly during the last twenty years, such as Luton, Corby, and Kettering. These are ugly enough in all conscience, but they are not definitely deleterious to health; they are not, that is to say, for the most part slums, and they should, I suppose, be allowed to continue their development. But to pursue these topics would take me outside the scope of this book, involving me in the obligation to deal with the development and siting of industry, a task with which, mercifully, I have no competence to deal and which I propose, therefore, to permit myself to shirk. Let it, however, be said that the development even of Doncaster and Crewe must be subject to certain conditions and protections which have not been accorded to towns which were developed earlier. These conditions should by now be familiar to readers of this book.

If a town is to grow, it should, it is obvious, grow in accordance with a planned scheme which (1) determines in advance both the amount and the rate of growth so that the town does not sprawl shapelessly over the surrounding country; (2) assigns a clearly defined boundary between town and country so that when a town stops, it stops; (3) makes provision for the need for rural areas on the outskirts—and rural areas do not mean merely exiguous green belts—and in the immediate neighbourhood of the developed town.

II. Nineteenth-Century Industrial England

Nineteenth-century industrial England has often been described with a wealth and range of denunciatory eloquence which I cannot hope to compass. I would recommend the curious reader to J. B. Priestley's book, *English Journey*, and more particularly to the passage on Shotton Bridge, taken as the type and supreme exemplar of those places which under the name of towns cover large areas of the North of England, places which ought not to have been built, but which, having been built, ought to be pulled down.

It is not difficult to justify this last statement; it is sufficient to remember the conditions in which these towns *were* built. In the early and mid-nineteenth century it was thought necessary to put up dwellings as rapidly as possible, without regard to beauty, health, convenience or amenity, for the rapidly growing armies of workers which the industrial revolution was concentrating in the mills, mines and factories. It is Middlesbrough's boast that it was 'run up' more quickly than any other town in the country. It looks like it!

On the general conditions in which and the conceptions from which these towns originated, I venture again to quote from G. M. Trevelyan's *English Social History* (Longmans):

'Still throughout the 'forties nothing was done to control the slum-landlords and jerry builders who, according to the prevalent *laissez-faire* philosophy, were engaged from motives of self-interest in forwarding the general happiness. These pioneers of "progress" saved space by crowding families into single rooms or thrusting them underground in cellars, and saved money by the use of cheap and insufficient building material, and by providing no drains—or worse still by providing drains that oozed into the water supply. In London Lord Shaftesbury discovered a room with a family in each of its four corners, and a room with a cesspool immediately below its boarded floor.'

Trevelyan quotes the following passage from the Report of Edwin Chadwick, one of the Poor Law Commissioners, written in the 'forties:

'The prisons' (he wrote) 'were formerly distinguished for their filth and bad ventilation; but the descriptions given by Howard of the worst prisons he visited in England' (which he states were among the worst he had seen in Europe) 'were exceeded in every wynd in Edinburgh and Glasgow inspected by Dr. Arnott and myself. More filth, worse physical suffering and moral disorder than Howard describes are to be found amongst the cellar populations of the working people of Liverpool, Manchester or Leeds and in large portions of the Metropolis.'

An Industrial Town on a Sunday

What these towns were in origin they still are in essentials. Some improvements have been made and sometimes they are extensive improvements; there are wider streets, better houses, occasionally a distinguished building, for example, the Libraries at Manchester or Leeds, or the universities at Nottingham or Birmingham. But these things are occasional and haphazard; they are not the rule, and the general picture of meanness, gloom and squalor remains. The most depressing sight I know is a moderate-sized industrial town, Bury, say, or Accrington or Sunderland or West Bromwich on a Sunday afternoon in February. It is six o'clock and a rain-laden wind is blowing along the streets. On the pavements groups of young men are standing; they are *just* standing—'loafing' is a good nineteenth-century word for it—looking at the girls and waiting for the pubs to open. A few couples walk by. Round the doors of the chapels gather little knots of people, the respectably pious, dressed in black and looking like crows. Nobody is laughing, nobody is singing, nobody weeping and gnashing his teeth, nobody pulling the place down; nobody even making fiery speeches exhorting other people to pull the place down; they are just standing amid the unutterable dreariness of their surroundings, the young waiting for the pubs, the old for the chapels to open. These impressions are psychological; the industrial towns of Victorian England are, I am suggesting, lowering to the spirit. 'Well,' you may say, 'but that is debatable; their inhabitants like them very well.' But they are also, I add, harmful to the body and that is not debatable. I have just[1] been reading a speech by Major Markham, M.P. for Nottingham, in which he averred that the pollution created by smoke had materially reduced the hours of sunlight in industrial towns and increased the duration and intensity of fog. 'We have', he said, 'produced in the hearts of great cities conditions so awful that the toll of death and diseases is probably greater than ever before in our history, save only during great plagues. It is a cruel commentary on civilization that the smokiest areas of the country show an infantile mortality rate double that of the sunny, small towns.' That is not a matter of opinion; it is a fact, a fact established by statistics. Nor is it hard to credit, when we are told that the amount of smoke dirt deposited in Sheffield is about five hundred tons annually per square mile.

And yet, I agree with my imaginary objector, the inhabitants of these places like them very well. Most of them do not know

[1] February 1945.

that their surroundings are dreary and, when their towns are attacked by people like myself, they passionately defend them. Even if they do not regard them as shining exemplars of the city beautiful, they look upon them as being at least places in which men may rub along very well to their own and everybody else's content. They are even proud of them, as I have found to my cost.

Journey to X

In the early days of the war it fell to my lot to go to one of these places—I had better not say which because of the civic pride to which I have just referred; I have grievously hurt it once and don't want to hurt it again—to make a speech. I had had a few days' holiday in the Lake District. The time of the year was late May, the weather had been fine and the Lake District at its best. All along the southern valleys were masses of bird-cherry blossom; the young leaves were all in different shades of green in the Borrowdale woods; there were still daffodils at Winster. I had had, I remember, one wonderful day in particular, going over Looking Stead, Pillar, Steeple and Haycock and so down over Middle Fell to Wasdale Head Hall; another, over Allen Crags and Glaramara. When the time came to go, the memory of these places was still vivid with me. I had a difficult cross-country railway journey to the north-east coast which involved waiting for a couple of hours at Penrith. Penrith is pretty awful, but it has a park near the station with a bowling green. Here I sat and watched the bowls and ate my lunch under a hot sun, a thing rarely done in Penrith before. For one thing, it is practically never hot enough; for another, Penrith is not the sort of place to attract migrant eaters of sandwich lunches. There were fine views of the Pennines to the east and still the spell was not broken. Then south by train to Appleby and south east to Kirkby Stephen, and so over the spine of the Pennines down to Barnard Castle.

Digression on the Appleby Country

I cannot turn my back or let you turn the page on Appleby without a word of recognition for its lovely but little known countryside. When we go to these north-western parts, the Lake District is so potent a magnet for us that few have time for the country that lies to the east of it; for the Sedbergh Hills, for Wild Boar Fell or for the country by Appleby. This last is the valley of the Eden, a wide, deep, slow stream flowing sometimes between meadows, sometimes between sloping hills covered by great trees, so that one is at times reminded of the Severn. Beside the Eden the valley is alive with streams running down from the high fells. A walk along the Hoff Beck, running north-wards into Appleby, takes one through some of the most delightful country of its kind in the North. The plain itself is broken up by small hills, while patches of heather country show themselves among the cornfields. There is a multitude of birds and every now and then there is an outcrop of rock to remind one that this is the North. How frequently the foothills of mountainous country offer the best walking, best both from the point of view of solitude and from that of variety, and how few walkers know it. Parts of the valley are highly cultivated with wide fields; there are little copses, gorse and heather commons and at the back the line of the Pennines with Dufton and Murton Pikes behind Keisley shutting in the view to the east with their lovely shapes. Ascend them and pass beyond eastwards over their tops and you find yourself in country as wild as there is in England. In the foreground is a tableland of moor; to eastward, north and south the fells stretch away as far as the eye can see. There is not much heather in these parts, the hills being mainly limestone and you can walk as you please without giving a thought to the 'keeper-curse'.

This Appleby country is specially distinguished by two things, the size and beauty of the trees and the quality of the light. Both oaks and beeches are numerous and grow to a size such as one does not often see in the North; looking only at them, you would think that you were in an eastern county. (My private view about this is that since the prevailing winds in England blow from the west, each line or layer of north-to-south trees acts as a screen to the line or layer to the east of it, so that the most easterly line—short, of course, of the wind-bitten wastes near the east coast—being the most screened and sheltered, grows the tallest. Is there anything in this, I wonder? Possibly,

possibly not.) As to the light, this has a curious, luminous quality—I have already referred to it in describing a railway journey along the Cumberland coast—which is experienced at its most striking on the west coasts of Scotland and Ireland. It is a light in which objects look insubstantial; they seem almost to float and the suggestion of unreality adds to the loveliness.

Continuation of Journey to X

To return to my journey, the railway over the Pennines is indubitably one of the finest in England. Up and up the train climbed, grunting terribly at about twelve miles per hour. To the north were the green hillsides of the Pennines with Cross Fell in the distance; to the south and west the views were wider, looking towards Wild Boar Fell and the hills above Sedbergh; behind and further to the west were the mountains of the Lake District and to the south in the far distance Whernside, Ingleborough and Penyghent. The weather still held, the sun shone from a cloudless sky, it was still spring, the world was still lovely and the spell still held, held to such purpose that when at last we came down to Barnard Castle, I was mused and dazed with beauty. Then eastwards to Darlington and Stockton and Eaglescliffe and Middlesbrough and northwards to Sunderland and Hartlepool, Jarrow and Hebburn.

As the horror of this man-blasted plain gradually crept about me, I came out of my daze to find myself in a tearing temper. What fools we were, I thought, meditating once again on a theme on which, I fear, I may already have enlarged. If we had initially been given Jarrow and Hebburn and Stockton and Middlesbrough and had gone to great trouble and labour and expense to substitute the bare hills of the Pennines, one could have understood and one would certainly have admired. But, in fact, it was the other way round. We had inherited not, indeed, here the Pennines, but a fertile coast plain—for the country behind Redcar is very pleasant and the Cleveland Hills are lovely—and we had gone out of our way spending an immense amount of time, labour and money to cover it up with Jarrow and Hebburn and Sunderland and Middlesbrough. Objectively regarded, it is an astonishing thing to have done.

'It Ought to be Pulled Down, of course'

The last twenty miles I did in a car—twenty miles of almost continuous squalor. The sun which had been shining all day from a cloudless sky disappeared behind a pall of smoke; the land was flat as a pancake and ranged along the riverbank were cranes, derricks and railway sheds; chimneys belched smoke; factories and mills were surrounded by acres of squalid yard; the road ran through miles of streets lined with little, mean houses, houses which were covered with a coat of grime. No single building distinguished itself, by reason either of its size or its beauty, from the mean monotony of the prevailing architecture. As the car penetrated deeper into this district, my heart sank. The contrast between what had been during the preceding seven days, between what had been even to-day in the places where man had largely left God's work alone, and between the places in which he had substituted his own, would have depressed anybody but a saint or a local inhabitant, for—and here we come to the point of all this—the local inhabitants did not at all share my horror. In the Town Hall there was a reception. There were the Mayor and the Corporation; there were smartly dressed men, noisy with heartiness, beaming with jollity and agog for speeches. I had not expected this. At least, I had not expected 'this' to be quite so grand and I was not dressed for it. In point of fact, I was still wearing the clothes in which I had been walking in the Lakes, a pair of flannel 'bags', stained, an old coat, torn, an Aertex shirt whose natural brownness could not wholly conceal its acquired dirt, and nailed boots. As I came stumping into the hall, I was made all too consciously aware of the deficiencies of my costume. I could see the company, so sleek, so black, so neat and so glossy, looking covertly down its nose at me so stained, so torn, so dirty and so clumping. What the women thought, only a woman could say. With the memory of the Lakes and their contrast to the place in which these people lived and with which they seemed content vivid in my mind, I, not to be outdone, **was** metaphorically looking down my nose at them, resenting their sleekness and blackness and neatness and glossiness, so **that**, what with one thing and another, the business of welcoming and complimenting being now over, when the Mayor opened the serious, conversational business with the words, 'Now, tell us, Dr. Joad, what do you thing of X?' I, speaking from out of my background, a background of beauty past and my immediate environment of ugliness present and taking the thing, as it were, for granted, replied, 'It ought to be pulled down, of course.' I will not describe—I have not the novelist's pen—the consternation with which this utterance of mine was greeted. I only fully grasped the size of the brick I had dropped and the height from which I had dropped it on the following morning when I read an account of what had taken place in the local paper. The account had been written by a friendly reporter, obviously anxious to do what he could to soften the uncompromising bluntness of my announcement and mitigate the resultant displeasure. 'His Worship the Mayor', he wrote, 'then asked Dr. Joad what he thought of X, to which Dr. Joad replied that, although, judged by the most exacting canons of architectural beauty, X might be held in some respects to fall short, nevertheless, he agreed with the Mayor that when the very extensive improvements which the Mayor had under consideration'—no, 'under active consideration—for the end of the war had been effected, then neither Venice nor Paris nor any of the far-famed cities of the Continent would "have anything on X".'

The Decaying Towns and Suburbs

In spite of the reporter, I do not know that I can conscientiously modify what I said. X ought to be pulled down, of course, and so ought Y and Z and many other towns in the North. And, equally of course, they won't be. Yet short of pulling down, something could be done to improve them which would at the same time help to halt the countryside's pre-war rake's progress. In the years before the war many of these places had become partially derelict. I think of Maryport, of Hebburn, of Jarrow. When new industrial developments occurred, they broke out in the bright and thriving Midlands, with the result that more life was sucked away from Maryport and Hebburn and Jarrow, which decayed still further. Inevitably, the new developments which took place in the Midlands and elsewhere were effected at the expense of rural areas. Industry descended upon a piece of land, ate it up and then moved on elsewhere.

This is the practice of the locusts, and the policy that permits it, a locust-policy. The right course, it is obvious, is to pull down or redevelop the derelict towns of X and Y and Z, instead of leaving them to rot, and to refuse to allow any new areas to be opened up so long as X's, Y's and Z's remain to be redeveloped. Pulling down, by the way, is not always involved. Industrial areas frequently contain large derelict open spaces which could accommodate considerable numbers of houses. The Ministry of Agriculture, for example, has recently prepared plans showing that all the houses which will be required during the next ten years by nineteen Local Authorities in the Birmingham and Black Country areas could be provided by reclaiming and utilizing 5,700 acres of derelict land within those areas. Even so, 1,200 acres would be left over for open spaces. No single acre of agricultural land need, therefore, in those areas be 'developed'.

When the derelict spaces do not suffice, there is nothing for it but to pull down built-up areas and then to rebuild. This course would, no doubt, be more expensive than that of developing new areas, but really it is the only thing to do with most of these places.

In a number of nineteenth-century towns there is an inner ring of decaying suburbs from which the life has long been ebbing. Outstanding examples in this class are some of the suburbs of London. Barnsbury, for instance, and Canonbury and Highbury and Edmonton in the north and Penge and Norwood and Denmark Hill in the south. Who does not know those once select suburbs of large, red, Victorian houses standing well back from the road, discreetly withdrawn behind their curtain of evergreens? They are very ugly, albeit often celebrated in the poems of Mr. John Betjeman; they are commodious and were comfortable. Now in many suburbs they are falling into decay. They subside into small private schools or the branch offices of Government departments; or, worse still, several families move in and they are transformed into tenements; or they stand empty. It would be better to pull them down and replace them by the small houses appropriate to our servantless age or even by blocks of flats, instead of leaving them to decay while the towns bypass them and spread out beyond over the country. But of this more in the next section.

III. Twentieth-Century Industrial and Dormitory England

The Dormitory Suburb

This is the England of the Great West Road, flanked by factories and intersected at right angles by other roads lined with pink houses, and streaming with cars. They are very light and airy, these houses. Their chief purpose, indeed, seems to be to exhibit as much window space as possible, so that their occupants, anxious to see and to be seen, have as little privacy as goldfish. They occupy themselves in this way, I suppose, partly in order to fill the emptiness and to mitigate the loneliness of their lives, for this England, the England of the factory and the spreading dormitory suburb, is a lonely England and lacks almost all those places of meeting in which human beings have traditionally gathered, known their neighbours and felt the stirrings of civic consciousness. There are no assembly halls, no theatres, few churches, no civic centres; in many garden cities there are no pubs or very few. There are only those awful isolating cinemas where the inmates sit hand in hand, absorbing emotion like sponges in the dark and, so far from knowing, do not even see their neighbours. These spreading suburbs have no heart and no head, organs which above all others are essential for the generation of a social consciousness. But their problems and those of the lonely women who there live their stranded lives, do not belong to this book which is about the country and the relation of the country to the towns.

From this point of view, I have three objections to bring against this new industrial and dormitory England: (1) It intervenes between the dwellers in the first and second Englands and the country, since by building itself round the fringes of the towns, it causes the towns to spread and the country to recede; (2) Owing to the fact that it is unplanned, it spreads over a disproportionate amount of land which it eats up at the expense of the country; (3) It is liable to break out anywhere on the surface of the English countryside.

Is there any recommendation that the country lover can make in regard to this twentieth-century England? Only one, and that, I am afraid, is unpopular. It is that instead of living in sprawling dormitory suburbs men and women should in the future consent to bunch and live in flats. I have ventured to put this as bluntly and uncompromisingly as possible, in order that I might evoke at the outset the full blast of the opposition which this proposal always arouses. Let me, having done so, proceed, so far as I can, to mitigate it.

(1) I am writing from the point of view of the country and from this point of view only, and I recognize that until the population gets smaller it will, assisted by the car, spread all over the country *unless it can be induced to bunch.*

Garden Cities, Satellite Towns and the Demand for Neighbourliness

(2) The alternative is satellite towns. But these, even when they take the form of Garden Cities, eat up too much land and, as far as I can see, evoke no enthusiasm among those who live in them. Most English people are town dwellers with the instincts and interests of town dwellers. How incorrigible these instincts are, the persistent return of evacuated adults to 'blitzed' areas when the 'blitz' was at its height—they would insist on coming back, as often as the Local Authorities insisted on sending them away—affords convincing testimony. As town dwellers, they want the close intimacy of town life, the proximity of neighbours whom one knows, the meeting with common friends with common interests in shops and pubs, the chats on doorsteps, the feeling that fellow members of one's species and one's kind are all about one. These, after all, are the conditions in which three out of every four human beings in this country have lived for the past hundred years. Is it any wonder that men and women coming from this background find the country dull and lonely, and at night-time terrifyingly dark? The country, they feel, is all very well to visit occasionally, especially in spring and summer, but it is emphatically not a

place to live in. When it comes to living, people and not fields are what most of us want to find about us; houses and not trees what most of us want to see when we open our front doors in the morning.

'Well, what do you think of it, mate?' I once heard a resident ask a workman newly imported to the Garden City of Letchworth, as they walked together from the station.

'Not much,' was the answer. 'Nothing but trees everywhere. What do they want with trees?'

This, no doubt, is an extreme expression of a townsman's view which I take to be none the less typical.

'Where would you like to live,' a Manchester workman was once asked during a Mass Observation interview. 'In the town or in the country?'

'In the town.'

'In what kind of town?'

'In Manchester, of course.'

'What, in Manchester just as it is?'

He thought for a moment; then, 'I would like to live in Manchester built just like Edinburgh,' he said.

The two considerations I have mentioned seem to me to tell overwhelmingly against the Garden City conception as a model for the housing of most of the inhabitants of England, when it comes to the question of rebuilding after the war.

Unpopularity of Flats

And so I come back to the idea of flats. Now, I know very well that the English working man does not like flats; that he wants a garden; that his wife does not like flats—how, she wants to know, is she going to get the perambulator up the stairs?— that flats outrage all the traditions of the English, who still have roots, albeit long-stretching ones, in the soil; and that it ill becomes one, who has devoted so many pages to making the worst of a life cut off from nature and the soil, now to recommend as a model for housing after the war the most artificial kind of dwelling that mankind has yet devised; also, and finally, that blocks of flats look horrible, being for the most part a cross between a barrack and a prison . . . and so on, with much more in the same vein. I am sensible of the weight of these objections. Nevertheless, I am not convinced. How are they to be answered? 'Most of your criticisms', I should insist—and I am imagining myself as confronting the flat critic—'are due to the fact that you have never seen a decent block of flats in your life. Your ideas are derived from the tenements, which private enterprise, and, I am afraid, all too often Local Authorities, have put up in our big towns to house the workers.'

Unrepentant Advocacy of Flats

But suppose you had seen those workers' flats which the Municipal Council of Vienna put up in the great Socialist days, which seemed in their beauty, their elegance, their convenience and their comfort such an outrage to the workers' betters—who were the workers, they wanted to know, that such places should be built for them, and out of public funds, too?—that Dolfuss and his homegrown Fascists had to knock them to pieces with their guns when they downed the Socialists in 1934. The walls are windows, long stretches of glass, through which the dwelling rooms get the maximum amount of sun. The roofs are gardens with perhaps a café, where you can get a cup of tea or a drink. There are stairs certainly, but there are also lifts, and if you don't want to take your perambulator up in the lift, there is a lobby at the bottom of each flat, in which the tenants can leave their perambulators.

The centre of the courtyard is a lawn in the middle of which a fountain plays. Round it are seats and shelters facing the sun and giving protection from wind and rain, where one can take one's ease with one's neighbours on a fine summer evening. There are sandpits for the children and fenced-off spaces for the babies. Admittedly, the worker has no garden. At least he has no garden at his back door, but—and now we come to the great asset upon one's estimate of the importance of which the whole case for flats stands or falls—by bunching the population up into flats, we have contrived enormously to reduce the area over which they are housed, with the result that, instead of sprawling far and wide over the surrounding country, our cities are cut off sharp and clean from the surrounding country.

THREE ENGLANDS AND WHAT HAPPENS TO THEM

The Garden and the Allotment

The medieval city was confined within a city wall; it is at a similar model that, as I see it, we too should aim. Within the wall is the town, outside the wall is the country; outside the wall, then, is one's garden or allotment, larger than the stretch which surrounds the middle-class villa, much larger than the backyard which is all that has hitherto been vouchsafed to working men, and within easy walking distance, a quarter of a mile or, at most, half a mile from his dwelling. In other words, he has given up a skimpy bit of garden at his back door for a substantial plot of land a short walk from his house. I advocate flats only in those cases where very large numbers of people must be housed in a comparatively small area, but, granted acceptance of the principle of 'the city wall', the principle, that is to say, of the town that stops short instead of sprawling over the countryside, there are, it is obvious, other methods of applying it.[1]

The Terrace

There is, for example, the terrace. Many residential areas in our noblest towns, in Bath, for instance, or in Norwich, are built in the form of terraces. The terrace, like the street, is a row of houses adjoining each other and is, therefore, an appropriate mode of building for a town. The dweller in a terrace enjoys neither more nor less privacy than the dweller in that modern abomination, the semi-detached house; he has neither more nor less garden. But, as opposed to the modern sprawls of semi-detached houses, terraces can be planned as a whole—the terraces in Bath or Hove or Edinburgh are beautiful examples of eighteenth-century and early nineteenth-century planning—and they are not wasteful of space. The terrace, then, conforms to the 'city wall' conception, and, because it is economical of space, brings the countryside and incidentally the allotment close to the doors of the terrace dweller. But I see that, seduced

[1] Since the above was written, I am glad to note that no less a person than the Minister of Health, my friend Mr. Aneurin Bevan, has pronounced in favour of similar proposals for very similar reasons.

THREE ENGLANDS AND WHAT HAPPENS TO THEM

by Bath and Hove, I am wandering from dormitory suburbs, Great West Roads and industrial horrors back again into our more delectable towns. Moreover, I have for too long left the country; it is time to return to it.

Chapter Ten

THE FOURTH ENGLAND AND WHAT HAPPENS TO IT

IV. Country England

'I find a smell in our native earth better than all the perfumes of the East.'—LORD HALIFAX.

This is the England that I care for and on whose behalf this book has been written. Yet I do not know what to say of it. Certainly there is nothing new to say of it, nothing that has not been said dozens of times by richer and abler writers than myself. Some of them, Hudson, for example, knew it better than I can ever hope to do; so did Cobbett and both of them were masters of the art of describing what they saw. There are novelists, Hardy in particular, whose vision was backed by a detailed knowledge to which I can never aspire and there is a bunch of contemporary writers who have taken to the country, Henry Williamson, for example, Adrian Bell, and H. W. Freeman, whose novel, *Joseph and his Brethren*, is the best that has been written about English country life in our time. All these know more about the processes of agriculture, and certainly not less than I of the changing English seasons and the changing English scene. And then there is our nature poetry, the loveliest and most abundant in any literature known to me, stretching from the Elizabethans, with their first, fine lyric rapture, through Pope and Dryden and Thomson of *The Seasons* and Blair and Young, culminating in the new vision that was vouchsafed to the Lakeland poets and so on through the nineteenth century in Clare—how good he is—Francis Thompson, Meredith and Hardy—I exhort the reader to look again at some of Hardy's nature poems, more particularly those in *Later Lyrics and Earlier*—to the group of young poets born of the last war; W. H. Davies is, to my mind, the best, but Blunden and Edward Thomas and Hodgson are all first rate.

Why, then, try to write more about the English country? I can think of no sufficient reason, though I have two excuses to plead. The first is that I have seen such a lot of England and enjoy writing about what I have seen.

Walking through England

It is a commonplace that to see a countryside, as it should be seen, you must go on foot and during the last thirty-odd years I have walked over a large part of England. I suppose I know the south best, and of the south Surrey and Sussex, particularly south-west Surrey and west Sussex. I have walked in Kent but think it overrated. Much of it is flat; hop fields are rarely beautiful and orchards only for a short time in spring. I have lived in the New Forest, and in northern Hampshire I know well the bare upland country stretching from Alresford in the east to Whitchurch and St. Mary Bourne in the north-west. I am weak on Wiltshire and on Dorset except for the coast, but know Devon well both south and north—I was at school at Tiverton—and also south Cornwall, where I spent my schoolboy holidays. I am strong on Monmouth and fairly strong on the Welsh Border counties. I wish I knew more of them. I have referred to them already in this book, and here content myself with again putting it on record that Herefordshire, Shropshire, Radnorshire and Montgomeryshire contain the largest tracts of first-rate unspoilt country that are left to us south of the Peak and the Yorkshire Dales. (The country round Bishops Castle, for instance, is superb in every direction.) Incidentally, I know well the country of Kilvert's Diaries.

Like many Londoners, I know Bucks and, unlike most of them, I know the further reaches, the Chilterns round Christmas Common, the plain of Aylesbury—I used to go frequently to Aston Clinton, but the R.A.F. at Halton have ruined all this country—also Fingest, Turville and Stonor. I know Bix Bottom and Maiden's Grove. I even went on one occasion to those forgotten ends of the old Metropolitan line at Quainton Road and Verney Junction. The names had always intrigued me and I once travelled the whole length of the railway to see what they were like. It was an unrepaying journey. I am weak on the Midlands which I rate low in the scale of England's beauty. I have, however, been much in Worcestershire, particularly in the Bredon Hill country, know my Cotswolds as well as another and have walked on the borders of Lincoln, Rutlandshire and Northants. I know what remains of Charnwood Forest. Part of my knowledge of the Midlands is derived from canals.

On Canals

I have praised walking and riding as ways of seeing the country; let me here put in a word for canoeing along canals. If I were a better man, I should have gone on barges, but I have not the patience to be for so long inactive and slow. I have tried it, been introduced to some very queer company in the process —Mr. Rolt in his admirable book, *Narrow Boat,* will tell you about it—and obtained a glimpse of a way of life, that of the bargees, which has come down to us unchanged from pre-industrial revolution England. Nevertheless, barge travelling is not my 'cup of tea'; you have too much time to think about yourself, to look within and, if you are me, to feel afraid of what you find there.

The great advantage of canals is that they take you through the empty spaces of a forgotten England, away both from the England of the factories and the industrial revolution and the new England of the arterial road and the spreading dormitory suburb. It is an England that has been left behind, an England that has been starved and drained and emptied. I have travelled along a canal in Warwickshire where forgotten manor houses sit brooding on the banks and have rowed for miles up another in Staffordshire which, running through Tettenhall, which is west of Wolverhampton, northwards by Penkridge to Stafford, takes one through some of the most deserted countryside in middle England. Another branch, called the Shropshire Union, runs northwestwards into Shropshire; but this I have never followed. I have canoed in high June down a canal that runs through Oxfordshire and Gloucestershire to join the Thames and the Severn. The country on its banks is lovely.

I am glad of and see hope in canals; I cannot believe either that they will ever again be useful or that, when they have become completely derelict, it will occur to anybody to fill them up. Our untidiness has its advantages; there will always be tow-paths to walk on. And yet—such is the principle of evil in things —even canals, it seems, need some treatment to keep them in good heart. If they are left only to themselves, things will go wrong with them; their towpaths will sink and subside into them, the connections between their towpaths and their bridges may be disrupted, or they themselves may dwindle into ditches of stagnant water carrying broken bottles and dead cats. Therefore, let us prescribe for them the minimum of attention necessary to keep them as they are.

The East and the North

I am weak on the eastern counties, though I know the coast of Suffolk and the Essex–Suffolk border country where I think are the loveliest villages in England outside the Cotswolds— Lavenham and Sudbury and Long Melford and, in Essex, Finchingfield and Bardfield; how lovely they are and by what merciful dispensation of providence has industry left and never returned to them. Norfolk and Lincolnshire I know scarcely at all. I am ashamed of my ignorance of the former and have sworn to repair it before I die, resolving in particular to go to Blakeney and Wells and see the birds. There is lovely country round Sandringham, but this I have only seen from a car. Of my ignorance of Lincolnshire I do not repent at all. This county strikes me as depressing, at times rather frightening; there is so much of it, stretching as it does in all its dreary fer- tility for nearly a hundred miles along its mournful coast. 'Go to Market Rasen' they say, 'where you can rise and see the Wolds. They will make you change your mind.' I went to Market Rasen and saw the Wolds. They would rank as middling second-rate country in Sussex. In compensation Lincoln has the loveliest cathedral in the country. Indeed, I have fan- cied that the works of man most nearly approach the divine where the countryside, fertile and dull, bears upon it most clearly the imprint of the human, so that, looking at fields of cabbages or sugar beet from the midst of which Ely and Lincoln lift their lovely heads, one is tempted to say that here man made the country and God the towns.

The North. Escape by Hellifield

Yorkshire I know well, as well indeed as a man can know what is, in effect, a sub-continent. I have always maintained that it contains more good country than any other English county—not perhaps very difficult, considering the amount of country that it contains of every kind. The east Yorkshire moors going northwards from Malton are bordered on their southern edge by lovely villages, Lastingham, for example, and Hutton-le-Hole. This, I think, is my favourite part of Yorkshire. It is a great country for walking and in three or four days I have covered the whole sweep of these moors, from Appleton-le-Moors in the south to Guisborough and Rosebery Topping in the north. I know the Dale country fairly well. Time and again I have been on a journey to the North, blenched at the prospect of the industrial towns in which I was to speak, and escaped from the train to play truant for a day on the moors. Where does one make one's escape? Why at Hellifield Junction, of course. Most Yorkshire trains find their way sooner or later to Hellifield Junction and by going to the north end of the platform and walking eastwards across the railway tracks, contriving, I hasten to add, to give up your ticket somewhere on the way, you can walk straight away on to fields which in a mile or so become fells. At Bookilber Farm you find yourself at the beginning of the wild country and, if you walk on to Rye Loaf Hill, you will have had almost as fine a day as you will get anywhere in the Dale country. Almost, but not quite. Swaledale, especially the wild upper reach by Keld, Dentdale and Litton Dale are all better. And who knows Mallerstang? Very few, thank the Lord. The Forest of Bowland is first-rate country for walking and the villages, Newton, for example, and Slaidburn in the Hodder Valley are a delight.

Derbyshire I know; but it is not a favourite county. There is pleasant country round Ambergate and Crich, but in Dovedale and the Manifold Valley you are never without the feeling that you will meet somebody round the corner. The Peak District I have already tried to describe; it is wild and savage rather than beautiful.

All the mountainous country of England and Wales I know, except the Cheviots.

Of the Lakes I have already written at length, but throughout this book I have laboured under the consciousness of faults of omission in regard to the mountains of North Wales. I once lived for a time in the foothills behind Penrhyndeudraeth and climbed all the hills from Cnicht to Hebog and from the Mynydd-Drws-y-coed range, which nobody knows but the rock climbers of Cwm Silin, to the Moelwyns. I rate this country second only to the Lakes, second, because the hills are more spread out and the valleys, when you come down to them, less lovely.

But this which I intended merely as an indication of a quarter of a century's fairly extensive walking shows signs of degenerating into a mere catalogue of names. I put an end to it here, excusing myself for my inability to resist the temptation of mentioning so many places by pleading the pleasure that their mention brings.

The Pleasure of the Names

Over much of this country I am too old now to walk extensively again and of recent years I have tended increasingly to gravitate to two or three loved spots. Thus, there is a nostalgia in reminiscence and to write the names is to remember the places for which they stand. This, then, must be my first excuse. For, indeed, I have loved very dearly the English countryside, loved its changing skies, its soft contours, its infinite variety of scenery, loved it in all the seasons, loved it in February, loved it even in late July and August—though in these brooding months, with all the leaves the same colour and the flowers gone, it is at its least lovable—loved it, above all, in October and early May, loved it so much that, again and again, going abroad for a holiday, I have come scuttling home before half of it was done in a frenzy of nostalgia for the sights and sounds and smells of the English countryside.

Now—and here I come to my second excuse for this chapter—this country that I know so well and have loved so much is threatened. If existing tendencies continue, if the various societies that exist for their obstruction or mitigation continue in the future to be as impotent as they have been in the past, and if the Government fails to introduce a comprehensive plan for the layout of the country as a whole, a plan, moreover, whose operation shall be compulsory and not merely permissive, then, so far at least as southern England is concerned, this countryside that I have known will in fifty years' time have largely ceased to exist.

The Country Houses

The country house set in its park belongs already to the past. Before the war it was increasingly the prey of girls' schools and mental homes. When the war came, it was seized by the Forces or by Government departments and was made to harbour Ats, Wrens, Waafs, soldiers, sailors, airmen, clerks, generals and their staffs, while the family either departed or retreated disconsolately to two or three rooms in one of the wings. The family will never come back; they won't have the money and they won't have the servants. In some cases they may stay on as tenants of the National Trust, opening their state rooms to the visiting public on a couple of days a week in return for the privilege of continuing to live rent free in what was once their own house. These, however, are likely to be the exceptions and the fate of most country houses will be to subside into schools, hospitals, homes and permanently evacuated offices.

As schools they do very well—Stowe and Bryanston are good examples—and they are well qualified to serve as the homes of the new public schools which we shall need after the war, if we are to give a public school education to all who are able to profit by it. It seems desirable in any event that the Young People's Colleges envisaged in the Butler Act should be in the country.

But—let us make no mistake about it—the peculiar glory of these places, the peculiar flavour that we sense in them and the peculiar pleasure that we take in them will have departed. For the country house stands for a whole way of living, a way of living that in the second half of the eighteenth and the first quarter of the nineteenth century generated the most civilized men and women that England has produced. And just as their society was a civilization, so the country houses were themselves works of art, the best in the way of indigenous art that England has given to the world since we ceased after Purcell died at the end of the seventeenth century to produce great music. How lovely they are as they stand in their great parks, with their flat Georgian faces or their classic porticos, the reminders of an age when life was gracious and leisured and men were not so busy saving time that they had no time to spare, nor so continuously in movement that they had robbed their lives of most of the purposes and pursuits for which movement is justified.

But the way of living has passed and will not return. These, its monuments, still stand, as alien from the spirit of the present age, as the Abbeys and Monasteries with which the piety of Christendom adorned the face of England in the Middle Ages, commemorators of the vanished age of faith, as the country house commemorates the vanished age of reason.

But the country houses do at least stand, even though their atmosphere, distilled by a couple of centuries of gracious living, has evaporated. What of the parks in which they stand?

Parks

I am no great lover of parks. Like many things in the country, like views, for instance, or some woods, they are better to look at than to be in. Entered, they are apt to be disappointing: 'How lovely,' you say, 'the park looks. Let's go in.' And in you go; but really there is very little more to be enjoyed in the visiting than you have already enjoyed in the viewing. The short grass, of course, is pleasant to walk on as well as to look at, but the great houses are better seen from a distance and deer are singularly boring beasts. There are no flowers and often there is little undergrowth.

I believe that, short of wild country, the most repaying country to walk in and to be in is that which has been mixed with the spirit of man. It is in work that man mixes his spirit most harmoniously with nature. Next to country that has been worked in, is country that has been played in. Cultivated fields, then, and the surroundings of villages are best and after them I would rank copses that have been shot in and streams that have been fished in. But the park is none of these things. There it is, very stately and dignified like an old dowager whom all respect but few can love. Nevertheless, we *do* respect stately old persons, and our present treatment of parks is, therefore, all the more lamentable. Most of them are in occupation by the military. There they are cutting down the timber, gashing the fields and the meadows with their tanks and lorries, dumping their tents and their huts upon the unprotesting surface of the land and, sensitive as ever about being overlooked, surrounding themselves with the inevitable environment of sentries, fences and barbed wire. When the war is over, the parks will be cut up and sold for building sites. We have been sufficiently socialist to destroy by taxation the class which in the past has preserved the amenities of the country, but we are still too wedded to the capitalist principle of *laissez-faire* to interfere with the purposes to which the land is put by those to whom it is sold. Presently, the familiar rows of bungalows will make their appearance and the pink roofs of villas will perk up amid the few permitted trees. Perhaps the best thing that can happen to a park is to be situated sufficiently near to the outskirts of a town to be taken over by a Municipality and maintained for the benefit of citizens, as has happened to Kenwood, for example, to the north of Hampstead Heath or to Roundhay Park on the north-eastern outskirts of Leeds. Where this is done, everything depends on the degree of enlightenment that the Municipality brings to the administration of the area which it takes over. Does it, for example, follow the lamentable habit of the L.C.C. in cutting and lopping great trees and then affixing waste paper baskets to what remains of them; does it, as the L.C.C. does, dot the place with refreshment huts and booths, put up fences, sow the grass with sprouting notice boards, drive roads through what were once fields and paths through what were once copses, paths which it proceeds to cover with asphalt or strew with ashes? Or can it rise above the townsman's conception of a Municipal Park complete with seats, flowerbeds, shelters and bandstand and bring itself to leave the place alone? Municipal bodies show considerable variations of enlightenment in these respects. I would give the Leeds City Council almost full marks; what a lovely place they have been content to allow Roundhay Park to remain. But I would give the L.C.C. considerably less than half marks for their administration of Kenwood.

The Threatened Countryside

Now these tendencies which are at work upon the parks are also in various degrees at large throughout the English countryside as a whole. In most places they are still in their infancy, but unless the forces which have generated them are arrested, I do not see what is to prevent them from relegating the English countryside that I have known and loved to the category of past things. No village will remain unspoilt; none, that is to say, that has not yet been spoilt by us will remain unspoilt. There will be no little pubs in which the townsman can still hear the rustics talk; there will be no farmhouse with its inglenook, home-made teas and rows of hams hanging from the rafters in the kitchen; no shepherd's hut, no secret places in the hills, no hidden sources of the streams. In a word, there will be no place that is different, for our civilization will have ironed out with the dead hand of its suburban uniformity the little differences and individualities that have survived from a more varied past. Many of these things will, no doubt, be maintained as museum pieces, but the life that has sustained them will have passed away. Or they will be imitated. Or they will be transferred bodily to America where English fields in process of being ploughed by Suffolk Punches harnessed to mother-of-pearl ploughs will be exhibited, neon-lighted, by New York hostesses anxious to provide smart guests with a new thrill.

In Appendix VI there is a *résumé* of the relevant provisions of the Town and Country Planning Act which was passed in the autumn of 1944. The most noticeable thing about this Act is its omissions. It does *not* give the power to purchase land, to sterilize land from building, to protect it from industry or to preserve it for agriculture. Or, rather, such powers as it bestows upon Local Authorities in these respects are permissive and not compulsory; they may exercise them, if they so decide, but they are not compelled to exercise them. The Act does *not* embody the recommendations of the reports of the Barlow, Scott and Uthwatt Committees, nor would such an Act be passed unless there was a public opinion to demand it. How, then, is the public opinion to be created?

Advertisements

One of the greatest evils which our civilization has inflicted upon the suffering countryside is the evil of advertisements which are ugly, discordant, glaring and unnecessary. There is scarcely a lovely old village in the country whose sheds, walls and bridges, the gable ends of whose houses and the fronts of whose shops are not plastered with advertisement posters, advertisement boards and advertisement plaques which—of doubtful value to the pocket of the advertiser—are certain ruin to the beauty of the village. For most of the other evils that afflict the countryside, for sprawls of houses, uncouth hydro-electric schemes, factories, quarries and pylons, there is at least some justification on the score of local utility or national necessity, but for the advertisement there is no justification. Two or three pounds' worth of wood, tin and paint are permitted to ruin a village—not, God be praised, irretrievably, since the cost of the removal of the offence would be trifling—for no better reason than that no person in authority has cared enough about beauty to prohibit these outrages. Is there a chance that authority will come to care?

As I write, there has been a debate in the House of Lords on a motion by Lord Mottistone requiring the Government to ensure that all planning schemes for the countryside should contain provisions for preventing disfigurement by ugly signs and advertisements. He demanded that there should be specific legislation directed to this end. Replying for the Government Lord Woolton pointed out that not only do planning schemes usually contain precisely these provisions, but that two Acts passed in 1907 and 1925 designed to regulate advertisements already exist. They do; but the powers which they give are, once again, permissive.[1] They do not *demand* that no hoardings containing advertisements should be put up, or that any should be taken down. Their legislative effect is confined to making the disfigurement or obscuring of a landscape *one* of the deciding factors when a case is put for the removal of a hoarding. Who decides whether there has been disfigurement or not? Answer, the licensing justices. Clearly a matter of opinion is here involved and it is very far from being beyond the bounds of possibility that local justices might not regard as disfigurement an advertisement which to the reader or writer of this book does most clearly disfigure. One feels no surprise on hearing that only in a few cases have these Acts actually been brought into operation against an offensive hoarding. Lord Woolton also appealed to advertisers to restrain themselves in the future from committing the many offences against good sense and good taste of which he and other noble lords complained in the past. The appeal does more credit to his heart than to his head; for few advertisers are remarkable either for taste or sense. Moreover, the situation is such that even if most of them possessed both, the vulgarity and ostentation of the few would suffice to ruin many a good landscape and quiet street. The case of advertisement hoardings illustrates the difficulty of preserving beauty by legislation. If only people cared sufficiently for beauty to send a letter to every firm whose display of posters on roads, by rivers, on hills, or even along railway lines they resented, saying that they would on no account purchase the articles so displayed, the advertisements would quickly disappear. In fact, of course, people get the advertisements they deserve. It is difficult to see how they are to get more seemly advertisements in the country or none, until there is a public opinion which demands more seemly advertisements or none. But how, I repeat the question, is such a public opinion to be created?

'Beautiful England' Photographs

On this topic I shall have something to say in a final chapter.

[1] Appendix VII contains a summary of their provisions, an indication of the respects in which they are defective and recommendations designed to make them effective.

Meanwhile, let me cite as an earnest of the discussion to come an obligation which I would lay upon all producers of 'beautiful England' photographs and writers of 'beautiful England' articles, the obligation, namely, never to publish a photograph showing the loveliness of the English country without also and at the same time publishing opposite to the first photograph a second showing the outrages that have been perpetrated upon it. *The Times* before the war used to publish very soothing pictures of the English countryside which with enormous ingenuity managed to avoid all those areas which have been spoilt or ruined, which picked out the twelfth-century church but not the twentieth-century bungalow, the lane but not the by-pass, the open downland but not the enclosed poultry run, the farmyard and the farm building but not the barbed wire, the concrete post and the tin shack—which dwelt in a word on the survivals of the past and not on the encroachments of the present. The *Manchester Guardian* used to do the same thing and papers like *Country Life* and *The Field* make such pictures part of their stock in trade. All honour to them; it is well that beauty should be recorded by beauty's friends, but not well that no mention should be made of beauty's enemies. For my part, I would make it a penal offence to do the one and not the other and, since I have here returned by a roundabout route to the subject of the beauty of the English countryside, and since I have put myself under a self-denying ordinance not to ramble any more at large about the country, at least in this book, I propose to permit myself the final indulgence of dwelling for a moment on two pieces of country which I happen to know well. Taking them as illustrations of the problem that confronts us, I want to describe them, to say what should be done to them and to say what, in the absence of appropriate legislation, will, in fact, be done to them.

Two Tracts of Country

(1) *The Surrey Hills*. The first is in Surrey, that tormented and maligned county. Because the northern slice has been eaten up, people believe that the whole is defiled—the 'facile suburbanity of Surrey', I read. This belief is a delusion; in the southern half of the county and more particularly in the south-western

corner of it, there is lovely country which is also deserted country. I am writing this in the middle of Witley Park. Looking round, you would say there was no house for a couple of miles; nor is there.

It is not, however, of this tract of country that I wish to write but of that which runs southwards from the Dorking-Guildford Road in the direction of Leith and Holmbury Hills. It consists in part of a series of parallel valleys along the bottom of which run small streams, broadening out from time to time into a string of little lakes. On each side are ridges topped by trees which begin by being oaks and beeches and then, as one goes southward and the soil gets sandier, pines and larches and spruce. These valleys are great places for spring flowers. Year after year I have found primroses in them both in December and in January. The scenery here is small but exquisite; it is like a miniature, reminding one of a Japanese willow plate pattern. And because it is so small it can be very easily spoilt, because it is lovely it offers a severe temptation to those who would rifle and ransack, for it is fatally easy to reach from the road where the motors run, and is in fact continuously invaded not only by motorists straying with picnic baskets from the road, but also by parties of ramblers who sing raucously in the woods and leave litter round the camping places and caravans which they pitch under the lee of the hills. Builders and developers have long cast acquisitive eyes upon these valleys; more recently, engineers and military men have been 'at them' and left their traces behind in the shape of huts and pylons and poles and wires and concrete and posts and rifle ranges. A certain amount of defilement there has already been, yet, for all its fragility, this tract of country is still singularly untouched. Go southward behind the Rookery; you will see a lake, a row of exquisite poplars, a long meadow running up a winding valley between hills and on each side ridges topped by gracious lines of beeches; it is a perfect bit of country and the odd thing is that nobody has as yet 'got at it' at all.

If you go further south, you will find yourself in a barren, sandy tract of pine, heather and bracken. I have walked all over this country north of Leith, Holmbury and Pitch Hills which push their three sandy snouts into the clay of the Weald.

I used to like it more than I do—as I get older my preference grows for cultivated country and here there is no cultivation, nor is there even the scantiest grass for cattle. As is usual in pine country, there is very little undergrowth, there are practically no animals and few birds, but it is good country for walking over in winter and the circumstance of there being no cultivation and no big estates enables the walker to wander at will and revel in a fine feeling of loneliness and desolation. From the hills there is a good view southwards over the Weald. Go further south still down the faces of the hills, and you find yourself in a rolling parklike country, very lush and lovely, with lakes, streams and hazel and chestnut woods in which the primroses and bluebells, very early here, are the loveliest of spring sights. The drawback to this country is that it is parcelled out into a number of large estates and it is difficult to walk over without being beset by angry keepers and gardeners.

Now all this country should be preserved precisely as it is. It is at the very door of twentieth-century London and is very properly invaded at week-ends by ramblers' clubs, unofficial parties of friends, young men and their girls and solitary walkers. You can see them on a Sunday morning in their hundreds on the platforms at Waterloo and Victoria bound for Holmwood and Dorking and Gomshall and Chilworth and Horsley and Clandon. I do not know how they could be better employed. I do know that if this country is allowed to go, Londoners will have sustained an irreparable loss.

That it will be allowed to go is, I fear, all too likely. Up the little valleys to the north of the hills motor roads will be driven; along the roads, houses will be built; on the hills, motoring hotels will spring up; in the middle of the pines and the heather, country clubs and stockbrokers' houses will establish themselves. The ridge running up to and including the top of Leith Hill is National Trust property and inviolable, but I expect the tops of the other hills will presently be crowned with tea stalls and shanties after the model of the Worcestershire Beacon.[1] Cars will be parked along the grass glades in the valleys running between the hills. In the wealden country to the south the big estates will be broken up and parcelled out among commuting

[1] See ch. ii, p. 34.

Londoners. And that will be the end of this part of the wild country of Surrey.

(ii) *The South-West Corner of the Downs*

The other area which I want very briefly to describe is the ridge of the western end of the South Downs and the country that lies southward behind the ridge. Twenty years ago the area chosen might have begun twenty-five miles to the eastward on the Downs behind Steyning, running westward by Chanctonbury Ring above Washington and so over Storrington Down and Rackham Hill and Amberley Mount to the Arun Valley. I think it is Belloc who, writing always of Sussex as if it were the crown of England, writes somewhere of the country round Amberley and Bury, where the Arun runs through the Amberley Wild Brooks, as the jewel in the crown. Sussex, he has suggested, is the type, the Platonic Idea as it were, of England; it is of Sussex that the men of Southern England think, when in exile they think of England and call to mind the countryside that they most love. Now what Sussex is to England and Englishmen, so the country round Amberley is, Belloc suggests,[1] to Sussex and Sussex men. It is the magnet that pulls them all; the spot to which the needles of all their compasses point. I agree. But upon the eastern end of this paradise the hand of the twentieth century has been heavily laid. The blight of Worthing has spread northwards to Cissbury; behind Storrington there is a horrid mess of bungalows called The Sanctuary, and Bury Hill is a training ground for climbing motors. And so I must advance the confines of my area westwards and begin at Bury Hill, thence westwards over Burton and Bignor Downs. Here is wild country in the middle of which Gumber Farm stands four miles from the nearest house; then, turning in a right angle northwards above Lavington past the Bishop's Ring to some of the most deserted country on the Downs above Graffham and Heyshott. To the south are Charlton Forest and Singleton and another ridge of Downs running southward to East Dean. On the other side of Cocking Gap the Downs are not less deserted. I have ridden for most of the day from Cocking over Linch and

[1] In *The Four Men*.

Elstead Downs and so by Beacon Hill to Harting Down and then westward again on to Buriton, and not once met a human being. But the glory of the Downs does not lie along the ridge. Most people having walked along the northern escarpment, whence you get a great view of the Weald, think they have seen the Downs. Many, indeed, plan walking tours on these lines, proposing for example, to traverse in a week the whole length of the ridge from Beachy Head above Eastbourne in the east to Butser just over the border into Hampshire in the west. They have, we may suppose, been reading that pleasant little poem of Kipling's, 'The Run of the Downs':

> *The Weald is good, the Downs are best—*
> *I'll give you the run of 'em, East to West.*
> *Beachy Head and Winddoor Hill,*
> *They were once and they are still.*
> *Firle, Mount Caburn and Mount Harry*
> *Go back as far as sums'll carry.*
> *Ditchling Beacon and Chanctonbury Ring,*
> *They have looked on many a thing,*
> *And what those two have missed between 'em*
> *I reckon Truleigh Hill has seen 'em.*
> *Highden, Bignor and Duncton Down*
> *Knew Old England before the Crown.*
> *Linch Down, Treyford and Sunwood*
> *Knew Old England before the Flood;*
> *And when you end on the Hampshire side—*
> *Butser's old as Time and Tide.*
> > *The Downs are sheep, the Weald is corn,*
> > *You be glad you are Sussex born!*

For my part, I find such ridge walking dull and monotonous. Views, as I have already remarked, once seen and wondered at are not really looked at again; there are few flowers and birds on this northern edge, and the immediate foreground lacks variety. Presently one begins to feel that one is walking for exercise. The great glory of the Downs lies in the spurs which they thrust out southwards—in these and in the valleys and folds between them. Here there is a greater variety of tree and copse, a bigger range of bird life; there are farms and little streams in the valleys and you are less likely to meet people than on the ridge itself.

East Marden and Compton and Eartham and Chalton, to take a few names at random, are places which nobody visits, while the little inn at Hook's Way derives its *clientèle* from no known source, since there are scarcely half a dozen houses within a two-mile radius. Chilgrove with its Green is beautiful and so is the southward going spur of down which ends in Bow Hill with its view over Chichester Harbour and Kingley Vale, mysterious with its groves of yew. All this, to my mind, is among the most beautiful wild country in the south of England. Beautiful in its views, in its great trees and the lovely ranges of its hills. I ask nothing better for it than that it should be left alone. It is difficult, however, to feel optimistic in this regard. It has two enemies, the cars and the builders.

Cars on the Downs

It was in the summer before the war that as I went up Amberley Mount I came upon a small Austin car perched on its very top. I rushed indignantly up to remind the owner of that neglected law[1] that forbids the motorist to park his car more than fifteen yards from the highway. Within sat a young man and his girl. Were they enjoying the air? They were not; the windows of the car were shut. Were they looking at the view? They were not; their backs were turned to it. Were they making love? Nothing of the sort. What, then, were they doing? The car carried a portable wireless set; this was turned on and, as I opened the door to put my head in to remonstrate, I heard a voice. The young man and his girl were sitting on the top of Amberley Mount listening to the Fat Stock Prices over the wireless. . . .

Cars, after the war, will be more numerous and more powerful; no stretch of the ridge of the Downs will be inaccessible to them and, since few drivers when they reach the top will know any better what to do with themselves than the owner of

[1] The Road Traffic Act 1930 which makes it an offence to drive a motor vehicle elsewhere than on the road, but permits parking within fifteen yards of a road provided that the parking is not on a footpath or bridle way.

the Austin, it is not too much to expect that much of the loveliest and most isolated country in the south of England will be ruined within the next two decades by riders in cars who have parked their metal boxes on the ridges of the Downs for the express purpose of listening to Fat Stock Prices announced by radio.

The other enemy is the builder. I have said all that I have to say on this subject in previous chapters. I have described the view from the Malvern Hills in Chapter II and expatiated on the outbreak behind Rottingdean in Chapter VIII. It is precisely this fate that I fear sooner or later for the whole length of the Downs. Indeed, I do not know what in the years to come can prevent it. We can plan on paper and say that there should be no building in such and such areas; we can give Local Authorities power to prevent it either by the purchase of the land or by taking out restrictive covenants upon it; we can buy· up pieces of land which are threatened and comparatively self-contained and hand them over to the National Trust,[1] but until we get a comprehensive plan for the country as a whole, which prescribes in regard to the South Downs what I have urged above it should prescribe in regard to the Leith Hill area, namely, that there shall be no change of any kind and in particular no building of any kind, and which threatens whoever may disregard this prohibition with the penalties with which we seek to deter the breakers of any other law, the South Downs will continue to be in danger and in a hundred years' time will, I suspect, be past saving. Is there, one wonders, any prospect of such a plan? The answer to the question depends upon the development of public opinion and the public's scale of values. To this I now turn.

---

[1] After fifty years' effort, and as a result of gifts, bequests and appeals amounting to millions of pounds, the National Trust now owns about 110,000 acres. This is about one-third of 1 per cent of the total land surface of England and Wales. Under recent legislation even this may be requisitioned for Government purposes (e.g. forestry).

Chapter Eleven

THE PROBLEM

An Evicted Landowner

I drove recently in a car from King's Lynn, loveliest of the Norfolk towns, to Hunstanton. I wanted to see something of the Norfolk countryside, but there was snow inland and mist on the coast so my vow to see Norfolk before I die has still to be fulfilled. My driver had once owned a small place on the borders of Sandringham. As we approached the royal estate he explained how he came to give it up.

When, as he put it, 'George V went democratic', he decided to open parts of the Royal Park on certain days of the week. As a result there could on these days be seen a large and ever growing stream of cars approaching, parking at and departing from Sandringham. Presently, there were char-à-bancs coming, I was assured, from as far afield as Newcastle. To welcome and accommodate their inmates tents, stalls, booths and huts sprang up near the main entrances. Ginger beer, cakes and oranges were sold, and the paraphernalia of tea making installed; there were picture postcards and cigarettes and, inevitably, there was litter and there was noise. 'In the end,' said my driver, 'the whole place was swarming with townees. There was no peace and I had to leave.'

'It will be worse after the war,' said I.

'It will indeed,' he agreed. 'If I were a younger man I would leave the country.'

'What would you do if you had your way,' I asked, 'to stop this sort of thing and keep the country as it was?'

'I'd sterilize them,' he said.

'Sterilize who?'

'Why a lot of these people from the towns. Stop them breeding. There are altogether too many of them.'

I have reported this conversation partly because it expresses in an extreme form what many people feel, partly because it

ΠΑΝ

throws into high relief the problem which causes them to feel as they do. It is because I understand why they feel as they do and share their feelings, that I have become acutely conscious of the difficulty and the urgency of the problem.

The Problem Stated

I agree, in the first place, with my driver that until the population of England is smaller, very much smaller, the countryside is and will remain in danger. I don't, however, subscribe to his recipe for diminishing either the population or the danger. I share, too, his hatred of most of our towns and of the behaviour of many, perhaps most townspeople when they are in the country. The effects of their impact upon the country and upon the way of life traditionally lived in it are, I agree, appalling. Unless these effects are prevented they will, I think, destroy the country. Yet I am not content to say with him, 'Bloody townees, they ought to be sterilized!'

On the contrary, I think the 'townees' have every right to go into the country and to enjoy it. I want to see more of them going and I want to see them going more often. Like many other Englishmen of my type I have Tory tastes and Radical opinions and my tastes are often at war with my opinions. On this question of the future use of the country the two fight a continuous pitched battle. The fact that this conflict goes on makes me, I like to believe, not only more acutely aware than most of the problem with which the post-war generation will be faced but also more sympathetic than most of those who *are* aware with the aspirations which give rise to it. I am neither so obstinately pig-headed in regard to 'townees' as my driver, nor so narrowly ignorant of my driver and his ways as are most 'townees'. Let me, then, try to state the problem, as I see it, in a series of propositions:

(1) I love the English countryside and wish it to be preserved.

(2) I want others to love it, too; one always, I think, wants to communicate one's enthusiasms and share one's tastes. Apart from this, I think that it is beautiful and the love of beauty is, I hold, a good.

(3) It seems to me to be an elementary requirement of social justice that others should be given the opportunity to enjoy this good.

(4) I see, moreover, that whether they are given it or not, they will in the future take it and take it increasingly.

(5) I know that in so taking it they will destroy the thing that I love and that I want them to love.

I want in this last chapter to consider how this result may be prevented. I do not want the historian of the future to record of us the melancholy verdict that it is only those peoples who do not love the countryside who are likely to retain a countryside worth loving.

Broadly speaking there are three ways of dealing with the problem: (a) So far as building is concerned, to restrict the towns within certain specified areas. (b) So far as the public is concerned, so to educate them and familiarize them with the country that they learn to care for it and to treat it as it should be treated. (c) Until this result is achieved, to minimize the extent of the damage and the area of devastation by canalizing the invasion from the towns along certain channels.

The Bearing of the Population Question

Of the propositions enumerated above, (4) seems to me to be the most immediately relevant. On general grounds I hold that there are far more people in this country than can be conveniently and comfortably accommodated. I think we should be happier, if we were fewer. Consider for a moment the figures. In the time of Queen Anne we were 5½ millions; we were just under 9 millions in 1800; by the beginning of the twentieth century we had risen to 32½ millions and we are now over 46 millions—this is the figure for England, Wales and Scotland. Somebody has estimated that if the birth-rate had remained at the Victorian level of 32 per thousand, we should in the year 2000 A.D. be numbering 200 millions.

As everybody knows, the birth-rate has declined and is declining, declining to such effect, that, if the present birth- and death-rates remain constant, from 1950 onwards we shall begin to be fewer and, as time goes on, our numbers will diminish with increasing momentum. Sensational figures have been quoted as, for example, that in rather less than two hundred years' time the population of Great Britain will have sunk to 6 millions, the figure, incidentally, at which it has stood through most of our history. For, though everybody regards the decline as a disaster, it merely constitutes a return to the normal. It was the Victorian age that constituted the abnormality, an abnormality whose full effects we have still to suffer.

The Industrial Towns and the People

For, it is here relevant to ask, what was happening to our swelling numbers during the century when the population was running up from eight or nine to between thirty and forty millions? In answer to this question, I would refer the reader to any book describing conditions of housing and employment in the industrial towns of the nineteenth century; to the quotations from G. M. Trevelyan's *English Social History* given in Chapter I as an indication of what those conditions were, and to the town which evoked my immediate reaction—which I contend would be the reaction of any objectively minded civilized man—'it ought to be pulled down, of course',[1] to illustrate what they still are. For my part, I hate these industrial towns and the way of life for which they stand, but I have already sufficiently indicated the grounds for my feeling and must resist the temptation to agitate myself and bore the reader with their repetition. For more than a hundred years we tied our swelling population to the industries which these places nourished and penned them in the places where the industries were carried on. We let them off and let them out on only five days a year, the five Bank Holidays, and we paid them so ill that, even if they had had the time they would not have had the money to enable them to seek out and to make acquaintance with the country. For these abounding millions the price that was paid in terms of human life and human values for man's increasing mastery over nature was, in Trevelyan's words—I make no apology for again quoting Trevelyan—'a divorce from nature that was absolute, and so too was the divorce from all dignity and beauty and

[1] See ch. IX, pp. 184, 185.

significance in the wilderness of mean streets in which they were bred whether in the well-to-do suburb or the slum'.

Meanwhile, those who were making money out of the expenditure of other men's labour in the places in which man's control over nature was greatest were using it to escape from the ugliness, the racket, the stench, the foul air and the overcrowding which control over nature cost to places in which nature still retained more or less complete control over man. Such, for a century and a half were the conditions in which the swelling population, whose dimensions afforded pride to statesmen, endured its existence.

But the penning of this overgrown population in the industrial towns had one beneficial effect. It enabled a country which should comfortably contain eight or nine million people to nourish a population of from forty to fifty million, without too much overflow into and destruction of its countryside. In fact, it was not until after the last war with the coming of the second industrial revolution to which reference has been made above,[1] that the effects of maintaining a population of forty-five million in an area appropriate to seven or eight began to be felt. The *full* effects have still to be felt.

Post-War Invasion

Let us assume that after the war there is a fairly high level of prosperity. Men and women, we will suppose, are assured of comfort and a competence on six or seven hours' machine minding a day; they have high wages and staggered holidays, and a mass-produced car, selling at about £200, has made its universal appearance.

Is it not clear that the scale of the invasion of the country by the towns will be beyond anything that most of us have experienced and beyond what most of us have imagined?

There are two methods by which the country can meet the invasion which threatens it. The first is to dig in its heels like a mule, lower its head like a bulldog and growl, 'These bloody townees, they ought to be sterilized'—in other words, to be as obstructive as possible. The second is to foresee and make pro-

[1] See ch. I, pp. 15, 16.

vision for the invasion, to educate the invaders and to canalize their inflow until they are educated. From this point of view the next fifty years are crucial. In fifty years' time either the tides of modernity and ugliness will have engulfed us completely or begun to recede. England, in other words, will have either been irretrievably ruined or the effects of a declining population coupled with those of increasing education will have begun to make themselves felt. It follows that there is laid upon the men of my generation a peculiar responsibility; not only have we the effective power in the community but we have also the knowledge of England as it was. We are, indeed, the last generation who knew England as it was before the flood gates were opened and the waters of change poured through. We have known, then, what the values are that we must seek to preserve. Most of those who have grown up in the last twenty-five years have not this knowledge or they have it in less degree. They have not been able, as we have, to take for granted the background of an England where the *tempo* of living was slow, where there was a strong consciousness of locality, where there was peace and where there was solitude.

That Good Taste is not Natural but Acquired

The gradual disappearance of this background over the last fifty years cannot be without effect upon the consciousness of this and the last generation. Good taste of whatever kind is not instinctive but acquired. This is true of the perception of beauty in art. 'Taste', said Sir Joshua Reynolds, 'does not come by chance or nature; it is a long and laborious process to acquire it. It is the lowest style only of arts, whether of painting, poetry or music that may be said, in the vulgar sense, to be naturally pleasing.' It is true also of the perception of beauty in nature. We do not naturally love the highest when we see it. What we *naturally* do is to litter it with rubbish, build hotels on its peaks and transmit picture postcards of it to our friends. Now it is only from intercourse with nature that the knowledge and the love of nature are born. There is nothing remarkable about this principle, nor is its application to nature peculiar. If we are not fully developed men and women, we cannot enjoy the pleasures proper to mankind. Thus if we have not refined and developed our senses of seeing and hearing by intercourse with beautiful sights and sounds, we cannot appreciate great pictures and respond to great music; if our minds have not been trained, we cannot be moved by intellectual curiosity or feel the thrill of discovery in the realms of science and philosophy, or enjoy the pleasures of intellectual intercourse; if our spirits have not been cultivated by prayer, enriched by meditation and sharpened by the constant endeavour to increase in virtue and the love of God, we cannot, so the religions tell us, fully enjoy the benefits of God's goodness and love. And if anybody chooses to think that these are high-falutin' examples, I refer him to that teaching of his own experience, which assures him that it is only in so far as he knows something about a thing that he can feel an interest in it—only in so far as he knows about machines that he enjoys being shown machines; only in so far as he has some acquaintance with farms or horses that he enjoys being shown his friend's crops and stables; only in so far as he knows something about food and wine that he will be able to appreciate those mysteriously concocted dishes served to him in the little restaurants of Montparnasse. Not only is the love of what is beautiful acquired by contact with its object; it is maintained by it. If you don't hear good music for a month, the finer points escape you at your first famished hearing. The lover long deprived of his beloved finds that the first raptures of sexual renewal are brutish, the satisfaction of a need less human than animal, rather than the refinement of sense, the refreshment of spirit and the fusion of personalities. The starving man forgets that he is also a gourmet. So when we are ill or worried or in fear of the Gestapo or marooned on desert islands, it is our tastes for Bach fugues, Beethoven quartets and Château Yquem that are among the first to fall away from us.

For these reasons, I do not think that it is predominantly to the young of the present or to the not so young of the immediately past generation that we must look to maintain the guardianship of England's beauty, partly because they have not known it at its best, partly because they have lived hurried and harassed lives. Apart from a small and diminishing class of landowners and farmers, there are the townsmen, the ramblers, campers, climbers and naturalists. These care for it and visit it again and again on Saturdays or at week-ends to walk and camp and climb and watch, but they form a comparatively poor and unimportant section of the community. Compared with the industrialists and the planners they have no political power and in Parliament, where the policies of the nation are determined, their influence counts for little.

That the Argument for Beauty is the Argument that Cannot be Used

The influence of what is called the 'amenity interest' is, indeed, very small. Politicians, of course, give lip service to beauty as they do to virtue. They speak eloquently of the beauties of the English countryside and express their desire that they should be preserved. They are also jealous for English traditions, are sentimental about English farmhouses and pubs and speak affectionately of quiet, remote and unspoiled places that nobody knows. There have never been so many books on 'Beautiful Britain' or so large a sale for them. Yet none of these sentiments weighs in the scale against the modern values of efficiency, which in this connection means rapidity of transport, and development, which means somebody's claim to make profits. I have already referred to the fact that when one is negotiating with a public body or a Government department, pleading with them *not* to put a cement works in the Edale Valley or to plant firs and pines on Lakeland hills or to drive a road over a pass or to make a suburban sprawl round a town, the argument for beauty and solitude is the one argument you can never afford to use. If you bring it up, you will be told that the place is, indeed, beautiful but that if it is opened up, more people will be able to enjoy the beauty. If you speak of solitude it is pointed out to you that *ex hypothesi* very few people enjoy the threatened spot—if they were not few, it would not be solitary—and, therefore, that the loss of amenity involved by the quarry, the factory or the big hotel, will not be widely felt. Thus, when Midhurst Common was threatened by the brickworks of the Midhurst Brick and Lime Company the managing director contended among other things that the amenities of Midhurst Common could not be regarded as important, since so few people enjoyed them. He had, he assured us, 'no lack of appreciation of the value of the amenities', but, he added, 'my experience is that the Common is not a popularly patronized pleasure resort. I spent the major part of the day there on Good Friday last with the express purpose of testing my previous impression on this point, and I did not encounter more than half a dozen people.' It did not occur to the managing director that those who wished to preserve Midhurst Common did so precisely because it was a place in which it was still possible not to 'encounter more than half a dozen people'. It was in fact precisely the fewness of the people that constituted the attraction of the place to the few. If everybody enjoyed the pleasures of Midhurst Common, nobody would enjoy them because there would be no beauty left to enjoy. You cannot appreciate solitude if a multitude is busy appreciating solitude at the same time.

Considerations of this kind are lost upon developers and industrialists. Hence, we have to speak to them in their own language, adducing or inventing good commercial reasons for our plea; saying, for example, that the Lakeland firs and pines are bad for the Herdwick sheep, or that the cement works will be inaccessible and the transport of their products excessively expensive, or that the hydro-electric schemes for harnessing the waters of Scottish lochs will not employ as many people as their promoters anticipate and that they will not be local people, or that if more land is taken for the erection of factories on the outskirts of London or Birmingham, more people will live too far from their daily work, or that even bigger and better targets will be offered for long-range bombardment by the V2's of the future.

Poor arguments, indeed, but what others can we use? It is idle to speak of the beauty of colour to a blind man, to bid a deaf one to appreciate Mozart, or to expect the cat not to upset the pieces on your chessboard.

These are some of the reasons which induce a feeling of pessimism in regard to the preservation of the values lauded in this book.

Discourse on the Value of Beauty

That they are, indeed, valuable few of us, I suppose, would on reflection deny. There is in general to-day a wide disagreement as to what things are good and the kind of life which it is right that men and women should try to lead. Yet where so much is doubtful of this, at least, most of us feel reasonably assured, that the experiences which intercourse with nature and solitude bring are, indeed, valuable, that a life which embodies them will be fuller and richer than a life which does not; and that, if the community of the future denies them to its citizens, it will have been content to demand for them less than the best.

Professor Trevelyan has put this better than I can hope to do. 'The race bred under such conditions' (the conditions of the industrial town divorced from nature) 'might', he writes, 'retain many sturdy qualities of character, might, even, with better food and clothing, improve in physique, might develop sharp wits and a brave, cheery, humorous attitude to life, but its imaginative powers must necessarily decline, and the stage is set for the gradual standardization of human personality.'

Some Conclusions

I propose in summary of these rather rambling observations to draw four conclusions.

First, there is little hope for the preservation of England's beauty until more townspeople are so trained and educated that they learn to recognize and to care for it.

Secondly, intercourse with beauty itself constitutes in the last resort the only effective method of training and education. If for the reasons I have given, beauty continues to diminish, we may expect the capacity to appreciate and to care for it to diminish too. This is to start a vicious circle as a result of which, unless present tendencies are checked, a generation will arise which, having never known unspoiled natural beauty, will not be aware of what it is that it lacks. What is more, it may even come to suspect, perhaps to persecute or to incarcerate as mad, such few survivors from an earlier time as remember the beauty that there once was and lament its loss. The reader will, perhaps, recall H. G. Wells's story, *The Country of the Blind*, in which the blind people, resenting as an eccentric monstrosity the sighted stranger who finds his way into their territory, propose to put out his eyes.

Thirdly, a new factor is introduced by the prospective decline of population. This means that within fifty years the country will either have been destroyed past reclaiming or that the worst of the danger will have passed. As our numbers continue to diminish, the threat will grow less, until ultimately we shall be too few to constitute a serious menace.

Fourthly, for this reason the next fifty years are of crucial importance. It follows that upon those of us who are acquainted with and sensitive to the values I have tried to describe, a special obligation is laid. We are the high priests of the temple of a half-forgotten cult, the tenders of a sacred but dying flame. Upon us is placed the obligation to keep it alight, until such time as we can hand on our charge to our successors. It falls, in short, to us to hold the pass until democracy can safely be let through. But here, at the imagined spectacle of myself as priest and acolyte, I am mercifully assailed by an irreverent ribaldry. The sentiments, no doubt, are noble, but they should, I tell myself, be mentioned only with the greatest circumspection, as, abashed by my own magniloquence, I hear the still, small voice that whispers, 'Fiddlesticks'.

Some Suggestions

I hasten to quiet it by a number of concrete suggestions, interim suggestions designed to tide us over the next fifty years, until the battle has either been irretrievably lost or the effects of a better educated and smaller population have begun to tell.

(1) *Legislation*

The first suggestion is one that I have already made by implication in this book. It is that such legislation as is passed affecting the countryside should be made compulsory and not permissive. It should not give powers which departments and authorities may use, if they please; it should confer powers which they must use. Nor are the powers in doubt. If all the recommendations of the Scott and Barlow Reports—the most immediately relevant are cited in Appendix VI—were passed into law, then, provided we are also given an Access Act on the lines indicated on pages 127, 128, provided also that all areas rendered valuable by reason of their natural beauty or wildness are transferred to national administration, there would be little more to ask. I have seen it sometimes argued that compulsory legislation is undemocratic since instead of indicating some step which Local Authorities may take *if* they so desire, it prescribes a step which they *must* take whether they desire it or not. I agree that this is indeed its effect but until objection is raised on the same ground to legislation prescribing compulsory education, compulsory sanitation and the compulsory punishment of crime, I shall conclude that the assumption of certain legislative functions by the State is a necessary condition of the national well-being. I add that in certain familiar spheres everybody knows and agrees that this is so.

(2) *Service upon Local Authorities*

Meanwhile, those people—and they are many—who share the views of the author—not all of them, of course, but those relevant to the preservation of England's beauty from desecration or destruction—should make it their business to serve on Local Authorities. As long as we are content to leave Local Authorities to be staffed and administered by tradesmen or persons otherwise 'interested' in 'development', we must expect 'development' to occur. Public beauty will continue to be exploited for private profit, until the goose that once laid the beautiful eggs will at last have been well and truly killed, the whole face of England will look more or less alike and there will be no more money to be made by anybody out of the surviving vestiges of its former beauty.

The views I have expressed in this book fall roughly into two categories. I want beauty preserved but I also want the townsman to enjoy it. Now most of those who share my views on the first point abhor those which I have expressed on the second. Like my friend, the Sandringham ex-estate owner, they want 'townees' sterilized, though they don't say so. Failing sterilization, they want them kept out. But there is another class of country lovers and preservers, a class to the furtherance of whose interests this book is mainly addressed, who do not share this attitude to 'townees'. For they are mainly 'townees' themselves who have been going to the country at week-ends and for holidays all their lives. Many of them have grown into country-goers under the auspices of such bodies as the Ramblers' Association, the Youth Hostels' Association, the Camping Club of Great Britain and Ireland, the Holiday Fellowship, the Co-operative Holidays Association or the Cyclists' Touring Club; or they belong to no organized body at all but go to the country with a few friends; or they go alone. Sometimes though not often—for usually they have not much money to spare—people of this kind have week-end cottages in the country; sometimes—though this is very rare—they actually live in the country.

Now this class of countrygoer is apt to be indifferent or apathetic where the protection of his country-going interests is concerned. It is not hard to understand why. He goes into the country to escape from public into private life; to throw off, not to put on responsibilities; to find his real self in intercourse with nature, or to develop it in the company of his friends. Not only does he not want to be bothered with committees, memoranda, reports, minutes, meetings, appeals; he does not want the country he is learning to care for to be associated with and so to remind him of these things. When he goes to the country, he wants to be apart from them and he wants to keep the country-going side of him apart from them. It is precisely in this 'apartness' that, for him, the value of the country lies. It is an ill thing to ask such a man to serve on committees that he may devote himself to the protection of the very thing which he wishes to keep unsoiled by committees. Yet the request must be made.

While urban authorities are in the hands of tradesmen whose conception of the country is modelled upon that of the Municipal Park complete with bandstands, iron railings, asphalt paths and baskets for litter; rural areas are run by landowners and farmers, one of whose main concerns is to keep the townsman at arm's length. It is upon these latter that public-spirited lovers of the country who nevertheless do not wish to monopolize the country should serve.

Perhaps when they are too old to do much walking, they may consent to give part of their old walking time to public work designed to ensure that those walkers' joys in which they have delighted in the past may be preserved for others in the future.

(3) *The Education of the People*

Thirdly—and here I come to the public itself—I do not see how to avoid using the word 'education'. One shrinks from it, of course; it is a colourless word, much associated with platitude, and until it receives content denotes very little. And in this connection the content is particularly hard to give. It is easy to speak of instruction in such things as botany and natural history in schools, to advocate the giving of little moral talks on the avoidance of litter, to warn the young against the uprooting of wild flowers. But to a town child botany and nature study and the non-uprooting of wild flowers mean little or nothing in the abstract. Even when they are eked out by occasional conducted walks with teacher, there are usually too many on the walk and the walks themselves occur at too infrequent intervals, or the children themselves are too uninstructed to derive much benefit from these rather formal occasions. And what, one wonders, in the mind of a child does 'a walk with teacher' stand for? As for the talks on litter, does the injunction not to drop orange peel and newspaper really mean anything to a town child? You might as well tell it not to throw stones. If all children could be brought up wholly in schools in the country, one's pessimism in this regard would be less.

Country children may be brutal and loutish but they don't make the same mistakes in their treatment of nature as the occasional visitor from the towns. Given continuous daily contact with nature in early childhood, there is always the chance that one out of every ten town-born children may find himself or herself sufficiently content to wish to stay on in the country as labourer or land girl, that one out of every twenty may be so caught by the spirit and beauty of nature as to remain in and with it as naturalist, artist, mystic or as mere walker. My own theory is that in most of us the aesthetic sense does not begin to flower until puberty is reached. It is at sixteen or seventeen that the soul opens and the girl or boy reads poetry, listens to music, awakens to beauty and feels the stir of romance. It is pre-eminently at this age that we should try to catch them and to help them to appreciate natural beauty and all that it stands for. Hence, I welcome a memorandum containing proposals for a code of countryside manners which the Ramblers' Association have recently drawn up and submitted to the Ministry of Town and Country Planning.

(4) *Interim Canalization and Butlinization*

Fourthly, there is a suggestion for interim canalization. By 'canalization', I mean so directing and confining the crowds of people who will swarm over the countryside when the war is over, that the areas affected may be circumscribed. That large parts of the country must be sacrificed after the war, I take for granted; the problem is to ensure that the devastated areas shall be so limited by canalization that the problem may be mitigated though, of course, not solved. Here Mr. Butlin has shown us the way.

I consider that the opposition which Mr. Butlin's camps have provoked among country goers and country lovers who share the views expressed in this book is short-sighted. Apart altogether from the question of beauty, there is also the question of happiness and in this connection I hold that Mr. Butlin is a public benefactor who has been responsible for a very considerable increase in public happiness.

The issues here raised have been thrown into high relief by Mr. Butlin's action in taking a stretch of the Welsh coast near Pwllheli with the express intention of putting there a large holiday camp. The camp had been erected but not opened when the war broke out. It was taken over by a Service Department which subsequently announced its intention of returning the property to Mr. Butlin when the war was over, so that it might revert to its originally intended purpose as a holiday camp with all the well-known Butlin specialities, including fun for all and all for fun. This proposal raised in an acute form the issues which I have here briefly discussed. A number of eminent persons, including Mr. Tom Jones and other jealous guardians of their native land, took the lead in sounding the alarm. Rumbling with apprehension, as if they were the Welsh national bowels, they painted terrifying pictures of hordes of Butlineers invading the solitudes of Snowdon. Mr. Butlin replied. The rumblings are premonitory of a coming storm, for there really is an issue here of first-rate importance which will break out on us, unprepared as usual, with considerable violence after the war. It is the issue which has been raised by implication throughout most of the foregoing book.

England and Wales are a small country with forty-two and a half million inhabitants. After the war most of them will, for the first time in their lives, enjoy holidays with pay; moreover, they will be staggered holidays, covering most of the summer months.

Before the war holiday camps achieved enormous success and were developing rapidly. After the war, with new armies of paid holidaymakers to cater for, their development will be even more rapid. Many of such unspoiled stretches of the English and Welsh coastline as remain will be absorbed by them and, it may be, some wild mountain country as well.

Those of us who love the solitude of wild country have duly shuddered but we, after all, are few and holidaymakers are many. It is, then, reasonably certain that, whether we like it or not, Mr. Butlin will have his way.

And what, after all, have we to urge against Butlinization? A holiday camp supplies a certain sort of delight which is best enjoyed in company. I say 'delight' but, in fact, it is a whole way of life that is offered, complete with riding and swimming, with tennis and dancing and shopping, with 'mateyness' and heartiness during the week and religious services and more 'mateyness' on Sunday.

'No doubt, and very nice too in its way,' say the objectors. 'But establish a camp community on the outskirts of Colwyn Bay or Southend and these pleasures can be enjoyed equally well, and nobody will be a penny the worse; establish it on a wild stretch of coast and, though the pleasures of the Butlineers will be no greater, a whole world of loveliness will have been destroyed, carrying with it in its destruction the possibility of experiences to whose value no assessment in terms of pleasure can do justice.'

It is wrong, they urge, to exploit the snobbish prestige that still attaches to natural beauty in order to bring to country that is wild and solitary those who wish to enjoy not wildness and solitude but something else, namely, the pleasures of a Butlin camp; for, inevitably, beauty shrinks at the touch of heartiness, nor is it possible that Snowdon should tolerate a Ye Olde Pig and Whistle Inne at its base—still less at its summit—and remain the mountain that we love.

Answer to Anti-Butlineers

These arguments sound convincing, but I believe them to be short-sighted. Let us, first, view the situation not from the point of view raised in this book that, namely, of the preservation and enjoyment of the country, but from the point of view of the happiness of townspeople. From this point of view, Mr. Butlin appears as an angel of light.

The old-fashioned working or lower middle class holiday was a dreadful thing. A little family bloc was dumped down in a couple of back rooms in a back street; the sea was half a mile away and out of view; there was no company but their wearisome own and with that they were bored to tears; the wife nagged, the children whined, while the husband lounged and craved for the girls on the prom. Or the whole family sat listlessly on the beach. An ill-tempered landlady provided bad food, badly cooked, and when it was raining there was nothing to do but sit in the bedroom. If the family went to a cheap boarding house they were turned out to fend for themselves, rain or no rain.

It is against this background that the Butlin camp with its varied assortment of pleasures must be viewed. Nor are the pleasures purely passive. The camp aims at the development and expression of personality. There are games and competitions, there are amateur theatricals, there are discussions and debates, there is the self-government of communities by their members.

Men and women whose lives are spent in monotonous routine jobs experience for the first time on these holidays the joy of the awakened mind, the exercised talent and the pouring out of energy in vivifying initiative and strenuous endeavour. They do not passively receive; they actively contribute and, so contributing, find the outlet for personality which their working lives deny. Also they develop their social senses.

All this, I think, is to the good. The goods which accrue lie outside the scope of this book. I mention them because, even if no other goods were involved, these would, in my view, be sufficient to justify Butlin camps.

Now consider the Butlin camp from the point of view of the preservation of country and coast. From this point of view, it constitutes a pre-eminent example of what I have called canalization. For a holiday camp concentrates 4,000 persons in a single bloc who would otherwise straggle in long lines of frowzy bungalows and ambiguous con-urbanizations along many miles of coast. Look at Shoreham or Peacehaven. From this point of view—I hope the inelegance of the metaphor will not set readers against me—the camps perform the same office as a drainage system. Just as a sewage farm accumulates and concentrates refuse and prevents it from spreading, so does the camp concentrate those very elements whose unchecked spread would overwhelm the countryside.

But why, it may be asked, should not the concentration take place at Colwyn Bay or Southend, areas which, in the eyes of Mr. Butlin's critics, are already devastated? The answer is because the campers should be given their chance, a chance to open their eyes to the fact and presence of beauty which only contact with beauty can bestow.

Why, Mr. Butlin pertinently asks, should the campers who look at bricks and concrete all the year round be required to look at the bricks of Blackpool and the concrete of Colwyn Bay in their holidays? Why should they not look at Snowdon? There is a magnificent view of it, by the way, from the Pwllheli camp. 'You say it is a good thing that men should learn to love natural beauty. Well, I', says Butlin, in effect, 'am helping them. You cannot, after all, jump overnight from the Blackpool holiday in a mob to the mountain holiday with two or three. You must first be given the opportunity to see mountains and then perchance you may feel their spell and learn to love them. Well, my Pwllheli camp performs the office of a kindergarten for future mountaineers. There is the view of the Snowdonian range opening out every morning to greet them when they get up and, if they desire to improve the acquaintance, there are motor coaches to take them into the mountains.'

I can see no answer to this argument for how, one may ask, are the dwellers in Bootle who are also the holidaymakers of Blackpool to see natural beauty? How, as they live their ordinary lives of work and of play, are they to come by the chance to discover whether their eyes will open to it or not? Mr. Butlin gives them that chance. If the eyes of only one in ten, nay of one in twenty, are opened, then his camp and all that it stands for is justified. Hence, subject to the operation of whatever planning and siting controls may be in operation after the war, I am in favour of an extension of the Butlin camp movement and an increase in the number of camps.

(5) *The Agencies of Light*

There are a number of agencies which seek to do deliberately what Butlin does on occasion by happy accident. They fall into two classes. First, propagandist and administrative; second, practical. The propagandist and administrative are bodies which exist both to preserve the countryside and to educate people in the right attitude towards it. Prominent among them are the National Trust, the Commons, Footpaths and Open Spaces Preservation Society, the Council for the Preservation of Rural England and the Standing Committee on National Parks.[1] It is not easy to praise too highly the men and women who do the work of these bodies. There is no money in this work, little publicity and no glory. Nobody praises a country-preserver and, with one exception,[2] nobody ever bestows upon him an Honour. He spends many wearisome hours

[1] See ch. v, p. 106.
[2] Sir Lawrence Chubb, the admirable Secretary of the Commons, Footpaths and Open Spaces Preservation Society; he was also the founder of the Ramblers' Association and the first secretary of the National Trust.

on committees and deputations for which nobody thanks him, and for fifty years past his work has been as unrepaying as it has been exacting. For during these fifty years he has fought in the main a losing battle and it is rarely that he can comfort himself with the assurance that his efforts have been graced with the reward of achievement. He can, therefore, have absolutely no motive for his prolonged and exacting activities except the best of motives, public spirit and love of the country which he desires others to share. For these reasons it is difficult, I venture to repeat, to praise too highly those who give their time ungrudgingly to the work of these bodies.

Having said so much, I feel emboldened to mention two defects from which this work suffers. First, the bodies have little or no money; secondly, they are timid and unwilling to flout public opinion or to exceed the bounds of gentlemanliness in their protests against operations which threaten the countryside they exist to preserve.

In so far as the first of these defects is concerned, the only remedy is to be found in a more generous provision of funds by those disinterested elements in our public life which were responsible for their formation. But voluntary effort cannot any longer suffice. The work of the National Trust, the C.P.R.E. and the Commons Society should no longer be left to the public-spiritedness of voluntary bodies, but should be accepted by the State as one of its responsibilities. For if there is any substance in the arguments used in this book and particularly in the considerations advanced on pages 539–541, the work which they do is the responsibility of the community as a whole.

Their timidity is largely due to the fact that those who have time and inclination to devote themselves to this work are mainly old and mainly well-to-do. For my part, I should like to see more young people concerning themselves with the work of country preservation; young people who are not so well-to-do, who have the fires of discontent in their bellies and the cause of the disinherited at heart. Until the work of these bodies is taken over by a new Ministry of Amenities, there lies, I submit, a direct challenge to young people to assist in its performance. Young people are already largely concerned in the administration of the Youth Hostels Association and the Ramblers' Association, but these belong to the category of what I have called practical bodies.

These are bodies actually engaged in the work of bringing townspeople into the country, of accommodating them and of teaching them how to get the most and the best out of it while they are there. They are the bodies to which reference has frequently been made in the foregoing pages, the Ramblers' Association, the Youth Hostels Association, the Co-operative Holidays Association, the Camping Club of Great Britain and Ireland and so on.

These bodies I wish to praise and to urge more people to join them that they may become stronger than they are. It is only in the last resort through strength of public opinion that the changes advocated in this book can be brought about. I would also urge that the State should strengthen them with grants of money. In making this suggestion, I do not propose here to retraverse the ground covered or to summarize the conclusions reached in this book. I content myself with reaffirming that if it is good that young people should go to the country, it is good also that, when they do so, they should be enabled to enjoy the best that the country can give without violating the spirit or destroying the virtue which makes the gift possible. (I have already said enough about the so-easily-put-up-backs of people living in the country. I assume, too, that these should not be 'put up' more than is absolutely necessary.)

It is in the light of these considerations that the value of the work done by these bodies can best be gauged. The Ramblers' Association encourages people to go to the country and organizes in clubs those who have not the wish or the determination to go alone, or who do not sufficiently know their way about the countryside to be able easily and happily to go alone. The Youth Hostels' Association provides them with accommodation, the Holiday Fellowship and the Co-operative Holidays Association both with accommodation and with organized rambles and expeditions.

All these bodies do admirable work but could do more if they had more money. Their experience would, moreover, be of first-rate value to a Ministry of Amenities to which had fallen the responsibility for the care of National Parks and should in the early stages be enlisted to assist in their administration. It would also be useful in connection with the organization of a scheme for the training and education of young people during a possible compulsory sojourn of six months or a year in wild country. Assuming that the State ultimately takes over many of the country houses which their owners are no longer able to occupy, in order to prevent them from falling into the hands of private builders, it could not put them to better use than to hand some of them over to the Y.H.A. to administer as additional hostels.

I hate suggesting this, yet as hostels they will be neither better nor worse off than as schools, institutions or mental homes—their spirit will long ago have evaporated in any event—while, if they are used as hostels, there is a good chance that their parks may survive. It seems to me, moreover, that there is a certain appropriateness in the last surviving monuments of a way of living in and loving nature that is now dying or extinct serving as the links between the old way and the new.

If in the new age they could play their part in fostering the appreciation and love of nature in the descendants of those whose labours enabled their owners to build and to enjoy them in an age which is past, they would help to repay some part of the debt which in the course of our long history the disinheriting few have contracted to the disinherited many.

Appendices

Compiled by Francis Ritchie

(Hon. Assistant Secretary of the Ramblers' Association)

Appendix I

NATIONAL PARKS

National Parks Abroad

The first great national park, the Yellowstone, in the United States, dates from 1872. In 1916 the National Park Service of America was instituted to look after 'those areas of unusual scenic beauty set aside by Congress to conserve the scenery and the natural and historic objects and the wild life therein, and to provide for the enjoyment of the same in such manner and by such means as will leave them unimpaired for the enjoyment of future generations'. In the State of New York, which has a very high population density, the great Adirondack 'park' covers 3,000 square miles and includes 500 miles of walkers' trails. In addition there are in this State alone more than forty smaller parks.

In Canada the first national park was established in 1885. Australia and South Africa possess several national parks of long standing. New Zealand, which is little larger than Great Britain, has one huge 'park', Fjordland, of 3,500 square miles.

In Europe, Sweden, Switzerland, Italy, Poland and Holland are among the countries which have established national parks or reserves.

National Parks at Home

National Parks were first subjected to Government 'inquiry' in 1930, when a Committee presided over by Lord Addison reported in favour of creating a number of 'parks' and propounded two modest schemes to that end. Nothing was done. Several official pronouncements have, however, since been made which seemed to imply that the Government accepted the principle of National Parks.[1]

[1] Lord Portal (then Minister of Works and Planning): 'It is clear that no national planning of the use of land would satisfy the country, if it did not

NATIONAL PARKS

In May 1945, two further Government reports were issued, *National Parks in England and Wales*, prepared for the Minister of Town and Country Planning by Mr. John Dower, and *National Parks—A Scottish Survey*. The following account is largely based upon these two reports.

Definition

National Parks are defined, in relation to Great Britain, as extensive areas of beautiful and relatively wild country in which (a) landscape beauty is preserved, (b) access and facilities for open-air enjoyment by the public are amply provided, (c) wild life and buildings and places of architectural and historic interest are protected, while (d) established farming use is effectively maintained.

Selection of Areas

This 'relatively wild country' forms more than one-third of Great Britain. In England and Wales it covers some 12,000 square miles out of 58,000; in Scotland no less than 21,000 square miles out of 30,000. Many of the areas comprised in these two areas are unsuitable—they are insufficiently beautiful (e.g. the

provide for the preservation of extensive areas of great natural beauty and the coastline.'—21–4–1942.

Lord Jowitt (then Sir William Jowitt, Paymaster-General): 'Is there anyone who really doubts that a district such as that' (the Lake District) 'ought to be a National Park. . . ?'—29–4–1942.

Lord Portal: 'I reiterate what . . . I said about National Parks; they are all important for the future.'—6–11–1942.

Mr. W. S. Morrison (then Minister of Town & Country Planning): 'My Ministry is determined that the amenities of the country shall be preserved, and I have it in mind that we should set apart certain areas as National Parks.'—13–10–1943.

Scott Report: 'The establishment of National Parks in Britain is long overdue.' 'Within the first year' of peace 'the demarcation of National Parks and nature reserves (should) be completed, and the National Parks Authority set up.'—August 1942.

A White Paper on Control of Land Use prescribed as part of the Government's programme of reconstruction 'the preservation of land for national parks and forests, and the assurance to the people of enjoyment of the sea and countryside in times of leisure'.—June 1944.

industrial Pennines), too small (Cannock Chase and the Malverns), or devoted to other interests not wholly compatible with the purposes of National Parks (afforestation, mining or quarrying, or military ranges). There still, however, remains far more potential national park land than would be required under the most generous scheme.

Areas Suggested

After careful surveys Mr. Dower suggests the following regions:

First List—Parks to be established immediately	Approx. square miles	*Second List—Parks to be established at a later date*	Approx. square miles
The Lake District	860	Craven Pennines (Wharfe, Aire and Ribble)	380
Snowdonia	320		
Dartmoor	310	Black Mountains and Brecon Beacons	470
Peak District and Dovedale	530	Roman Wall	170
Pembroke Coast	100	Exmoor and North Devon Coast	280
Cornish Coast (selected parts)	180		
	2300		1300

Twelve other areas are mentioned which, though less outstanding than the above are, nevertheless, recommended for National Park treatment.

	Approx. square miles
The Broads	120
North Yorkshire Moors and Coast	460
Dorset Coast and Heaths	200
Berkshire and Marlborough Downs	240
North-East Cheviots (Till and Coquet)	300
North Pennines (South Tyne, Wear and Tees)	640
Swaledale Pennines (with part of Wensleydale)	240
Howgill Fells (upper Lune Valley)	280
Merioneth Coast and Mountains (including Berwyns)	660
Plynlimmon	400
Radnor and Clun Forests	420
Elenith Mountains (Elan, Towy and Cothi)	440

NATIONAL PARKS

The South Downs and the New Forest would have been included, had not Mr. Dower been satisfied that facilities for their enjoyment will be adequately safeguarded by the relevant Local Authorities and the Forestry Commission.

Scotland

The Scottish Report names five districts in order of preference with three more as 'reserves':

	Approx. square miles
Loch Lomond, the Trossachs	320
Glen Afric, Glen Cannich and Strath Farrar	260
Ben Nevis, Glen Coe and Black Mount	610
The Cairngorms	180
Loch Torridon, Loch Maree, Little Loch Broom	500
	1870
Areas mentioned as 'Reserves'	
Moidart, Morar, Knoydart	410
Glen Lyon, Ben Lawers, Schiehallion	140
St. Mary's Loch	180
	730
Total	2600

Administration

It is recommended that the authority responsible for the administration of National Parks should be a Commission specially appointed by and responsible to the Minister of Town and Country Planning.

Special duties of the Commission would include:

Landscape Preservation and, where possible, enhancement of landscape beauty.

Maintenance of Farming Use.

Ample provision of Access (freely over commons and uncultivated land; by footpaths and tracks in agricultural land; by road *to* and *around*, but not *through* national parks, except where roads already exist).

Encouragement of and in some cases provision of suitable accommodation for visitors.

Participation with the Local Authorities concerned in 'Executive Joint Planning Committees' for each area.

It is emphasized that each National Park must be treated as a single area for the purposes both of planning and of administration.

Appendix II

ACCESS TO MOUNTAINS AND MOORLAND

The Problem

In most civilized (and uncivilized) countries, but not in Great Britain, there is a public right, legal or traditional, to roam at will over uncultivated mountain and moorland. Although in certain parts of Great Britain, such as the Lake District and most of the Welsh mountains, the walker normally enjoys the freedom of the hills, from others, notably the Peak District and Scotland, he is rigorously excluded. It is in the Peak District, a natural playground for the enormous urban populations on its fringes, that the prohibition upon access is most acutely felt, but the problem is widespread and the principle involved is universal. An uncertain privilege or tradition of access, operating over part of the country only and always liable to be withheld, does not meet the present-day needs either of walkers or of farmers and landowners.

The Sporting Interest

The strongest opposition to any general measure for providing access to mountains and moorlands has usually emanated from the 'Sporting' (i.e. grouse shooting and deer stalking) interests. The main reason for this opposition is to be found in the enormous acreage of what are normally termed 'rough grazings' devoted almost exclusively to these pursuits, for sheep are excluded as well as walkers. Sir R. G. Stapledon in *The Hill Lands of Britain* gives figures of about 4½ million acres for authenticated grouse moors commanding high rentals and of over 3¼ million acres for deer forests. From the great bulk of this land the public is rigorously excluded on the unproven ground that their presence would interfere with 'sport'.[1] Sir R. G. Stapledon, who is perhaps the foremost authority on the improvement and farming utilization of hill land, goes on to say that 'sport has blinded men's eyes to the other uses to which highly esteemed sporting land could be put'.

The issue roused by the sportsmen's opposition was summed up by Mr. Dower in his Report on National Parks as follows: 'When the issue is seen as a broad question of principle—whether the recreational needs of the many should or should not outweigh the sporting pleasures of the few—there can be little doubt of the answer: that walkers should, and sooner or later, will be given freedom of access over grouse moors.' The same conclusion applies to the Scottish deer forests, with which the Dower Report was not concerned.

Water Catchment

The exclusion of walkers from water gathering grounds is discussed in the following extract from a Memorandum submitted to the Ministry of Town and Country Planning by the Ramblers' Association:

'Many water undertakings oppose access to uncultivated lands in catchment areas on the grounds of increased dangers of water pollution. Much of this opposition we consider to be based on undue conservatism, and to be without scientific warrant. In practice there are many anomalies and wide variations in restrictions upon ramblers. There are reservoirs with public motor roads alongside, and others with popular footpaths over the adjacent moorlands. On the other hand some authorities have gone to the length of dismantling the farms and denying any right of access. In the past some authorities have forbidden access for rambling to catchment areas, but have let the moors for grouse shooting.

'The Ramblers' Association suggests that this alleged danger

[1] For instance, Ilkley Moor, a popular urban common open to the public, is also a grouse moor and after many years of public access it continues to produce consistently good 'bags'. The grouse are understood still to be plentiful on the Langshaw and Blacka moors near Sheffield, to which the public have access.

of pollution and the possibility of overcoming it without rendering derelict wide stretches of wild country should be investigated by an impartial committee.'

The Need for Legislation

The reasons for the complete failure of the Access to Mountains Act, 1939, to meet a need which is widely felt are explained in the text (pages 128–131). As Mr. Dower states in the White Paper on National Parks already referred to:

'The Act did not come into force until after the war had started; no use has yet been made of its provisions, and it seems distinctly doubtful whether it ever can or will be used on any effective scale. On the most hopeful estimate, the cumbersome case-by-case procedure required by the Act would have to be kept hard going for many years, before anything like a general right of access over all uncultivated land could be secured. If the popular claim to walk freely over mountains, moors and other uncultivated land and the popular need for a full measure of such health-giving recreation are admitted (and the Act clearly implies such an admission), then there is a strong case for the early introduction of new legislation to start, like the original Bill, from the other end—to confer public rights of access over *all* uncultivated land (suitably defined) by direct and immediately operative provision; to subject it to appropriate general regulations with penalties for abuse; and to establish a case-by-case procedure for determining any particular areas of uncultivated land for which special conditions are desirable, or even complete exception from the general rights of access. There is good precedent for this approach in the automatic application of Section 193 of the Law of Property Act to commons in urban districts.'

It has been argued (with some force) that the terms 'mountain, moor, heath, cliff and down', referred to in the original Bill, as the land to which access would apply, are incapable of legal definition. For them should be substituted the phrase 'uncultivated rural land'—which is what they were *intended* to cover. For this purpose cultivated land might be defined (roughly) to include all arable land, in crops or temporary ley, permanent grass land (as opposed to rough grazings), land used for horticulture or forestry, and land and gardens attached to a dwelling house.

Changes Required

The following provisions should be included in any new legislation on 'access':

1. The Minister responsible for administering the Act should be the Minister of Town and Country Planning (in Scotland the Secretary of State).

2. Appeals against the inclusion of land within the scope of the Act on agricultural grounds should be made jointly to the Ministers of Agriculture and of Town and Country Planning.

3. Where, following an appeal, access is withheld either wholly or in part, the present provisions of the common law regarding trespass should remain.

4. No public authority or voluntary organization should be put to expense in gaining access to suitable land.

5. With the necessary allowances for any differences in the two legal systems, the new legislation proposed should apply to Scotland as well as to England and Wales.

6. Section 193 of the Law of Property Act, 1925, granting automatic access for air and exercise to all urban commons, should be extended to include rural commons as well. These commons amount to approximately $1\frac{1}{2}$ million acres. Most of them are rough and hill grazings; in fact, it is estimated that of the 5 million acres of rough grazings in England and Wales, about one quarter are grazed as common land. The transfer of the administration and 'regulation' of these lands to the Law of Property Act would be a valuable contribution to the wider problem of access to *all* uncultivated land.

7. Though the fact should not debar access, suitable warning should be given by means of red flags, etc., on the (comparatively few) days when grouse shooting is in progress. In practice most walking is done at the week-end and most shooting in mid-week.

8. Signposts, notices, etc., should be unobtrusive and kept to a minimum, and there should be little or no increase of 'made' tracks.

Postscript to Appendix II

Access to the Scottish Deer Forests and Grouse Moors

[I cannot resist the temptation to add to the above a postscript giving a brief account of the depopulation of the Highlands in the past and indicating the obstacles which impede access to this extensive tract of wild and lovely country in the present.

The postscript consists of an article by Edwin Royce entitled 'Bens and Glens and—the Lairds', which appeared in the Autumn 1945 issue of the magazine entitled *Out of Doors*. My thanks are due to the author and to the Editor for permission to reproduce it here.—C.E.M.J.]

'Until the year 1707 the two countries of England and Scotland were governed by separate Parliaments, but in that year the Act of Union brought about the coalescence of the two Parliaments into one representative body. Hence the frequent references to Scots Law in legal questions and—sometimes—truly remarkable differences in English and Scottish interpretation of the Law. 'Under the old Celtic tenures,' says Sismondi, 'the only tenures by which the lords of Sutherland derive their right to the land, the Klaan, or children of the soil, were the proprietors of the soil.' Burton, in his *History of Scotland*, writing on the state of the Highlands at the beginning of the sixteenth century, says: 'Instead of the land nominally belonging to the head, it belonged, so far as there really was property in it, to the holders and cultivators of it, while their head or chief had concern, not with it, but with them, as living beings, over which he held absolute rule.'

The first Jacobite rising was in 1715, but the doom of the clans followed the crushing of the second rebellion at Culloden in 1745, the famous 'forty-five'. The slaughter on the battlefield was followed up ruthlessly by 'Butcher' Cumberland and the Law Officers: the head of many a Scottish chieftain rolled on Tower Hill, whilst exile or death was the fate of their humble followers. And English landlords, or men with Hanoverian sympathies, lorded it over the land of the heather and the flood. In the fell clutch of time and circumstance this great Scottish tragedy has been idealized into the Bonnie Prince Charlie 'romance'.

The slaking of Sassenach vengeance was thorough and lasting. The clans were dispossessed, the carrying of arms forbidden and the wearing of the kilt proscribed. Scotland remained in complete political subjection under the Dundas despotism until 1806. The English landlords, flushed with their triumphal Enclosure Acts wangled through the Westminster Parliament, made hay in the two countries, whilst their sun shone so bounteously. Justice was being done, rough justice on the customary 'baronial' model.

Large profits had been made in England by sheep-rearing, following the intensive cultivation of English lands made possible by the thousands of Enclosure Acts. The obvious thing to the new landlords was to convert their extensive Scottish estates into multiple large-scale sheep farms. There was a slight difficulty— the peasants and crofters already living on those lands. The solution adopted was to evict them to the number of 15,000. They were removed, forcibly in many cases, from the interior glens (where there was the most fertile soil) to the sea coasts, the argument being that it was desirable for these poverty-stricken folk to have two sources of 'income'(?), the sea and the land. To make sure the evicted did not return, their humble dwellings were set on fire, or the huts unroofed, often with ill people inside.

Here is an episode from the Sutherland Clearances, notorious for their extent and brutal methods. 'Donald Munro, Garvott, lying in a fever, was turned out of his house and exposed to the elements. Donald Macbeath, an infirm and bedridden old man, had the house unroofed over him, and was in that state exposed to the wind and rain until death put a period to his sufferings. I was present at the pulling down and burning of the house of Wm. Chisholm, Badinloskin, in which was lying his wife's mother, an old bedridden woman of nearly 100 . . . I informed the persons about to set fire to the house of this circumstance and prevailed upon them to desist until Mr. Sellars came. On his arrival I told him of the poor old woman being unfit for removal, when he replied: "Damn her, the old witch, she has lived too long, let her burn." Fire was immediately set to the house and the blankets in which she was carried out were in flames before she could be got out. She was placed in a little shed and it was with great difficulty they were prevented from firing it also.' (Page 26, *Highland Clearances*.)

Many of the displaced folk went to Canada and their descendants still recall what happened in Sutherlandshire. There is a well-known song, 'The Canadian Boat Song', with this chorus:

> *Fair these broad meads, these hoary woods are grand,*
> *But we are exiles from our fathers' land.*

News spread slowly in 1814–18, but when the disgraceful events became known in England, the Leveson Gower family (Duke of Sutherland) of those days had an awkward time. They enlisted the services of several 'Whitewashers', one being Mrs. Harriet Beecher Stowe, of *Uncle Tom's Cabin* fame. Whitewashing was even attempted as late as 1883-4 by the Crofters' Commission. When Alexander Mackenzie published his book on the Clearances (about 1881) an effort was made in influential circles to get it suppressed. Even in 1932 *The Field* is so ashamed of the circumstances that it contends the stories which have come down to us are 'untruthful'.

Deer and sporting rights (after the passing of the Game Laws) soon became more profitable than sheep. When this occurred, 'deer forests were to a large extent substituted for sheep runs', the plunderers having retained their loot. Scotland contains some $12\frac{3}{4}$ million acres and nearly four million acres were reserved as deer forests in the second half of the nineteenth century. Deer stalking is a real sport, not an artificial affair like shooting tame pheasants, or the slaughter of driven grouse by stout gentlemen cowering in a line of butts, and is also an expensive sport. Nor should the untravelled reader picture a Scottish deer-forest as a densely-wooded series of hills; the greater part of the Caledonian 'forests' is a treeless waste, hardly capable, during a British summer, of supporting its stock of deer. During the winter, artificial feeding is necessary. Only for a couple of months during the year is this vast tract of waste inhabited, and then only by gillies and sportsmen.

Deer forests are costly amusements. They are rented for the season, two months (12th August to end of September) and £4,000 was asked in 1924 for the season for an Argyllshire forest of 33,000 acres of mixed land. An analysis of twenty estates gave an average of £44 per stag as rent only, to which must be added all incidental expenditure.

Deer are elusive beasts and, animated doubtless by the spirit of fair play, our plutocratic sportsmen were soon demanding the exclusion of the rest of the world from their expensive deer forests. One part—the sanctuary—is never entered except under very unusual circumstances. Paths, roads even, were closed (the writer has been bullied for being on a *road*—Glen Cona, Morven—in 1926), rights of way interfered with, and a species of terrorism instituted, all in the interests of sport.

In 1845, Glen Tilt was the scene of a right of way dispute, due to the action of the sixth Duke of Atholl in interfering with the passage of a party of botanists, under the leadership of Professor Balfour, who had been collecting plants on Ben Macdhui. The Dukes of Atholl have an amazing record (see *Our Old Nobility*) and the Duke's object on this occasion was not money but the sacredness of his deer forest. Anyone who has been through Glen Tilt would recognize at once that the pass, rising only to 1500 feet between hills more than double that height, must have been a thoroughfare between the valleys of Dee and Tay from the days of prehistoric man. The obstinate Duke went to law and lost, but still interfered with walkers. The Balfour incident is described in lively style in a delightful poem by Professor Maclagan, of Edinburgh, under the title 'The Battle of Glen Tilt'; the poem is reproduced in full in *The Ramblers' Federation Handbook*, Manchester 1937.

The attack on the walker intensified all over the north of Scotland. The Duke of Leeds stopped the Luibeg route up Ben Macdhui; a ferry boat which crossed the Dee near Braemar was removed; the longest and highest pass in Britain—the Larig Ghru in the Cairngorms—came under the ban; the Shiel Inn, by Loch Duich, was closed to keep climbers out of Kintail, and other inns were deprived of licences; the Cluanie Inn in Glen Moriston was forbidden to accept visitors arriving on foot. Children in the Braemar area at one time subsisted on tinned milk because the local fodder was required for deer; cottagers were threatened with dire penalties if they took in visitors or supplied refreshments. The most famous walk in Britain, that across Scotland through Glen Affric and Glen Lichd, was made impracticable except to the strongest walkers by more inn closing, the distance being increased to fifty miles between possible accommodation. That wonderful stretch of hill-country around Loch Maree, including the Torridon hills, Liathach, The Teallachs (the finest mountains on the British mainland), was to be attained only by peril and hardship, in the year of Jubilee. The list can be continued indefinitely; see the late Dr. E. A. Baker's *Highlands with Rope and Rucksack*, and remember that for years his was a voice crying in the wilderness for access to mountains.

About 1890, an American millionaire, W. L. Winans, bought a forest of 200,000 acres (over 300 square miles). It extended through Strathfarrar and Kintail and was patrolled by an army of sentinels, making it almost impossible to travel from north to south or vice versa. Excisemen were not allowed to search for illicit stills (perhaps the only good the Highlands got out of the occupation) and the millionaire prosecuted a crofter because his children's pet lamb strayed on the vast unfenced area dedicated to the stag. All this was perfectly legal and would be equally legal in 1945.

Winans is no longer with us, but there are more deer forests than in his time, and the restoration of the right of public access to mountains and moorlands is yet to come. It is not permitted to the tourist of 1945 to land on the island of Rum without the owner's permission; he will be stopped by the crew of the MacBrayne steamer, if he attempts to go ashore. The shooting tenant in Glenmore (Cairngorms) as recently as 1932, attempted to put pressure on the Forestry Commission to cease granting permission for the driving of cars over the Sluggan Pass, maintaining that the road was only a right of way for pedestrians. The old evil is latent only; given suitable opportunity, it will come again. As Scotland has been exploited in the past by the wealthy, so she will be in the future, until the inordinately wealthy cease to exist. Not quite the wish-fulfilment it would have seemed in 1939. Everybody is going to be poorer and £4,000 for two months' shooting (price for 1924, remember) will not materialize readily. Moreover, hydro-electric schemes and factories mean some reduction of the four million acres, not to mention a more harassed life for the deer.

Epilogue

Advertisement from *The Field* and *Country Life* for 26th September 1936:

WYVIS, ROSS-SHIRE
for Sale

11 miles from Novar and 39 from Inverness. This well-known forest extends to 23,000 acres. Deer stalking and grouse shooting of high quality. Excellent lodge ... commanding lovely view.

A most attractive estate without tenants.

Full particulars from XYZ'

Appendix III

FOOTPATHS

The Present Position

1. In few cases can it be said with certainty that a path is a public right of way. A legal right of way can be presumed to exist only where there has been a decision to this effect by the courts, or where the path has recently been laid down under a Planning Scheme, or as the result of an act of 'dedication' on the part of the owner of the land.

2. Owing to the appalling complexity and uncertainty of the law the Local Authority is rarely willing to institute costly legal proceedings to settle disputed cases. (A case recently settled in Cornwall was under active dispute for seventeen years; while an unsuccessful attempt to prove a path to Stonehenge cost £3,000.)

3. Under the Rights of Way Act, 1932, it is necessary in order to establish a right of way to prove uninterrupted public use of a path 'as of right' for twenty years—forty years in the case of land privately owned—a matter of extreme difficulty.

In disputed cases no statements are allowed to be taken in evidence from tenants or employees of the estate through which the path runs. Crown land is in any event excluded from the operations of the Act.

4. Owners, occupiers and Parish, Rural and County Councils all have limited, overlapping and generally only *permissive* powers in regard to the upkeep of footpaths. As a result, paths become obstructed, blocked up and overgrown while stiles and bridges are broken down and not replaced. Paths are, in effect, often lost to the public because the responsibility for upkeep and repair is not squarely laid upon any one authority.

5. Ambiguity in the wording of the Highway Act, 1835, has led most County Councils to disclaim liability for the repair of

paths unless they can be shown to have been public since 31st March 1836.

6. Parish Councils upon whom the duty of maintaining footpaths is primarily laid are frequently composed of or dominated by interests opposed to their free use by the public.

Changes Required

1. *The Establishment of a Footpaths Commission*

The appointed custodians of footpaths having so largely shelved their responsibilities, partly no doubt because of the involved nature of the problem, partly because of their preoccupation with more important matters, for example, roads, the responsibility should be placed elsewhere. Cross-country footpaths should no longer remain under the general control of the Ministry of Transport, the Government department at present responsible, but should be transferred to the Ministry of Town and Country Planning.

The establishment by the Ministry of a Footpaths Commission to exercise general responsibility in all matters affecting footpaths, including their establishment in the first instance and their subsequent maintenance and repair, is the solution propounded by the Ramblers' Association and accepted and endorsed by the Scott Committee.

2. *The Establishment of a National Record*

1. Liability for repair and maintenance is frequently refused because the authority or occupier concerned disputes the existence of a right of way. The first duty of the Commission is, therefore, to supervise the preparation of a national record of all existing footpaths and bridle-ways.

2. Local Authorities should be instructed to prepare lists and maps of all paths believed to be public. (Under the Rights of Way Act, 1932, several have already done so with varying degrees of completeness.)

3. These provisional lists and maps should be published or otherwise made available for inspection.

4. Landowners, residents, preservation societies and ramblers should have the right to recommend additions or deletions from the list.

5. The Local Authority would embody such of these as appeared to have substantiated their right to inclusion and on which agreement had been reached.

6. Disputes outstanding at this stage should be referred to the Footpaths Commission for arbitration, with a right of appeal against its award to the High Court on questions of law.

7. Without a thorough recasting of the law relating to the dedication of highways, such arbitrations must necessarily be based upon existing legal provisions. But pending the general recasting here proposed, certain adjustments in the public interest should be made in the existing law. In particular, the long period of usage required for a presumption of dedication should be lessened.

8. Dates and periods would be specified for completing the various stages indicated above. The list finally established would provide for the first time an indisputable legal record of our public footpaths.

3. *The Creation of New Paths*

1. Granted an agreed list of existing paths, it would be possible to estimate what new footpaths are required. It is probable that many unacknowledged paths will have come to light during the survey and that new requirements will therefore be comparatively modest. They will fall into three main categories.

2. 'Through Routes' such as the Coastguards' Path and the Pennine Way (see page 89). In these cases, the main requirement will be for a number of connecting links between existing paths. (It is estimated that footpaths already exist covering more than three-quarters of the 250-mile Pennine Way.)

3. Footpaths to serve as links, generally quite short, joining unconnected villages, valleys, etc.

4. Footpaths on the outskirts of towns and urban concentrations.

5. Provision for the footpaths referred to in 3 and 4 can be

made in local planning schemes, which from this point of view would require the approval of the Footpaths Commission.

6. Provision must be made for the inclusion from time to time in approved planning schemes of further paths rendered necessary by building development or population changes.

7. The longer 'Through Routes' (see 2) constitute an aspect of national planning and should be the direct concern of the Footpaths Commission and the Minister of Town and Country Planning.

4. *Repair and Maintenance*

1. It has been shown that in practice the repair of paths is often nobody's business. A statutory obligation to undertake all necessary repairs should be placed upon County Councils, who have since 1929 been the Highway Authorities. The delegation of power to Rural and Parish Councils should not be deemed to absolve the County Council from its responsibility.

2. The law should be altered to require such improvement of foundrous paths as will make them passable in wet weather.

5. *Obstructions*

1. As the law stands, the Highway Authority has a duty to ensure that paths are kept free from obstruction, but frequently refuses to act except at the request of the Parish Council. Steps should be taken to ensure that the machinery for removing obstructions is used.

2. Barbed Wire. It is unlawful under the Barbed Wire Act, 1893, to place barbed wire so that it may injure any person or animal lawfully using a right of way; if it is so placed, the Highway Authority can require the occupier to remove it, failing which, it can be forcibly removed at his expense.

3. Bulls. County Councils are empowered to make by-laws prohibiting the keeping of bulls over one year old in fields traversed by a right of way. Instead of being permissive, this restriction should be embodied in the law of the land. The following counties have NOT adopted any bull by-laws:

Beds.	Northants	Anglesey
Cambs.	Northumberland	Brecon
Durham	Oxfordshire	Carmarthen
Ely, Isle of	Peterborough, Soke	Denbighshire
Essex	Rutland	Flintshire
Kent	Shropshire	Pembrokeshire
Lincs (Kesteven)	Staffs	

4. Ploughing. A path may only be ploughed if this has been the custom 'from time immemorial'. The public then has the right to retread the way. But much additional ploughing has been permitted under the Defence Regulations (see pp. 80, 81).[1]

6. *Miscellaneous*

(i) Signposts. The Highway Authority is under an obligation to provide a signpost where two or more ways meet. This duty, in so far as it applies to footpaths, has in practice been largely ignored.

(ii) Trespass. Deviation from the strict line of a path is technically a trespass, which, however, incurs no legal penalty unless damage is committed—except where the trespass occurs on the property of certain statutory authorities. Railway companies, for example, are sometimes empowered under their special Acts to prosecute trespassers. In practice the casual and harmless trespasser has nothing to fear from the law. If told by the owner or agent to leave, he must do so, but he may demand to be allowed to go to the nearest highway or public path.

(iii) Enforcement. The Footpaths Commission should be empowered to receive and investigate complaints of non-observance of any of the statutory obligations regarding footpaths, and to ensure that the functions of the respective authorities are properly carried out.

Note. The Scott Committee's demand for a special Commission

[1] Since this was written the Defence Regulation authorizing the ploughing and diversion of footpaths has been revoked (November, 1945). All paths should now revert automatically to their original course, and further ploughing up becomes illegal.

to deal with footpaths' problems seems a reasonable, if novel, request. It may be, however, that other methods of meeting the need will be found. Provided that the job is done, it matters little who does it, but experience has shown the need for some form of statutory sanction.

Appendix IV

THE COAST

I. Building

1. The salvation of the coastline from disorderly development and ultimate ruin lies in the immediate and rigid application of the highest standards of town and country planning. Development of some sort on a large scale is inevitable. But a single badly sited house, bungalow or shack, a single house of discordant material can ruin several miles of coastline.

2. Planning in 'rural' coastal districts is backward and Local Authorities lack the finance and power to carry out the measures which the situation demands. For the whole county of Pembrokeshire a 1d. rate only produces £1,021 annually; for West Cornwall £872. (1937 figures.) A number of general principles governing coastal planning must, therefore, be laid down and enforced by the Minister of Town and Country Planning, on the assumption that the coast is a national rather than a local possession and that the nation as a whole should meet its share of the cost.

3. Any new buildings, whether permanent or temporary, must be grouped and zoned. Unless this is done, the whole coast will sooner or later resemble the stretch from Poole to Christchurch, from Prestatyn to Llandudno, or from Littlehampton to Newhaven where for over thirty miles the line of buildings is more or less continuous.

4. *Permanent Buildings.* The erection of permanent buildings should be subject to the following conditions:

(i) The careful 'zoning' of coastal land and the prohibition of all building development in agricultural and 'amenity' zones.

(ii) A strict interpretation of the Restriction of Ribbon Development Act, 1935, which prohibits building within 220 feet of the centre of a classified road, and

(iii) An extension of the principle of this Act to apply to the coastline. A prohibited belt wider than 220 feet will, however, often be required, varying in width according to the contours, the rate of erosion and the nature of the land.

5. *Temporary Buildings*. The erection of huts, shacks and caravans has in the past been completely uncontrolled. The imposition of reasonable but rigidly enforced regulations in respect of water supplies, sanitation, litter disposal, etc., coupled with the above-mentioned regulations affecting permanent buildings, would tend to 'group' these erections, instead of permitting them to sprawl in a broken line along the coast. Definite camping grounds should be allocated and camping outside them restricted by the application of the powers of Section 269 of the Public Health Act, 1936.

6. A long-term policy should provide for the compulsory acquisition and demolition of individual permanent buildings whose ugliness is exceptional, or which, because of their commanding position, spoil long stretches of coast. Temporary buildings falling within these two categories should be removed *in the near future*. Little hardship would occur as they could usually be erected elsewhere.

7. As a general rule houses should not be built on the seaward side of roads running close to the coast.

II. Access

The Foreshore. Ownership of the foreshore, that is to say, of the land between high and low water mark, is usually vested in the Crown and its recreational use by the public is traditional. But in some cases it is vested in or has been leased to private individuals and public access has been stopped or permitted only on payment of a charge.

1. The right of the public to the free enjoyment of the foreshore should be established, legally, practically and universally.

2. No part of the foreshore should be parted with by the Crown except by way of lease to Local Authorities or to the National Trust, who would administer it for the public benefit.

3. The foreshore already parted with should be regained.

THE COAST

Walking along the Coast and Cliffs

The Scott Report recommends 'the reopening of the old coastguards' path as a right of way for walkers round the whole coastline of England and Wales except where existing buildings or other constructional development including newly raised sea walls of earth construction render this impossible, in which case inland detours should be clearly indicated'.

Very long stretches of this path are already public rights of way. These should be linked to constitute what would become the most popular footpath in the country. Inland detours should be reduced to a minimum and only in exceptional circumstances should the existence of a private garden running to the edge of the cliff be held to warrant such a detour.

Access to the Coast

Footpath access to the coast and the coastal path is often much restricted, and increased provision should be made for approach by footpaths. Car parks should be provided at a reasonable distance inland to prevent 'casual' parking on sand dunes, uncultivated cliff land, etc.

Erosion

Access to and walking along the edge of the cliffs has often been endangered or prevented by cliff falls, and there is need for legislation to provide the shortest possible detours where breaks in the path occur. In planning many parts of the coast it is essential to provide a belt of open land running inland from the coast which would be sufficiently wide to allow for possible losses of land due to erosion on the edge of the cliffs.

Military Occupation

This is dealt with in a separate Appendix. (See Appendix IX.)

Responsibility for Administration

Finally, the responsibility for the planning and supervision of the entire coastal belt should be specifically laid upon the Ministry of Town and Country Planning.

Appendix V

AFFORESTATION

The Present Position

The Forestry Act, 1945

This Act reconstitutes the Forestry Commission and makes it responsible to the Minister of Agriculture. Otherwise the provisions of earlier Forestry Acts remain largely unaltered, which means that the Commission is still responsible for the execution of forestry policy.

The Act, however, provides wide additional powers for the compulsory acquisition of '*any land* which in his' (i.e. the Minister's) 'opinion is suitable for afforestation or for purposes connected with forestry'. The only exceptions relate to 'land which is the site of any ancient monument or other object of archaeological interest', or which forms part of a park, garden or pleasure ground, or which is the property of a Local Authority or statutory undertaking.

Defects of the Act

There is no protection for common land or for land held by the National Trust. The Act specifically authorizes the compulsory acquisition of the latter, 'notwithstanding that such land is held inalienably by that Trust' under the National Trust Acts. There is no reference in the Act to the Minister of Town and Country Planning.

Forestry Policy

The old Commission has in effect been reappointed, and its Report on 'Post-War Forest Policy', 1943, stands, therefore, as the official statement of the policy advocated by the Commission.

It recommends that of the three million acres of existing woodland, much of it in private ownership, two million should be selected for development and control (directly or indirectly) by the State, and that an additional three million acres should be afforested within the next fifty years.

Between 1919 and 1939 the Commission acquired 714,000 acres, of which 434,000 were planted. Activity on a vastly increased scale is, therefore, contemplated.

The desirability of these proposals can be considered only in relation to figures indicating the classification of various types of land for Great Britain as a whole. The following figures are taken from the latest Agricultural Returns, 1938.

AGRICULTURAL RETURNS, 1938

	Approximate million acres	
	England & Wales	*Scotland*
Agriculture	25	5
Heaths, etc.	$5\frac{3}{4}$	$12\frac{1}{4}$
Woods and Forests	2	1
Non-agricultural[1]	$4\frac{1}{4}$	$\frac{3}{4}$
	37	19

The following figures indicating a different basis of classification have been prepared by the Land Utilization Survey for England and Wales.

Good Farmland	$16\frac{1}{2}$
Medium Farmland	14
Mountain and Moorland	$4\frac{1}{2}$
Lowland Heaths, etc.	$1\frac{1}{2}$
Chief Towns	$\frac{1}{2}$
	37

The Commission's Report further estimates that the total afforestable area, in addition to existing woodlands, is 4·2 million acres. About 80 per cent of this area is in hilly country,

[1] The term 'non-agricultural' has not been defined, but it includes roads, railways, towns and villages, derelict and waste land, and some mountain land not grazed.

that is to say in Wales, the North and North-West of England, and the southern uplands and Highlands of Scotland. Nearly half is in Scotland.

A certain proportion of this four million acres must be deducted as unsuitable owing to lack of transport facilities or for some other reason. Rather more than three million will then be left.

If the Commission has its way, it follows that practically every part of Great Britain capable of afforestation will be taken for that purpose, irrespective of any wider considerations touching the best use to which the land could be put. Such considerations include the rights of commoners, the recreation of the public, its access to and freedom on the hills and the preservation of natural beauty.

Changes Required

At present there is no indication that the demands of the Forestry Commission are considered in relation to other needs, least of all to the needs of the walking public. Hence the essential requirement is to co-ordinate these demands with other needs and to subject them to an overall plan for the most effective use of the land of England, Wales and Scotland as a whole. In the preparation of such an overall plan, the Minister of Town and Country Planning and the Minister of Agriculture are primarily concerned.

Appendix VI

TOWN AND COUNTRY PLANNING
Legislation and Machinery

I. National

There is general agreement, in which the conclusions of the Barlow, Scott and Uthwatt Reports concur, that the machinery for national planning should be dual:

1. An inter-Ministerial Committee under a Minister for National Development, to co-ordinate all aspects of national development, including transport, the location of industry, housing, water supply, forestry, and agriculture, with a view to ensuring that they shall follow a single unified plan instead of being separately dealt with under a number of plans emanating from different departments.

2. The Ministry of Town and Country Planning, which should reform existing legislation, supervise and maintain adequate standards in local planning, and undertake direct responsibility for special features of national planning, such as National Parks and the coast.

Location of Industry

The Barlow Report on the 'Distribution of the Industrial Population' recommends a policy of 'redevelopment, decentralization and dispersal' to remedy the social, economic and strategic disadvantages of large industrial concentrations. It recognizes that many towns and urban concentrations are too large for healthy living or economic well-being, and recommends that industrial development likely to cause further growth should take place outside such concentrations. Suitable industries should also be encouraged to 'disperse'. A national authority is advocated to examine existing and proposed planning schemes, and to study, advise upon and regulate the location of industry. Such an authority would be given special and immediate powers to regulate or refuse the establishment of additional industries in the London area.

The Distribution of Industry Act, 1945, would seem in its final form to be a half-hearted attempt to assist the Distressed or, as they are now called, 'Special' or 'Development' Areas. These, however, constitute only one aspect of a more general problem.

The Scott Report

The famous Scott Report on 'Land Utilization in Rural Areas', 1942, covers a wide range of subjects, many of which have received separate treatment in other Appendices. In general, it recommends the adoption of a 'Five Year Plan' to operate from the end of the war and to include the completion of the following projects:

Town and Country Planning Schemes covering the whole country, together with a revision of existing schemes.

A definite number of houses for rural workers.

A full survey of all villages and hamlets, and a plan for the provision of halls, playing fields and village colleges.

Programmes for the supply of electricity, water and gas.

The establishment of National Parks including the provision of hostels, etc.

The determination and signposting of all footpaths and bridle paths and the creation of long distance paths.

The elimination of unsightly advertisements, petrol stations, etc.

Rules for the control of access to the countryside, the use of commons and highways and other rights of way.

An educational campaign to promote a better understanding between town and country.

Compensation

Planning legislation, whether national or local, will remain largely abortive unless planning authorities are given adequate financial powers to enable them to carry out the intentions of the plan. In practice it has been impossible to collect the 'betterment' value of areas developed under planning schemes, value which the 1932 Act (see below) intended to provide a fund for the compensation payable to owners whose application to develop their land had been refused. A solution to this problem of compensation and betterment, whether on the lines propounded by the Uthwatt Committee or by some other method, is a necessary condition of any effective planning.

II. Local

The Town and Country Planning Act, 1932

This Act consolidated previous legislation and brought under control both built-up and rural areas. Section one states that the purpose of the Act is to make schemes 'with respect to any land, whether there are or are not buildings thereon, with the general object of controlling the development of the land comprised in the area to which the scheme applies, of securing proper sanitary conditions, amenity and convenience, and of preserving existing buildings or other objects of architectural, historic or artistic interest and places of natural interest or beauty, and generally of protecting existing amenities, whether in urban or rural portions of the area'.

By August 1941, schemes had been or were being prepared to cover about $28\frac{1}{2}$ million acres of England and Wales (about $\frac{3}{4}$ of the whole), but planning schemes were actually in operation in the areas of only 45 authorities, covering one million acres. The total number of separate planning authorities is 1,441, of which 1,021 have joined forces to constitute 179 Joint Planning Committees.

Restriction of Ribbon Development Act, 1935

Under this Act, the consent of the Minister of Transport is required before any building (other than an agricultural building) can be erected within 220 feet of the middle of any 'A' or

'B' road. By resolution of the local Highway Authority this restriction may also be applied to unclassified roads, in which event the Highway Authority may be required to provide funds for compensating the owners of the margins of the road. In conception and administration this is not a planning Act but an Act for the improvement of transport.

Town and Country Planning (Interim Development) Act, 1943

This Act brought under negative planning control all land not subject to a scheme under the 1932 Act, and, pending the operation of approved schemes, empowered the planning authority to postpone consideration of applications for development.

Town and Country Planning Act, 1944

This provided more effective machinery for replanning bomb-damaged or obsolescent industrial areas and gave powers for the compulsory purchase of land, including land required for 'overspill' development to offset 'decongestion' of other areas.

The Small Effect of these Acts

The legislation here summarized, if strengthened and made compulsory, supplies a reasonably adequate framework for local planning, provided that certain defects are remedied. Among the reasons for its ineffectiveness in the past may be cited the following:

1. Planning Schemes have been purely *local* in character, and have not paid regard to considerations arising outside the immediate area covered by the scheme.

2. There are far too many planning authorities, and some of them are too small to be effective. (For example, there are 218 authorities covering populations under 5,000. In the London Passenger Transport area planning powers were divided in 1939 between 133 authorities.) The Scott Report recommends that the planning unit should be the county or county borough

and its surrounding area, or a combination of Local Authorities comparable in area, resources and importance.

3. Use of planning powers has been optional. Local Authorities have been under no obligation to use them and many have not done so.

4. Planning authorities have been unable or unwilling to meet the compensation involved (see page 265).

5. Statutory authorities (gas, water, electricity, and railway authorities) and agricultural buildings have been exempt from planning control.

6. The legislation is designed to deal mainly with *urban* expansion, instead of providing for the correct use of *all* land. The schemes approved during the years 1934–8 were divided between the various 'zoned' areas as follows: residential, 51·7 per cent; industrial, etc., 8·5 per cent; open spaces and agriculture, 19·7 per cent. These figures seem to show an excessive provision for the expansion of towns.

7. There has been no integrated national plan into which the local schemes could be fitted. There is no integrated plan for the location of industry, the preservation of agricultural land, the co-ordination of road policy, water catchment areas, forestry and housing.

Appendix VII

ADVERTISEMENTS

Existing Legislation

1. *The Advertisements Regulation Acts,* 1907 *and* 1925

Limited powers are given to County Councils and to the Councils of Urban Districts with populations exceeding 10,000, enabling them to adopt by-laws regarding the display of advertisements. County Councils may delegate their powers to Rural District Councils.

The commonest form of by-law relates to advertisements of which the effect is to 'disfigure the natural beauty of a landscape or to disfigure or injuriously affect a view of natural scenery from a highway, or of an historic building or a monument, or of a place resorted to by the public on account of its beauty'.

Defects in Existing Legislation

These powers are inadequate in themselves and their operation is hampered by cumbersome machinery. The following are their main defects.

(i) A Local Authority need not adopt a by-law unless it wishes; having taken powers to control advertisements, it need not use them.

(ii) Urban and suburban areas are almost completely unprotected by legislation.

(iii) Advertisements so situated that there is no rural scenery to form a background are particularly difficult to remove; yet they may be in country areas with open and unspoilt country in front of them, to the right of them and to the left of them.

(iv) Notice of intention to erect an advertisement over twelve feet high in an area to which the by-law applies must be given to the Local Authority, but advertisements under twelve feet in height can be put up without notifying the authority.

(v) Moreover, the removal of an advertisement which infringes the by-law in other respects depends upon the chance of somebody being willing to take the trouble to report the case to the authority.

(vi) If an advertisement is for any reason considered to infringe the by-law, its owner is warned to remove it. On refusal he can be prosecuted by the authority who, however, is required to prove that the advertisement 'disfigures or injuriously affects a view of rural scenery from a highway or railway, or from any public place or water, or the amenities of any village, or the amenities of any historic or public building or monument or of any place frequented by the public solely or chiefly on account of its beauty or historic interest'.

The question of conviction will thus depend upon the varying aesthetic opinions of magistrates.

(vii) When proof of infringement of the by-law has been effected and the advertisement removed, there is nothing to prevent the erection of the same advertisement elsewhere or of another advertisement in the same place.

2. *The Town and Country Planning Act*, 1932

Control of advertisements may also be exercised under Town and Country Planning Schemes, the Act of 1932 providing that, 'Where it appears to the responsible authority that an advertisement displayed or a hoarding set up in the area to which a scheme applies seriously injures the amenity of land specified in the scheme to be protected under this Act in respect of advertisements, the authority may serve . . . upon the owner of the advertisement hoarding a notice requiring him to remove it within such period . . . as may be specified therein. . . .'

These powers are also inadequate, because

(i) The advertisement must first be erected before it can be decided that serious injury to amenities results from it.

(ii) The clause only applies to those areas which are covered by a Planning Scheme.

(iii) The difficulty of proving 'serious injury' remains.

(iv) Even where a Planning Scheme has been approved and is working—and very few, in fact, have reached this stage[1]—a period of five years' grace is given to existing advertisements before they can be removed.

The Present Position

Outdoor advertising was growing apace until the war, and its admittedly disastrous effect on both urban and rural amenities had not been mitigated by the above legislation. In rare and comparatively isolated cases some advertisements were removed by those authorities who operated the limited powers given to them, only however to be transferred elsewhere. Thus along the eighty-odd miles of highway from Manchester to Newby Bridge at the foot of Lake Windermere there were in 1938 755 large advertisements, including 103 hoardings each displaying several advertisements.

The regulations were, moreover, largely vitiated by reason of the fact that advertisements had first to be erected before it could be shown that they were injurious. The truth is, of course, that in most parts of the country *any* commercial advertisement is an anomaly which should not be permitted.

During the war many advertisements have disappeared owing to restrictions on paper, labour and timber, but there is little doubt that unless effective legislation is introduced in the near future, not only will these advertisements return but their number will be largely increased owing to the resumption of advertising campaigns by the big national advertisers and the natural desire on the part of billposting and signboard companies to share in these campaigns to the best of their ability.

Changes Required

As an immediate step, the Government should be persuaded to introduce a simple Emergency Bill prohibiting new com-

[1] See page 265 above.

mercial advertisements in any rural area other than essential advertisements permitted under the present by-laws, i.e. advertisements relating to the trade carried on at the premises displaying the advertisement, auction notices, notices of coming events and so on. This would at least have the effect of preventing the position in the countryside, where there can be no excuse for commercial exploitation of the public highway, from deteriorating, pending the adoption of a long-term policy.

As soon as Parliamentary time permits, further supplementary legislation designed both to clarify and to reform the existing position should be passed on the following lines:

(i) Commercial advertisements, other than essential local advertisements permitted under the present by-laws (see above), should be prohibited in the countryside, i.e. in rural zones defined as such by the planning authorities. (These should include all rural scenery and picturesque villages.)

(ii) In urban and suburban areas commercial advertisements should be restricted to sites licensed by the Local Authority and should be subject to limitations in regard to size and height from ground. Licences would be subject to review at periodic intervals.

(iii) Railway companies should be subject to the same control, so far as advertisements in view from public highways are concerned.

(iv) Sky writing and the carrying of advertising streamers from aircraft should be prohibited.

Appendix VIII

WILD FLOWERS, LITTER, AND
WILD BIRDS

Wild Flowers

Existing State of the Law

There are by-laws in nearly all counties designed to prohibit the uprooting of flowers. Their usual form is as follows: 'No person shall (unless authorized by the owner or occupier, if any, or by law to do so) uproot any fern or other plants growing in any road, lane, roadside bank or hedge, common or other place to which the public have access.' This law applies to all plants. Some counties issue in addition schedules of plants and ferns in special need of protection.

Changes Required

The law should be made uniform in all counties. Prohibitions, instead of being embodied in by-laws which it is open to authorities to pass or not to pass as they please, should be embodied in Statute Law, made universally applicable and widened to cover the systematic picking as well as uprooting of flowers. The police should further be empowered to exact a summary fine for the stealing, uprooting or wanton picking of wild flowers.

Litter

Existing State of the Law

County Councils have powers under by-laws to prescribe penalties for depositing litter or refuse on any 'highway, or roadside waste, any common, village green, park, recreation ground or other open space to which the public have access for the time being; or any tidal or other water abutting on such places'. The effectiveness of these by-laws varies with the degree of vigour with which they are enforced. Before the war there were several prosecutions in Sussex; in other counties none at all. But police action alone, however widespread, cannot be successful without a quickened public opinion.

Changes Required

The police should be empowered to impose a summary fine for the leaving of litter. Whether a fine is or is not imposed, should depend upon the nature and quantity of the litter. Breadcrumbs soon disappear and apple cores are not as obtrusive as orange skins. Wirework containers displaying the litter within are often nearly as objectionable as the scattered litter they have collected.

Refuse Dumps

Disposal of village refuse often presents a difficulty, but most countryfolk observe reasonable standards of decency in getting rid of tin cans and other unburnable rubbish. The best solution is usually a village tip discreetly hidden, or a trench which when full is covered with six inches of soil.

Changes Required

There are two unmitigated nuisances which should be checked by law: tipping into a river or stream in the vague hope that the water will carry the refuse away, and rubbish dumps made by urban authorities in the country to save expense.

Wild Birds

Existing State of the Law

It is an offence under the Wild Birds Act of 1880 to shoot or snare any wild bird except the Little Owl during the close season from 1st March to 1st August. Protection all the year round is afforded to bullfinches, goldfinches, kingfishers, lapwings, linnets, redshanks, and all owls except the Little Owl. This protection also applies to their eggs. County Councils have, however, powers to modify the provisions of the Act and as a result the position varies from county to county. In some cases full protection is given to nearly eighty species, a list of which will be provided by the Clerk to the Council.

An owner or occupier is allowed to kill on his own land any birds not included in a lengthy schedule to the Act.

Under the Protection of Birds Act, 1933, traffic in most live birds known to be taken and exhibited for sale is prohibited.

Unfortunately these regulations appear to be broken with impunity so far as the collection of the eggs and the shooting, trapping and poisoning of 'protected' birds are concerned. The effrontery of the egg collector is well known. Even worse are game preservers who order the destruction of any birds thought to prey upon their game. To quote Seton Gordon, the naturalist:[1] 'Golden eagles are shot as they leave the eyrie . . . the barbarous pole trap, although illegal, is still in use.'

Changes Required

A new Act is required, giving full protection to all birds and their eggs with certain exceptions and making such protection uniform throughout the country.

A keener public feeling, more private effort and more police action are required to enforce the law.

[1] *Wild Birds of Britain* by Seton Gordon.

Appendix IX

THE FUTURE USE OF REQUISITIONED LAND

The Requisitioned Land and War Works Act, 1945, provides machinery for:

1. The permanent acquisition by the appropriate Minister of any land on which Government war work has been done, or which has been damaged by Government war use.

2. The permanent stopping up of highways temporarily closed under the Defence Regulations.

3. The rehabilitation of requisitioned or damaged land, whether to be permanently retained or not, either directly or by reimbursing the owner with the cost of rehabilitation.

4. The establishment of a War Works Commission to advise the Minister upon any proposals to which objection is taken.

The Ministers concerned are the First Lord of the Admiralty, the Ministers of Air, War, Supply, Aircraft Production, Works, War Transport and the Postmaster-General.

Land

1. The Minister may compulsorily acquire land containing Government war works, together, if necessary, with contiguous or adjacent land, with the object of preserving the value of the works. Land which has diminished in value owing to government war works or war use may also be compulsorily acquired for the purpose of 'rehabilitating' it.

2. Every proposal for compulsory acquisition must be notified to the local planning authority, to persons interested in the land and to the press, and the notice must specify a period of not less than three months during which objections may be received. (In the case of industrial premises, and with the approval of the Board of Trade and the Minister of Town and Country Planning, this period may be reduced to fourteen days.)

3. Written objection may be made by any person having an interest in the land, and, if public amenities are threatened, by 'the local planning authority, by any local authority, or by a society or body having as its object or one of its objects the preservation of such amenities'.

4. Proposals to which objection is made must be referred to the War Works Commission, and before making their report the Commission must afford a hearing to the persons or bodies objecting, and in cases affecting planning or amenities consult the Minister of Town and Country Planning.

5. In the event of an unfavourable report from the Commission, the Minister may, nevertheless, in certain circumstances, after laying the report and a statement of his reasons for disagreeing with it before Parliament, proceed to carry out his proposals, unless either House objects within forty days.

6. No common land or public open space may be acquired without the express consent of each House of Parliament, unless the Minister of Agriculture in the case of a common, or the Minister of Town and Country Planning in the case of an open space, certifies that equivalent and equally valuable land is available and will be provided in lieu of the land taken. The Act does not authorize the permanent acquisition of land taken for agricultural purposes.

7. Notice of any proposal for compulsory acquisition must be given within two years of the end of the 'war period', as to which see below.

Highways

For the permanent closing of highways (including footpaths and bridleways) the procedure is broadly the same as the above, except that:

1. In all cases the Minister concerned is the Minister of War Transport.

2. Wider publicity is prescribed for the proposals, which are to be notified in two or more local newspapers, to every Local Authority concerned, including the Parish Council or Meeting, and by a notice set up at each end of the highway.

3. No order for permanent closure may be made in respect

of any highway that has ceased to be stopped up or diverted, or in respect of a footpath stopped up during the war for ploughing by order of a County War Agricultural Committee.

4. Provision may be made for the creation or improvement of an alternative route.

Definition of the War Period

The Supplies and Services (Transitional Powers) Act, 1945, provides that 'for the purpose of the Requisitioned Land and War Works Act the expression "war period" shall include any period after the expiry of the Emergency Powers (Defence) Act, 1939, during which this Act is in force'. In other words, the period during which requisitioned land may be retained is extended by five years, and the time limit for proposals for permanent retention will not end until 1952. This extension does not apply to highways.

Military Use of Land

The Act does not interfere with the powers for compulsory purchase for the purpose of the Defence of the Realm held by the Defence Departments under the Acts of 1842, 1854 and subsequently. These powers may still be used.